the speed of dreams

OTHER BOOKS IN ENGLISH BY
SUBCOMANDANTE MARCOS

the speed of dreams

SELECTED WRITINGS
2001–2007

SUBCOMANDANTE INSURGENTE MARCOS

EDITED BY CANEK PEÑA-VARGAS AND GREG RUGGIERO

CITY LIGHTS
San Francisco

Cover photograph of Subcomandante Marcos, San Rafael, Chiapas, Mexico, © 2005 by Daniel Aguilar/Reuters

Back cover photograph of Subcomandante Marcos © Yuriria Pantoja Millán

Cover design: Pollen

Text design: Gambrinus

LIBRARY OF CONGRESS CATALOGING-IN-PUBLICATION DATA
Marcos, subcomandante.
  [Selections. English. 2007]
  The Speed of dreams : selected writings, 2001-2007 / by Subcomandante Insurgente Marcos ; edited by Canek Peña-Vargas and Greg Ruggiero.
      p. cm.
  ISBN-13: 978-0-87286-478-8
  1. Chiapas (Mexico)--Politics and government--21st century. 2. Mexico--Politics and government--2000- 3. Ejército Zapatista de Liberación Nacional (Mexico) 4. Indians of Mexico--Mexico--Chiapas--Government relations.
5. Social movements--Mexico--History--21st century. I. Pena-Vargas, Canek.
II. Ruggiero, Greg. III. Title.

  F1256.M361413 2007
  305.897'07275--dc22

                              2007020188

City Lights Books are published at the City Lights Bookstore, 261 Columbus Avenue, San Francisco, CA 94133.
Visit our Web site: www.citylights.com

Contents

Editors' Note

BY CANEK PEÑA-VARGAS AND GREG RUGGIERO

In Chiapas, these are complicated times, in an even more complicated place. The desire for knowledge refuses simple answers and instead offers itself in the form of new questions. To a visiting traveler, valuable insights drift elusively through the air. In moments like these, expect to be disoriented, because this is a place where disparate worlds meet, mingle, or collide. A sign on the main road offers an explanation of what to expect:

MUNICIPIO AUTONO REBELDE ZAPATISTA — JUNTA DE BUEN GOBIERNO — CORAZÓN CÉNTRICO DE LOS ZAPATISTAS DELANTE DEL MUNDO[I]

This is Oventik, a zapatista *caracol*, a spiral-shaped path where travelers from around the world arrive, share questions, learn, and then return home. The zapatistas are here, standing before the world with their hearts in their hands—an invitation to solidarity. And here *she* is, a young and enthusiastic medical student, whose determined path takes her from Chile to Cuba, and now to Chiapas. She has come to embrace the heart of zapatismo and thinks she will find it at the center of this *caracol*, perhaps wearing a mask, perhaps smoking a pipe. Her time here is short, so she asks her questions quickly. "Have you read Marcos's latest communiqué? What did you think? Will he really ride his motorcycle through all thirty-one states of Mexico?"

Her questions receive a few brief, though friendly, responses, and then silence. The aspiring doctor struggles to slow her enthusiastic pace to the jungle's patient rhythm: the fog's wandering crawl, the sun's steady arc across the sky. Silence—followed by another question, which strikes to the source of her fascination. "Have any of you actually *met* Marcos?"

"Of course . . . we are all Marcos."

Another compañera had looked up and spoken. Her response turned a small crowd of heads; and now the group was looking at her and she was looking back at them. And there was an understanding. All of them, including the well-intentioned medical student, giggled at the absurdity of looking for the heart of a movement behind the mask of a single man.

When she addressed the Mexican National Congress in 2001, Comandanta Esther found it necessary to correct similar misunderstandings:

> *Some might have thought that this tribune would be occupied by Sup Marcos, and that it would be he who would be giving this main message of the zapatistas.*
>
> *You can now see that it is not so.*
>
> *Subcomandante Insurgente Marcos is that, a Subcomandante.*
>
> *We are the Comandantes, those who command jointly, the ones who govern our peoples, obeying.*
>
> *We gave the Sup and those who share hopes and dreams with him, the mission of bringing us to this tribune . . .*
>
> *Now it is our hour . . . And so it is I, an indigenous woman.*

There are many echoes of Comandanta Esther's lesson in this collection. The words that fill these pages reach beyond the signature of that renowned writer and insurgent, Subcomandante Marcos. Many of these words are signed by members of the zapatista guerrilla leadership, the Clandestine Revolutionary Indigenous Committee-General Command (CCRI-CG) of the EZLN: Comandates David, Eduardo, Tacho, Gustavo, Zevedo, Sergio, Susana, Omar, Javier, Filemón, Yolanda, Abraham, Isaías, Daniel, Bulmaro, Mister, Abel, Fidelia, Moisés, Alejandro, Esther, Maxo, and Ismael.[2]

In Chiapas, the indigenous command of the EZLN and representatives of the Good Government Juntas have revived a form of leadership, *mandar obedeciendo*, which means *to command by obeying*. This model of accountability is reflected in the process and product of zapatista writing as well. Communiqués or speeches might be signed by an individual, but they represent the voices of many.

"Through my voice speaks the voice of the Zapatista Army of National Liberation" are words one encounters often in zapatista speeches and writings. Despite the single signature at the bottom of each communiqué, zapatista texts have more than several authors. They have thousands, primarily indigenous, many of whom are illiterate, but all of whom contribute their work, their sweat, their leadership, their thoughts, and (all too often) their blood to the authorship of their own history.

The composition of zapatista communiqués is a collective process that includes as much action as writing. The words cannot be separated from the activity that animates them. Of course, indigenous zapatistas do not simply contribute sweat and blood to the movement. Their intellectual contributions travel through an intricate network of community councils, striving toward consensus through popular participation. This process is always present but not always overtly expressed in the now-classic sign-off: "From the mountains of the Mexican Southeast. Subcomandante Insurgente Marcos."

• • •

As editors and activists in solidarity with the zapatistas, producing this book presented several challenges. How to make a selection of the most poetic and philosophical texts from the vast trove of material produced by the EZLN? Which pieces will best communicate with English-speaking readers the questions, stories, and vision of the zapatistas' insurgent community? Limitations of time and space obliged us to limit our selection to pieces that had already been translated into English, and to those that were made public from 2001 to the present, the period of time following the publication of *Our Word Is Our Weapon*, to which *The Speed of Dreams* is a sister edition.

Originally written or spoken in Spanish and distributed by the zapatistas during public gatherings, through their Web sites, and through the Mexican daily paper *La Jornada*, most of the zapatista texts are translated into English by cultural workers and activists who translate as an act of movement solidarity and resistance. We are particularly grateful to the many years of translating rendered by "irlandesa." Many, if not most, of the writings in this book are based upon her translations.

The EZLN are prolific, and volumes of their public speeches, musical recordings, stories, and communiqués have been posted online as video and audio files, speech transcripts, and translated texts during the period this book covers, 2001 to the present. Along with the more allegorical, philosophical, and poetic texts, we also included some shorter examples of historical or logistical communiqués in order to reflect the poetics of praxis. Lacking the metaphors, imagery, and playful dialogue characteristic of the more "literary" pieces, these communiqués speak to the daily processes of building power, democracy, and sustainability within the autonomous communities. In a moment of self-consciousness, Subcomandante Marcos comments jokingly on his own dry tone: "I know that some of you will be thinking that this is starting to look like a government report, and the only thing missing is my saying 'the number of poor have been reduced' or some other 'Fox-ism.'"[3] Nevertheless, at times these logistical reports or linear histories inspire the imagination—the dream that another world is possible—in ways that metaphors and allegories cannot.

The Speed of Dreams begins with the March of the Color of the Earth, the EZLN's political march from Chiapas to Mexico City in 2001, and continues through to the Sixth Declaration in 2005 and its manifestation as a nationwide grassroots organizing effort, the Other Campaign, in 2006. Along the way, readers will notice a period of silence between 2001 and 2003. During this time, the zapatistas released few public statements. Instead, they focused on the task of building local networks of autonomy, communication, sustainability, and self-governance.

Readers may encounter new or unfamiliar terms, many of which we briefly explain with footnotes. However, we intentionally did not attempt to translate certain Spanish and indigenous words for which we could not agree on an adequate English translation. In the majority of these cases, we marked non-English words with italics. However, in several cases we chose not to italicize particular words as a way of introducing them to English. These immigrant words—as of yet undocumented by Merriam-Webster and the Oxford Dictionary—have no single-word English equivalent. In *Zapata and the Mexican Revolution*, historian John Womack illustrates the need to expand English vocabulary with the example of the word "campesino":

> *The word "peasant" does not normally appear here. I have preferred other words on purpose . . . I do not deny that there were and still are peasants in Mexico, but only affirm that by 1910 most families outside the cities there probably were not peasant; certainly most families in Morelos were not. What they were is clear in Spanish: "campesinos," people of the fields.*[4]

There are many words in *The Speed of Dreams* that are similar to "campesino" in that they resist translation. One example is the word "compañero" and its abbreviated form, "compa." The word means "comrade," "partner," "close friend," but no one of these can stand in for "compa" or "compañero." Rather than assimilate by translation or issue a temporary visa via italics, we chose instead to invite compañeros directly into English.

Another example is the word "ejido," communal land shared by the people of a community. There is no single-word translation for "ejido" and its variants: "ejidal," "ejiditario," etc. Considering Merriam-Webster has already included a definition for "hacienda," we found it important to introduce this alternative model of land use, one that references the historic struggle for Mexican land reform. Ejidos are one example of such an alternative, which prioritizes subsistence and collectivity as opposed to profit and hierarchy, and so we adopt rather than translate "ejido" as well.

In keeping with the EZLN's own use of the term, "zapatista" remains uncapitalized, except in instances where it appears as part of a proper name such as the Zapatista Army of National Liberation.

Special thanks go to many compas for their inspiration, support, feedback, and friendship throughout the editing process: Thank you Ren-Yo, Jacob, Maka, Karlita, El Pinche Simon, RJ, Juan, Miguelito, and Lydia. Thank you Roger Stoll for your dedication to the task of transcribing and translating zapatista music, making these songs accessible to the world. Thank you to organizations such as Estacion Libre, Movement for Justice in El Barrio, the Regeneración Childcare Collective, Pachamama, Pacifica Radio, and many others, whose actions lend flight to the words in this book, proving that international solidarity means global consciousness and local groundedness. Un abrazo fuerte to Laura Carlsen for her excellent introductory essay, and to Alejandro Reyes for his invaluable eleventh-hour help with translation. Finally, thank you Elaine, Stacey, Chante, Bob, and everyone at City Lights Books for supporting this project and making it a reality.

The texts in this book whisper and conspire. They do not simply recount historical events but inspire reflection, analysis, deeper connections, and direct action. They were spoken and written as acts of resistance and embody what the zaptistas call *caminar preguntando*, to walk questioning. *The Speed of Dreams* is thus an invitation to retrace and join the zapatista path of listening, connecting, questioning, resisting, dreaming—not just as isolated readers, but as compañeros in a global movement.

NOTES

1. ZAPATISTA AUTONOMOUS REBEL MUNICIPALITY—GOOD GOVERNMENT JUNTA—CENTRAL HEART OF THE ZAPATISTAS BEFORE THE WORLD
2. On December 2, 2000, it was announced that these twenty-three members of the CCRI-CG EZLN, together with Subcomandante Marcos, would comprise the zapatista delegation to Mexico City, the March of the Color of the Earth.
3. "Foxism" refers to the former Mexican president Vicente Fox Queseda. This communiqué excerpt is taken from *Chiapas: The Thirteenth Stele, Part Five: A History*.
4. Womack, John. *Zapata and the Mexican Revolution*. New York: Vintage Books, 1970.

An Uprising Against the Inevitable

LAURA CARLSEN

> *"'The inevitable' has a name today: fragmented globaliza-*
> *tion . . . the end of history, the omnipresence and omnipo-*
> *tence of money, the substitution of politics for police, the*
> *present as the only possible future, rationalization of social*
> *inequality, justification of super-exploitation of human*
> *beings and natural resources, racism, intolerance, war."*
>
> —Subcomandante Marcos

The indigenous insurrection of the Zapatista Army of National Liberation (EZLN) on January 1, 1994, produced shockwaves throughout the
world. For much of Mexican society, the response was twofold and
simultaneous: fear and exhilaration. The fear arose from finding that—
wholly unexpectedly—war had broken out *in* the homeland, and the
rush of exhilaration came with knowing that something had finally
thrown the train off its track.

The train in this case was the inexorable imposition of the neoliberal
model in Mexico. The 1988–94 administration of Carlos Salinas de
Gortari, a Harvard-educated member of the Mexican elite, had forged
its legacy as a classic example of neoliberal modernization. The pace of
trade and investment liberalization, as well as of privatization, was
unmatched in any other part of the developing world.

For Mexican social movements and the left, as elsewhere in the world, those rapid economic shifts meant a series of major defeats. Social farms and communal lands that had been a conquest of the Mexican Revolution were open to privatization; state-owned enterprises and basic services—including banks and telecommunications—passed to private hands in crony deals; government co-optation split opposition movements; fly-by-night production led to loss of leverage for workers; and major sectors of society were not only exploited but excluded in the vertiginous process of economic restructuring. Most damaging of all, a majority of Mexicans still believed that trade liberalization and foreign investment would pull the country into the first world, and many who didn't believe that had nonetheless come to view the neoliberal path as inevitable.

These privatizations and the reforms to the tax and financial structures had created, by design, a new and extremely powerful oligarchy that owed its existence and allegiance to its benefactor: Carlos Salinas de Gortari. Ironically, "modernization" consolidated a narrow elite with power comparable to that of the Porfirio Díaz dictatorship that preceded the 1910 revolution. With the signing of the North American Free Trade Agreement (NAFTA), which liberalized trade and afforded unprecedented privileges to transnational corporations, the stage was set for decades of corrupt control and "development" marked by a sharply unequal distribution of wealth and power, as well as loss of national sovereignty.

In this context, the left was on the defensive, and the prevailing metaphor was no longer revolution but survival—except among sectarian groups whose rhetoric is reality-resistant. On the eve of NAFTA's implementation, the promise of prosperity through free trade blasted through the airwaves on a daily basis; opposition voices barely registered as static compared to the main message hammered through the media.

The last thing anyone expected was an armed rebellion in a southeastern state of Mexico—a state that historically suffered the nation's highest rates of poverty, illiteracy, mortality, and sickness. A state where a large indigenous population had been controlled by rural bosses and corrupt politicians connected through the ruling Institutional Revolutionary Party (PRI). A state of great natural-resource wealth and immense poverty that had, through equal doses of bloodshed and dependency, historically maintained political stability despite sporadic attempts at rebellion.

It was in part the long list of contradictions present in the state of Chiapas that attracted the handful of Marxist urban guerrillas who joined a few indigenous leaders to form the Zapatista Army of National Liberation in 1983. They also were drawn to the depths of the Lacandon Jungle, where steep mountains, dense vegetation, and remote communities offered cover to slowly build a base without being detected.

In her excellent book about the EZLN—*The Fire and the Word* (forthcoming in English from City Lights)—Gloria Muñoz Ramirez describes how the organization grew during those first years. Testimonies from Subcomandante Marcos and members of the first villages reveal a painstaking effort to build toward insurrection, a trial-and-error process that grew family by family, village by village, region by region. Each time the EZLN grew, it developed a higher level of coordination within and among the villages and greater military strength in the mountains. But even more important, the villagers began to read their reality in a different way.

The villages in the jungle had been built on a history of resistance, so the idea of rebellion was not new among them. Mayan indigenous populations and mestizos relocated by agrarian policies mixed; many had participated either in land struggles or in the centuries-old battle of the indigenous population for cultural and physical survival. More recent history provided new experience, most of it in failed attempts to find ways to accommodate the new economic system through appropriation of productive processes and marketing. In *The Word and the Fire*, we hear one of the first members of the EZLN, Comandante Abraham, describe his experience:

> When the zapatista army first came to our villages, around 1984, 1985, we had already taken part in peaceful struggles. The people were already protesting against the government. When the clandestine organization arrived, they talked to us about

revolutionary struggle . . . An insurgent arrived with a pamphlet that had a political explanation of the national situation and there it said what exploitation was and all that.

We understood pretty much right away, because anyway we had participated in other movements, not in the revolutionary sense, but in struggles where we negotiated with the government for land, for coffee, for a road in the Lacandona Jungle in Montes Azules. Since we already experienced the repressions that the compañeros told us about, when the message of the EZLN arrived we were glad, and we felt happy there was another struggle to defend the security of the small farmers and the poor.

In some ways, the idea of armed revolt met with fewer obstacles among the indigenous villagers than it would have among perhaps most other segments of the population. This acceptance of taking up arms was not due to a propensity for violence, but rather to a combination of familiarity with death, recognition of having little to lose given the desperation of their daily circumstances, and frustration with the dead ends reached through other forms of organizing for social change. The political-military organization grew, until the EZLN villages called local assemblies to ask their members if it was time to rise up. The answer was a resounding *yes*.

Millions of words have inundated printed pages and Web sites in the attempt to explain what happened next. The armed conflict was brief. On January 6, 1994, in the first of a long list of communiqués, the EZLN set forth conditions for dialogue. On January 12, 1994, the government suspended fighting, and open warfare came to a halt. The zapatista insurgents had lost some 200 soldiers, but most surprising, they had captured headlines throughout the world and brought more than 100,000 people into the streets of Mexico City to support their demands and their call for peace.

A "movement of movements" had begun, and it marked the course of indigenous organizing, civil-society activism, and the antiglobalization movement into the twenty-first century.

II. THE WORD THAT SHAPES US

"It was words that created us. They shaped us and
spread their lines to control us."
—SUBCOMANDANTE MARCOS

In its review of its first twenty years of existence, the EZLN identifies three axes of struggle: (1) fire, which is the armed conflict and military aspects of their organization; (2) the word; and an overarching third axis of (3) popular organization. Although popular organization supports and defines all EZLN actions and strategies, between the first two axes, the word has been more important. More malleable than the sword and—in the age of Internet—"faster than a speeding bullet," the zapatista word has been crafted carefully into a weapon, a bridge, a dream, a story.

What is now recognized as a modern case study in political communication draws on several strengths. The most obvious to outsiders is the skilled pen of zapatista spokesperson Subcomandante Insurgente Marcos. With remarkable versatility and craft, the thousands of texts pouring from "the mountains of the Mexican Southeast" aim at distinct audiences and assume specific purposes. Some are intellectual and engage directly with leading writers of the times. These comply with what Marcos calls the critical-analysis role of progressive intellectuals: "to convert the word into both scalpel and megaphone." Others are formal political declarations, communiqués, and letters.

What has caught the attention of the world, for both their impact and their unexpected use of the genre, are the stories. These reveal a preference for parables over manifestos and often reflect indigenous ways of understanding the world. The zapatista stories have resonated in an antiglobalization movement asphyxiated by the commercialization of culture and starved for new foundational myths, not only for their literary quality but for their ability to spark the imagination. From conversations with Old Antonio, whose indigenous common sense invariably breaks through the rationalist constructs of the mestizo Marcos, to the sardonic truths of the beetle Don Durito, the subcomandante's zapatista stories have not only become the stuff of revolutionary

literature but constitute a direct challenge to capitalism's homogeniz-
ing culture.

Indigenous cultures in Mexico, as in most places in the world, are
built and sustained through oral tradition, and their literacy rates are
usually low. In remote communities, radio is often the primary means
of connection and information beyond the local sphere. In February
2002, the EZLN inaugurated Radio Insurgente—"The Voice of the
Voiceless." Broadcasting equipment has been established in several
communities, and the station has a recording studio and a Web site—
www.radioinsurgente.org—from which EZLN programs are down-
loaded and rebroadcast throughout the world. The station provides a
forum to communicate the progress toward autonomy in zapatista communities and promote the music and cultural activities created by them.

An important enabling factor in the shift from a primarily military
to a verbal battlefield was communications technology, especially the
Internet. Indeed, the zapatistas never would have achieved their current level of reception without the Internet. Free and available, the Net
has been the medium for creating armies of cultural workers to spread
the word. Volunteer translators grab the latest communiqués and send
them out in new languages within a day; Web activists post to listservs,
and their posts in turn multiply on other lists. Electronic media and the
decentralized, network-style organization of the antiglobalization movement resonate with the zapatista movement's nonvanguard style and
the independent initiative of its solidarity groups—and vice versa.

But the zapatista word and the movement itself cannot be reduced
to a propaganda machine. Although conservative analysts have accused
the movement of being a superficial form of mass manipulation, their
accusations reflect fear, and in some cases envy, more than a careful
reading of reality. The texts are written by an army in the mountains,
constantly defending itself and its communities against harassment
and hostile actions. Its language grows out of a daily praxis of living the
worst aspects of an unjust society while seeking to communicate to an
outside world. This set of circumstances has given the movement an
uncommon legitimacy from the outset.

Indigenous cultures that value the word as a constituent element of humanity and society have also lent weight to the zapatista word. Many of Mexico's indigenous peoples name themselves precisely for their capacity for language: the Zoques call themselves *O´de pöt* ("people of language"); the Chatinos *Chátnç* ("work of the words"); the Chols *Lak´ tyan* ("our word"). In indigenous communities, the integrity of one's word is considered essential to social cohesion and human dignity, although practice, as always, may deviate from the norm. The emphasis on truth, consistency, and sincerity contrasts markedly with modern conceptions of messaging and communication as a sales tool in a competitive marketplace of ideas.

When the guerrilla organizers first arrived in the Chiapas jungle and began work in the early 1980s, they expected to spread a fairly classic model of Marxist guerrilla "foco" organizing. According to Subcomandante Marcos in an interview with Yvon Le Bot, not long after gaining acceptance in several villages, the outside organizers found that the indigenous people they worked with complained: "Your word is too hard"—hard not as in difficult, but as in edgy, intimidating, impenetrable.

The language then underwent a metamorphosis in the chrysalis of the jungle, in which it shed much of the standard rhetoric of revolution. In the search for a common language, the guerrillas adopted simple terms, baseline ideals, and shared historical and cultural icons. "Democracy, freedom, and justice" took the place of socialism and revolution as central goals and demands, and Mexico's revolutionary heroes Emiliano Zapata and Pancho Villa stood higher than Lenin, Mao, or Che Guevara. Clearly, some of this thinking had occurred before the immersive contact with the communities (hence the name *zapatista*). But the capacity to listen and adapt fundamentally altered not only the language but the practice and the idea of the ultimate objective. When they adapted the rhetoric, it was because their perspectives were being altered by their chosen core constituency—the Mayan Indians of Chiapas.

Because it has been so effective, and because the military stage of the uprising was so brief, critics have accused Marcos of launching an "Internet war" that relies on selling false utopias to disaffected members of globalized society. Coming from the left, the skilled use of language is somehow considered a semantic sleight of hand. But as John Berger wrote in a passage cited by Subcomandante Marcos, words stir up currents only when they are deeply credible.

The zapatista word has found an echo, not only among indigenous people but among "civil society" in general, and not only in Mexico but throughout the world. It has gained credibility from a respect for the word that the indigenous rebels often contrast with the Mexican government's many retractions, contradictions, and false promises. The combination of the skilled use of language, a grounding in experience, and a cultural respect for the integrity of speech has enabled the zapatista movement to leap borders and acquire great moral authority within the antiglobalization movement.

III. THE PROBLEM WITH POWER

The zapatista movement proved the power of language to weave global webs of resistance at the same time that it rejected the language of power. From the First Declaration of the Lacandon Jungle on January 1, 1994, the EZLN announced its intention to defeat the Mexican Federal Army and march to the nation's capital to "allow the people to freely and democratically choose their own authorities." Unlike previous revolutionary movements, they did not announce plans to take power and install a new state.

Since then, and in the context of the switch from military to political means of social change, the zapatistas have deepened their commitment to building alternatives that empower from the grassroots rather than controlling, competing for, or often even confronting the formal power of the state.

Building autonomy is central to this process. Before the zapatista uprising, the Mexican indigenous movement had already formulated a concept of autonomy that focused on recuperating traditional forms of self-government in the community. This approach soon came to play a central role in zapatista discourse and practice. In the first stage, starting in 1996, indigenous autonomy became the unifying principle for forging a national indigenous movement and was the main demand in negotiations on indigenous rights and culture with the federal government. The idea was not that legislation could bring about the needed changes, but that constitutional recognition of indigenous peoples would offer a platform to strengthen and rearticulate their societies and would be a first step in a profound reform of a multicultural state.

When the Mexican Congress rejected legislation based on these agreements in April 2001, the EZLN entered a second stage of creating de facto autonomies within its territory. In July 2003, a series of communiqués announced a major internal reorganization in zapatista territories. The autonomous townships were coordinated under "Good Government Juntas" to help mediate conflicts, receive grievances against the "Autonomous Councils," monitor community projects, and organize solidarity efforts. At this time, five political and cultural centers, the Caracoles (meaning, literally, "snails"), were born at the sites of the previous centers, which had been called Aguascalientes.

Like the form of the snail's shell, the new centers represented a spiral path, inward to the heart of the communities and back out into the world abroad. The EZLN communiqué titled "Thirteenth Stele" describes the Caracoles as "doors to enter into the communities and for the communities to leave through; like windows to look out of and into; like speakers to spread our word and to hear the word from afar. But above all, to remind us that we must be vigilant and aware of the full range of worlds that fill our world."

The formation of the Caracoles and the Good Government Juntas explicitly seeks to deepen democracy and separate civilian self-government from the political-military structure of the EZLN. The thirteenth anniversary of the January First uprising showed the progress that has been made in this area. Over four days in the Caracol of Oventik, thousands of visitors and zapatistas gathered to celebrate the New Year and to witness the results of the period of internal reorganization. Representatives from the five Caracoles reported on their achievements and limitations in the areas of women's rights, defense of land and territory, production and marketing, communications, education, and health. The mere fact that so many members of the civilian base communities—including many women—

spoke in public about their experiences testified to the often imperceptible but profound advances in developing forms of grassroots democratic civilian government independent of the EZLN. Whereas the Other Campaign has been the visible and controversial focus of zapatista organizing from 2006 to the present, in those four days the world saw the other side of the process—the long-term *trabajo hormiga*, or "ants' work," of building autonomy in the communities and empowering zapatista villagers. The experiment is ongoing, but the results are already tangible.

Zapatista roots in indigenous culture and the movement's encounter with the communalist current of the Mexican indigenous movement helped forge a very different understanding of political power than conveyed by previous revolutionary forces. The maxim is *mandar obedeciendo*—"to rule by obeying." The National Indigenous Congress describes the guiding principles of this power as "To serve, not be served; to represent, not supplant; to build, not destroy; to propose, not impose; to convince, not defeat; to come down, not climb up." The principles of organization aim to develop grassroots leadership that is "horizontal, rotating, collective, inclusive, flexible, representative, plural, gender-equal and non-partisan."

Luis Hernández Navarro points out that the zapatista/indigenous formulation of power contributes to current debates on two major points. First, it rejects Weber's definition of *power* as a specialized sphere and formally related only to the state, in favor of a definition of *power* more along the lines of Foucault's—as a web of relations of force particular to any given moment and set of circumstances. In this way, it proposes taking power not by storming the National Palace but on the level of empowering citizens as social actors. Second, it redefines the relationship between power and morality. The Western interpretation portrays power as fundamentally pragmatic, in the best of cases *influenced* by moral precepts. This view is diametrically opposed to a concept of power as the privileged place from which to exercise morality, as found in many of Kant's writings.

Within the Indian movement, *to rule by obeying* leads to a different kind of organizational structure, as well, based on a loose network of assemblies, coalitions, liaisons, and forums that assure flexibility and serve to decentralize power—what Ramón Vera Herrera calls "the invisible web." More than an invention of the New Indian Movement, the conception of power arises out of "a series of particularly indigenous forms of organization, political conformation, justice and many kinds of human relationships that together make up the best of Indian peoples . . . their deeply reasonable intention is to distribute power evenly so it can do no harm—an idea implicit in the way they weave their clothes, mats and baskets and also in the design and dynamics of the constellations."[1]

The need to spread power—the Foucaultian vision—and the chameleon-like nature of power are basic themes in most feminist currents. Early feminist critiques of hierarchical power also focus on empowerment rather than taking control of centralized power. *To rule by obeying* and *empowerment* imply a profound reconstruction of power, both its content and its distribution. In this sense, women and Indian peoples share the experience of being the "other" usually located outside the realm of power. From there, or rather from a multitude of "theres," they construct a vision out of resistance, a rejection of the formal structures of domination and also of a hegemonic way of thinking and formulating the world that subordinates or represses all other ways. It follows that to build a deep democracy, the power of the state must fundamentally change and not just change hands.

The zapatista concept of democracy, like the indigenous concept seen in other countries of Latin America, challenges the liberal formulation by positing the central role of difference in society. It does not view citizens as indistinguishable cogs in a democratic machine, each with an identical function that corresponds to the exercise of individual rights— mainly voting to delegate representation. Rather, it sees "others" who are marginalized for diverse reasons by the economic system as the building blocks of a new world. These new social actors are not defined exclusively by their relationship to the means of production nor by immutable identity politics; "the other" posits a new way of affirming identity without congealing it. Ideally, all this comes together at some point, much as the magazine *Rebeldía* describes the zapatista Other Campaign: "Many collective actors begin to recognize each other as 'others' and begin to imagine what it would mean to be part of a political project that didn't try to homogenize or hegemonize."[2] Imagining, according to the zapatista philosophy, is half the battle.

This critique of power then goes beyond the nation-state and runs as deep as the human psyche and as broad as the entire architecture of global society. As such, it becomes clear that neither a revolutionary vanguard nor an elected government can confront a challenge of this magnitude. Both inevitably wind up reproducing the structures of domination, albeit with different names or appearances. For the zapatistas, the only solution is to build from the ground up something that will be defined along the way.

IV. EZLN IN MEXICO, LATIN AMERICA, AND THE WORLD

The Zapatista Army of National Liberation has had a tremendous impact on Mexican, Latin American, and global politics. Today it faces new challenges on all three levels.

The EZLN in Mexico: The Sixth Declaration and the Other Campaign

In June 2005, the EZLN came out with the Sixth Declaration of the Lacandon Jungle. The Sixth Declaration articulates a clear set of political definitions: it declares the movement anticapitalist (in those terms) and describes neoliberal globalization as a global war of conquest. It posits that "a new step forward in the indigenous struggle is only possible if indigenous people join with workers, peasants, students, teachers, employees . . . that is, all the workers of the city and countryside." It reclaims the label of "left," saying, "We believe that it is on the political left where you find the idea of resisting neoliberal globalization and building a country where there will be justice, democracy and freedom for everyone."

After a simple explanation of the problems generated by neoliberalism, the Sixth Declaration proposes to connect directly with people fighting back in Mexico and beyond. The objective is to free organized discontent from the reductive trap of electoral politics, which fails to offer alternatives to the neoliberal model. The second goal is to articulate and coordinate these struggles, and the third is to develop a more precise reading of the national situation from below, a constant in the zapatistas' four (1996, 1997, 2001, and 2006) forays out of the jungle.

The Sixth Declaration also announces the beginning of the Other Campaign. With presidential campaigns in full tilt, Subcomandante Marcos left Chiapas in January 2006 to tour the country and meet with groups that had signed on to the declaration. In scores of meetings throughout the country, he has registered their demands and activities: battles against environmental destruction, for workers' rights, against the ostracism and oppression of sex workers, and for indigenous civil and territorial rights. Organized groups of youths, punks, leftists, indymedia makers, small farmers, homosexuals, workers, women, and "others" have organized to receive the EZLN representatives.

Accustomed to swimming against the current, the zapatistas chose to denounce party politics just when a significant part of the left saw a ray of hope in center-left presidential candidate Andres Manuel López Obrador. López Obrador has criticized—without rejecting—aspects of NAFTA and neoliberalism, has called for a stronger role for government and national sovereignty, and has opposed the most politically sensitive privatizations, particularly of petroleum and the electrical system. On the other hand, the zapatistas correctly pointed out that López Obrador has not taken a clear stand against capitalism, neoliberal globalization, or U.S. domination, and that for his campaign manager he chose the man who helped orchestrate the congressional counterreform on indigenous rights. They also claimed that López Obrador undermined grassroots organizations as mayor of Mexico City and, before that, as president of the Party of the Democratic Revolution (PRD).

The harsh criticism of López Obrador and the split over the prospects of his candidacy to effect social change caused debate within the Mexican left. Although the zapatistas did not call on supporters to vote against López Obrador or abstain, leaving them free to decide, the Other Campaign was viewed by many as divisive.

When Felipe Calderón, the right-wing candidate of the National

Action Party (PAN), was declared victor in the presidential elections of July 2, 2006, by a mere half a percentage point, the EZLN was among the first organizations to denounce the fraud behind his election. López Obrador won the majority vote in the states visited by the Other Campaign before it was suspended in May following the violent repression of protesters in Atenco, so few analysts considered the Other Campaign a factor in Calderón's narrow, and highly questionable, victory.

The EZLN has, since its arrival on the Mexican political scene, criticized political pragmatism. In particular, the communiqués from the midterm electoral period in 1997, just weeks after the federal government went back on its word in complying with the San Andrés Accords, and criticism of the "practical vote" for right-wing candidate Vicente Fox by part of the left in order to defeat the ruling party reflect this view.

The zapatistas' criticism of the 2006 electoral campaigns took on a sharper tone as part of the new strategy to articulate the grassroots left and because the zapatistas viewed the first presidential elections as a siren's call that pulled progressive forces into an electoral process that continues to be fundamentally flawed and essentially illegitimate. Instead of seeing active electoral participation as a "necessary evil" or a bulwark against the right, they believe it detracts from the formulation of the more radical demands needed to address Mexico's problems.

The Other Politics of the Other Campaign explicitly distances itself from government and formal political power by committing "not to seek gifts, positions, advantages, public positions, from the Power or those who aspire to it, but to go beyond the electoral calendar. Not to try to resolve the Nation's problems from above, but to build FROM BELOW AND FOR BELOW an alternative to neoliberal destruction, an alternative of the left for Mexico."[3]

In a series of essays titled "The Pedestrians of History," Subcomandante Marcos describes the process of reflection that followed the first phase of the Other Campaign and the July 2006 elections. Regarding the Other Campaign, he notes organizational problems that at times allowed political and nongovernmental organizations to hijack the agenda at assemblies. He also points out that intellectuals, social leaders, and others on the left allied with López Obrador largely achieved their goal of "eliminating the voice" of the Other Campaign during the electoral period by blocking access to mainstream media and putting forth a message to discredit the zapatistas.

Those close to Mexican politics will not be greatly surprised at these maneuvers. What is unusual within Mexican political culture is the recognition of mistakes, the public rethinking and "walking and asking" that has come to characterize the zapatista "other politics."

The stolen elections of July 2006 threw off the calculations of the Other Campaign. Instead of facing a scenario that predicted a period of several years in which the people would become growingly disillusioned with a supposedly "leftist" government that did nothing to change the economic model, Subcomandante Marcos wrote that "the political crisis is already here." After selective consultations in July and August 2006, the Other Campaign called to accelerate the pace toward definitions, alliances, and delegation of specific tasks within the movement. Within the base communities, efforts to separate the military structure of the EZLN from the civilian governments moved forward, driven by the fear that power could take advantage of the fact that the public spotlight was focused on the conflict above to strike the EZLN. As Subcomandante Marcos said, the move was "aimed at insuring that the cost of the critique of the political class was 'paid' only by the EZLN and, preferably, by its military chief and spokesperson."

Following the elections, Subcomandante Marcos and an equally mixed female-male group of EZLN *comandantes* set out on a low-profile tour to continue the work of articulating local battles, discovering hidden pockets of resistance, and creating a map of Mexico Profundo, the deep Mexico, the underground Mexico, indigenous and nonindigenous, that will form the basis for new strategies for change. Citing both the pain and the heroism that had been revealed in the first phase of the campaign, Subcomandante Marcos stated the goal of the second phase: to build "a movement that unites the struggles against the system that plunders us, that exploits us, that represses and looks down upon us as indigenous. And not only us indigenous people, but the millions who are not indigenous: workers, peasants, employees, small business people, street vendors, sex workers, unemployed, migrants, underemployed, street workers, homosexuals, lesbians, trangendered people, women, young people, children, and the elderly."[4]

Zapatismo in Latin America: The State-Social Movements Debate

Social movements throughout Latin America are watching with great interest how the Mexican polemic progresses. Latin America has seen how the ascendance of center-left parties in recent years has led to a grand debate on whether this is a boon or an impediment to the aspirations of social movements for more profound change. The center-left governments of Brazil, Argentina, Uruguay, Venezuela, and now Bolivia have plunged those countries into uncertainty about how to relate to the state and the potential of governments to solve core problems of the poor in a globalized economy.

In this debate, the zapatistas provide lessons that cannot be seen as universal but that add theoretical and practical elements. One is their experiments with autonomy, self-government, and rejection of government aid in zapatista territory. Uruguayan analyst Raúl Zibechi notes: "The zapatista movement, since 1994, lit up the continent and the world with an uprising that did not seek to take power but to build a new world. It shows the importance of building autonomies (communal, municipal and regional) from below and more recently seeks to expand a poltical culture throughout Mexico that consists in listening as the point of departure for a non-institutional politics, always from below."[5]

The lack of a finished alternative model, a method the zapatistas call "walking-asking," is also seen by many as positive at this point in history. Colectivo Situaciones in Argentina notes that "public emergence [of the EZLN] on January 1, 1994, opened up a new sequence of struggles against neoliberalism [as a phase of capitalism] that didn't view the worldwide defeat of the socialist project as an obstacle for developing a revolutionary perspective but rather understood the lack of any political model for the future of society as a source of potential, and called for the creation and founding of a renewed notion of democracy, beyond the discourse of legitimating powers."[6]

For its part, the EZLN asserts in the Sixth Declaration, "Latin America, we are proud to be a part of you," and cites the shared political heritage of Che Guevara and Simón Bolivar. The EZLN does not, however, mention any contemporary figures that many associate with a new counterhegemonic movement in the hemisphere. In fact, when the EZLN was invited to the inauguration of indigenous leader and Movement toward Socialism candidate Evo Morales in Bolivia, it did not attend and did not even respond formally to the politician's invitation.

Zapatismo in the World: Decentralized Resistance

> "What we want in the world is to tell all of those who are resisting and fighting in their own ways and in their own countries, that you are not alone, that we, the zapatistas, even though we are very small, are supporting you."
> —SIXTH DECLARATION OF THE LACANDON JUNGLE

Like everything else, zapatismo has developed its own kind of solidarity. The tremendous groundswell of sympathy from abroad following the uprising was channeled into shared political commitments, respectful of the diversity in each person and group's role in society. "Don't copy us; we are not a blueprint or an example to follow. Create your own zapatista movement and we will walk together" was the message from Chiapas. European cities have established zapatista political and cultural centers, and groups and networks exist around the world that set their own agendas and decide on their own actions.

The creation of the Good Government Juntas and the Sixth Declaration both took steps to reorganize the EZLN's relationship with leftist, revolutionary, and antiglobalization forces throughout the world. International solidarity has been a mainstay for the survival of zapatista communities, and the constant contact with other groups oxygenated a movement enclosed in a remote part of southeastern Mexico, adding new political perspectives to their experience.

The reorganization clarified relations. The Good Government Juntas recognized the contribution of international civil society but applied new rules to solidarity by subordinating it to the priorities of the communities. The Sixth Declaration gets down to brass tacks in zapatista foreign relations: It promises to send maize and petroleum products to Cuba, crafts and organic coffee to Europe, and non–genetically modified maize to Ecuador and Bolivia. The quantities are insignificant, of course, but the symbolic point is to construct concrete relationships, outside the nation-state apparatus, that emphasize shared ideological commitments.

For the visitors that have streamed through the mountains and jungles since 1994, the zapatista experience continues to offer vision, hope, enthusiasm. Through praxis, an alternative view of politics and political change develops that at the same time serves to bolster action aimed at rebuilding the links that have been destroyed in people's lives and communities, and creating collective identities that go beyond wounded nuclear families and market-oriented societies and are founded on a sense of shared purpose. This vision has had particular appeal among youth in Mexico, Europe, the United States, and other parts of the world.

This book, *The Speed of Dreams*, is another way of using *la palabra*—the word. Not "The Word" with capital letters as if it were the only one, but instead as a little word that gains its force through the resonance it creates in many minds, in many hearts. It is a collection of musings more than manifestos, where at times the distance between hard-edged political analysis and erotic desire is no more than a paragraph break.

Because, after all, the human struggle for emancipation has many fronts and requires many tools. And building artificial fences between genres or disciplines of thought can be as oppressive as building fences between nations. *The Speed of Dreams* challenges the fences, inside and outside, and does so with humor and skill that convert the standard cult of revolutionary martyrdom into a wry celebration of humanity.

NOTES

1. See Ramón Vera, "Somos Más Que Todos Juntos: Tejido Invisible o la Construcción del Congreso Nacional Indígena," in Hernández and Vera, *Chiapas: La Nueva Lucha India* (Madrid: Editorial Talasa, 1998).
2. *Rebeldía* 35 (September 2005): 1.

3. "Sixth Decalaration of the Lacandon Jungle," Section VI, July 2005.

4. See part 1, section 5, of "The Pedestrians of History." For a complete English translation, see http://encuentro.mayfirst.org/communicado.html

5. Raúl Zibechi, *Dispersar el Poder: Los Movimientos como poderes antiestatales*, Tinta Limón Ediciones (Buenos Aires 2006), page 22.

6. *Bienvenidos a La Selva: Diálogos a partir de la sexta declaración del EZLN*, Colectivo Situaciones, Tinta Limón Ediciones (Buenos Aires 2005), pp. 13–14.

ZAPATISTA HYMN

[Himno Zapatista]

You can see on the horizon,
the Zapatista fighter,
showing the way
for those who follow.

REFRAIN
Let's go, let's go, let's go, forward,
out into the struggle!
Because our native land calls out and needs
all the strength of the Zapatistas.

Men, women, chidren,
will always be our strength;
peasants, workers,
always with the people.

(REFRAIN)

Our people demand
an end to exploitation now.
Our history calls us
to struggle for liberation now.

(REFRAIN)

There will be others,
to take up our task:
to live for our country
or die for liberty.

(REFRAIN)

Himno zapatista

Seventh Anniversary of the Zapatista Uprising

MEXICO, JANUARY 1, 2001

Through my voice speaks the voice of the Zapatista Army of National Liberation;

Indigenous Mexican Brothers and Sisters; Brothers and Sisters of Mexico and the World:

In this, the seventh year of the war against forgetting, we repeat what we are.
We, we are wind. Not the breast that inspires us.
We, we are word. Not the lips which speak us.
We, we are steps. Not the foot that walks us.
We, we are beat. Not the heart that drives us.
We, we are bridge. Not the lands which are joined.
We, we are path. Not the point of arrival or of departure.
We, we are place. Not the one who occupies it.
We do not exist. We only are.
We are seven times. We, seven times.
We, the mirror repeated.
We, the reflection.
We, the hand that is barely opening the window.
We, the world called to the door of tomorrow.

Brothers and Sisters:

Seven have been the reflections which the ancient mirror plucked in the second thousand and the twentieth hundred which have ended.[1]

In the first, we were wind from below, unexpectedly awakened. From very far back in time, fire made memory into breath. Fierce was the look and hard was the path. We, the dead of all times, returned, but this time in order to wrest a place in life.[2] With us, the mountain knelt down on the land and blew our history through the streets where the tyrant dwells.

With the second reflection, we were lips for the word and ears for the heart of the other. The fire remained quiet, and the heart learned to combine by broadening us. With shield and blade made, the word resisted, and betrayal was rendered futile.

With the spark of the third reflection, we made an agreement with the one who governs so that we who are the color and blood of the earth might have a dignified place with everyone. The one who governed did not honor his word. We, however, became a bridge for other worlds. Thus we learned that dignity is not the exclusive property of any nation and that goodness has many faces and speaks many tongues.

It was in the fourth reflection that those who govern and sustain us took the first step. One thousand one hundred and eleven times, our gaze looked upon the solitude we had finally defeated. Nonetheless, the stupidity that governs with blood wanted to block so much gazing. "Acteal"[3] is what we call the place where they will never close their eyes again.

The fifth reflection grew a resistance, making it a school and a lesson that gave direction. There, alongside the one who says he governs, are war, destruction, lies, and intolerance. Here are quiet dignity, rebel silence, and self-governance.

The sixth reflection traveled a lot, five times a thousand, to all the lands of those we call brothers. We asked of them; we listened to them. We held our word so that it would become fruitful and find its time.

The seventh finally came, and with it, the one that was already tottering fell. The other came, with many faces and without face, with names and unnamed, and completely anonymous, not the last, but indeed a ladder. To no one's regret, the one who never imagined that anything would be possible without his tutelage found himself alone and fell.

With the seventh reflection completed, the oldest of the first ones spoke to us through the mouths of our most recent dead. They spoke to us and they told us that seven was the moment to arrive at the earth that grows upward. Where the *señor* who talks a lot and listens little has his palace. Where the reason, which can guide the good law, dwells. Where the other who is different is our equal. Where struggle is the daily bread and salt.

Many times before this 7, it was already written:

> *"Come and see a wild nopal: and there you will calmly see a soaring*
>   *eagle. There he eats, there he grooms his feathers.*
> *And with that your heart will be content:*
> *There is the heart of the Copil*[4] *that you were going to wrench out,*
> *There, where the water turns and turns again!*
> *But there, where it was going to fall, you would have seen amongst the*
> *Crags, in that cave between reeds and rushes,*
> *That wild nopal has sprung up from the heart of Copil.*
> *And there we shall be:*
> *There we shall await and meet all peoples."*

(Taken from the anonymous Náhuatl poem "Fundación of México in 1325"[5])

Brothers and Sisters:

It has now been seven years of war against forgetting. Today, the one who governs says he wants peace. The one who preceded him said the same, but he did nothing about it; instead, he tried to destroy those who defied him by merely living.

That is why we wish to remind everyone, and the ones who are the government, that today there are still many injustices that must be corrected.

Before we return to dialogue [with the Mexican government], we demand the withdrawal and closure of seven military positions. Each of them represents an affront to the desire for peace among the great majority of Mexicans and hundreds of thousands of persons from other countries. The withdrawal of the military barracks at Amador Hernández was a good sign and a first step toward the dialogue table, but six positions remain.

Guadalupe Tepeyac remains.[6] On February 10, 1995, the residents of this community were stripped of everything they had by federal army troops. Preferring exile to serving the occupation troops, the residents of Guadalupe Tepeyac went to the mountain, and they are living there now. For 2,149 days, these indigenous Tojolabal have been forced to live and die far from their lands. A result of the Zedillo betrayal, this injustice continues today under Señor Fox's regime.

For dialogue and peace, on this seventh anniversary of the war against forgetting, we are inviting everyone to accompany us to Mexico City, seat of the federal legislative branch, in order to convince the deputies and senators of the justice represented by the constitutional recognition of indigenous rights and culture.

Brothers and Sisters:

For many years, those who took the government and served themselves with it tried to destroy the first blood of these lands. Seeing how the first seed abounded, they grew tired of fighting with us, with their terrible deaths, and then the great *señores* tried to kill us with forgetting.

But we indigenous resist.

We resist unto death that which killing kills.

We resist unto death that which kills forgetting.

We resist unto death.

We live.

We are here.

So it is ordered by our very first:

Our heartbeat unfolds in the 7.

It shall make echo

And bridge

And path

And place

And home

So that the first heart of this Patria[7] might live,

So that silence shall never again be accomplice to crime,

So that the word is not lost amid the noise,

So that solitude may be defeated and there be no borders for hope,

So that everyone's steps might have a dignified path,

So that no one may be without a place for sowing memory,

So that all may come and go, and that walls be not a jail, but shelter,

So that this country called Mexico may never again forget those whom they are with and for,

So that those who were previously outside and persecuted might be within, and with everyone, being who they are, but with everyone,

So that never again will a First of January be necessary to awaken and return memory,

So that the Mexican indigenous might be indigenous and be Mexican.

So it is ordered by our very first. It is seven now. Now time marks the time of the smallest.

The time of the indigenous of Mexico.

Brothers and Sisters:
We are the zapatistas.
We do not conquer. We persuade.
We are not served. We serve.
We are not a wall. We are a bridge.
We do not dictate the steps. We, we are the most small.

Brothers and Sisters:

It has been seven. This year our steps grow wider. Like seven years ago, but with words instead of fire, the hour of the Mexican indigenous is arriving once again. From them, with them, and for them, today we are once more lifting the flag of indigenous rights and culture. We shall continue fighting, because Mexico shall never again walk forgetting. The Patria will not be synonymous with exclusion again. The morning shall find us alongside all the different ones.

LONG LIVE THE MEXICAN INDIGENOUS!

LONG LIVE THE EXCLUDED OF THE ENTIRE WORLD!

LONG LIVE THE ZAPATISTA ARMY OF NATIONAL LIBERATION!

LONG LIVE OUR DEAD FOREVER!

DEMOCRACY! LIBERTY! JUSTICE!

From the mountains of the Mexican Southeast

THE CLANDESTINE REVOLUTIONARY INDIGENOUS COMMITTEE, GENERAL COMMAND OF THE ZAPATISTA ARMY OF NATIONAL LIBERATION

COMANDANTE DAVID AND SUBCOMANDANTE INSURGENTE MARCOS

NOTES

1. This translation may sound awkward, but it's a direct translation of the original: "Siete han sido los reflejos que el antiguo espejo ha sacado en el segundo mil y el vigésimo cien que terminan."

2. This line evokes one of the EZLN's earliest statements from January 1994 that began, "Here we are, the dead of all times, dying once again, but now in order to live." See http://blog.washingtonpost.com/mexicovotes/2006/06/amlo_the_populist_charmer_1.html

3. On December 22, 1997, fourty-five Tzoztil indigenous people were massacred while praying in their community church at Acteal. Among the victims were sixteen children, twenty adult women, and nine adult men. Seven of the women were pregnant. The victims were members of a local indignous organization, Las Abejas, which is sympathetic with the zapatista movement. The massacre was carried out by an anti-zapatista paramilitary organization.

4. According to the sacred Aztec narrative of the founding of Tenochtitlán, Copil—the nephew of the warrior god Huitzilopochtli—was captured and killed in battle by his powerful uncle. Copil's heart was torn from his chest and buried in the earth. A prickly pear cactus (*tenochtli* in Náhuatl) grew from the buried heart, giving its name to the Aztec city-state—Tenochtitlán.

5. For the complete text of the poem, see http://www.geocities.com/royflores/indigena/tenochtitlan.html

6. Guadalupe Tepeyac, a zapatista support village near La Realidad, was raided by the Mexican Federal Army in 1995 and then became the site for a well-fortified Mexican Army checkpoint. Two members from the EZLN support bases, Compañera Dalia and Compañera Felipe, wrote a letter called "The Story of the Resistance of Guadalupe Tepeyac," posted at http://flag.blackened.net/revolt/mexico/ezln/1997/resistance _encounter.html

7. The word *Patria* generally refers to a person's native land or country. It is often used by Latin American governments to promote varieties of government-centric nationalism. The word's etymology also suggests a patriarchal tradition of inheritance. In this case, however, the zapatistas seem to use *Patria* for another purpose: to reference the indigenous tradition of communal and ancestral connectedness to the Earth.

A Place in This Flag

Compañeros and Compañeras of the Support Bases, EZLN Militants and Insurgents:
Brothers from National and International Civil Society:

Through my voice speaks the voice of the Zapatista Army of National Liberation.

The oldest of our old tell that the very first of these lands saw that the *dzules,*[1] the powerful, had come to teach us fear and to make the flowers wither, and so that the flower of the powerful might live, they despoiled and bled ours.

Our oldest ones say that the life of the powerful has grown withered, that the hearts of its flowers are dead, that they stretched it all to the breaking point, and that they harm and swill the flowers of others.

Our first who came before us tell that the first flower of this soil took the color of the earth so that it would not die, so that the small might resist and guard the seed in their heart, so that, with heart like earth, another world would be born.

Not the very first world, not the world the powerful withered.

Another world. A new one. A good one.

"Dignity" is the name of that first flower, and many steps must be taken in order for the seed to find everyone's heart and, in the great land of all colors, for that world which everyone calls "tomorrow" to finally be born.

Today it is dignity that is raising, through our hands, this flag.

Up until now, there has been no place in it for us who are the color of the earth.

Up until now, we have waited for the others, who take shelter under it, to accept that the history that waves it is ours, as well.

We, indigenous Mexicans, are indigenous *and* we are Mexicans.

But the *señor* who speaks much and hears little, the one who governs, offers us lies and not a flag.

Ours is the March of Indigenous Dignity . . . the march of those of us who are the color of the earth.

Seven years ago, indigenous dignity asked this flag for a place within it.

Then we spoke with fire.

The *dzul*, the powerful, whose color is that of money that makes the earth reek, responded with lies and fire.

But then we saw other voices and heard other colors.

These others did not strike at the day, nor did they affront the night; their throats were not twisted, nor slack their mouths through which they spoke the word.

Brothers are those whose colors unite us.

With them, with the brother colors, today walks the color of the earth.

It walks with dignity, and with dignity it seeks its place within the flag.

The powerful have their government, but their kings are false.

Their throats are twisted, and slack is the mouth of the one who commands and orders.

There is no truth in the words of the *dzules*, the powerful.

Today we are walking so this Mexican flag will know that it is ours, and instead they offer us the cloth of pain and misery.

Today we are walking for a good government, and they offer us discord.

Today we are walking for justice, and they offer us charity.

Today we are walking for liberty, and they offer us the slavery of debts.

Today we are walking for the end of death, and they offer us a peace of deafening lies.

Today we are marching for life.

Today we are marching for justice.

Today we are marching for liberty.

Today we are marching for democracy.

Today we are marching for this flag.

Our voice does not reach alone to open the ears of the *señor* of much tongue and little ear, the one who governs.

There are many voices walking, so that the one who reigns will be silent and listen.

All the steps are needed, all the voices necessary.

With everyone, this is what we want: a place in this flag.

These steps of ours have a name; the voice we speak has a word: the March of Indigenous Dignity, the march of the color of the earth.

Compañeros and Compañeras of the EZLN:

For seven years we have resisted attacks of all kinds. They have attacked us with bombs and bullets, with torture and jail, with lies and slander, with contempt and forgetting. But we are here.

We are rebel dignity.

We are the forgotten heart of the Patria.

We are the very first memory.

We are the dark blood that illuminates our history in the mountains.

We are those who struggle and live and die.

We are those who say: "For everyone, everything; for us, nothing."

We are zapatistas, the smallest of these lands.

We salute the peoples who command and care for us. We salute their wise wisdom and their intelligence.

We salute our insurgent combatants, who are today keeping vigil in the mountain so that no harm will come to those of us who are today momentary light.

We salute all the zapatistas who today are speaking through our voice and walking in our steps.

We salute the zapatistas, the smallest of these lands.

As our ancestors resisted wars of conquest and of extermination, we have resisted the wars of forgetting.

Our resistance has not ended, but now it is not alone.

The hearts of millions in Mexico and on the five continents are now accompanying us.

Our steps go along with them now.

With them we shall go to the capital of the nation, which raises itself on our back and despises us.

Compañeros and Compañeras:

Señor Vicente Fox wishes to name these steps we are walking today.

"It is the march of peace," he says, and he keeps our brothers imprisoned for the worst crime in the modern world: dignity.

"It is the march of peace," he says, and he maintains his army occupying the homes in Guadalupe Tepeyac, while hundreds of Guadalupe children, women, old ones and men remain in the mountains, resisting with dignity.

"It is the march of peace," he says, and he plans to convert our history into merchandise.

"It is the march of peace," he says, and those close to him add in a low voice: "of lies."

That is what he says. But our steps speak other words, and they are true: This is the March of Indigenous Dignity, the march of the color of the earth.

Brothers and Sisters:

Today, February 24, 2001, Mexican Flag Day, we, the zapatistas, are beginning this march, the March of Indigenous Dignity, the march of the color of the earth.

Our steps are not alone.

With us go the steps of all the Indian peoples and the steps of all the men, women, children, and old ones in the world who know that all the colors of the earth have a place in the world.

We, the Mexican indigenous, have painted this flag.

With our blood, we painted the red that adorns it.

With our work, we harvested the fruit that paints it green.

With our nobility, we painted its center white.

With our history, we included the eagle devouring the serpent,[2] so that Mexico would name the pain and the hope that we are.

We made this flag, and nonetheless we have no place in it.

Today we are asking those above, who are power and government:

Who is the one who denies us the right that this flag might finally be ours?

Who is the one who flaunts forgetting, ignoring that, as we are the color of the earth, we gave color and protection to our flag?

For almost two hundred years this land has walked, calling itself nation and Patria and home and history.

For almost two hundred years it has been harvesting our blood and pain, our misery, so that Mexico can be Patria and not a disgrace.

For almost two hundred years we have been, and are, outside the house we built from below, which we liberated, and in which we have lived and died.

¡YA BASTA![3] says—and says again—the very first voice, we indigenous who are the color of the earth.

We want a place.

We need a place.

We, who are the color of the earth, deserve a place.

A dignified place in order to be what we are, the color of the earth.

No longer the corner of forgetting.

No longer the object of contempt.

No longer a source of disgust.

No longer the dark hand that receives charity and cleanses consciences.

No longer the embarrassment of color.

No longer the shame of language.

No longer sentenced to humiliation or death.

That is why this is the March of Indigenous Dignity, the march of the color of the earth.

And this march begins today, when the moon is new, so that the earth may finally harvest justice for those who are the color of the earth.

And today begins a march that is not only ours, but that of all of those who are the color of the earth.

The greatest and very first tremor begins today, the memory of that which made us nation, which gave us liberty and gave us greatness.

The March of Indigenous Dignity begins today, the march of the color of the earth.

With those who are the color of the earth, other distant colors are paying attention to what is beginning today:

The possibility that the other can be so without shame.

That the different might be equal in dignity and in hope.

That the world might finally be the place for all and not the private property of those who have the color and filth of money.

A world with the color of humanity.

Brothers and Sisters:

Those who are the government are laboring today to make this the march of the lying peace.

Those who govern are not alone in their lies.

Along with them are the steps of those who want our steps dead and the color of the earth forever dead.

Along with them are those who will not allow any color in the world that is not the color of money and its misery.

He who is the government yells and flails much; his breath smells of lies, and he wants us to take the fear he teaches as our own.

He wants to do us harm and to suck our strength.

But it will be in vain.

Along with all the colors, the flower of the color of the earth—which we are—will have a tomorrow, because it will have a flag.

With it and because of it, we, the Indian peoples, will at last have . . .

Democracy!
Liberty!
Justice!

From the mountains of the Mexican Southeast

CLANDESTINE REVOLUTIONARY INDIGENOUS COMMITTEE, GENERAL COMMAND OF THE ZAPATISTA ARMY OF NATIONAL LIBERATION

NOTES

1. *Dzules* is a Mayan word associated with people of Spanish or Creole origin. A Mayan poem in *The Book of Chilam Balam of Chumayel* offers a more detailed description: "The *Dzules* arrive. Their beards are red . . . They come from the East . . . They are white men" (translation by Suzanne D. Fisher).

2. An eagle perched on a cactus devouring a snake refers to the ancient indigenous prophecy in which the Aztec people were told by their deity Huitzilopochtli that they would find their promised land where they found an eagle on a nopal cactus eating a snake. Legend has it that, after wandering for hundreds of years, they found the eagle on a small swampy island in Lake Texcoco. This new Aztec home was named Tenochtitlán (meaning "Place of the Nopal Cactus"), the city that was to become Mexico City. The image of the eagle, cactus, and snake is the primary symbol on the current national flag of Mexico.

3. "*¡Ya Basta!*" translates as "Enough already!" and has been one of the zapatistas' primary slogans since 1994.

Recipients of the World, Unite!

MEXICO, JANUARY–FEBRUARY 2001

Sir, Madam, Young Man, Young Lady, Boy, Girl:

If you happen to find yourself reading . . . excuse me. I should begin again. Our best wishes to you. I am writing to you in the name of the men, women, children, and old ones of the Zapatista Army of National Liberation.

Now. If you happen to find yourself reading these lines, it is owing to two reasons that have to do with each other—or which are mutually, reciprocally related—or with coming and going, as when one says the one goes with the other and vice versa. It's like a table leg, which is a table leg because there is a table that has legs, and if it didn't have those legs, the table would fall down and it would just be a table on the floor (or in the mud, because here the floor and the mud are reciprocal, if you follow me). Or also like the paddle for a raft, which is a paddle because there's a raft that needs paddles (I already know that there are rafts without paddles, but I'm talking about a raft with paddles, so stop your rhetorical games). I know! I've come up with a verrry illustrative example! It's like a recipient who has a sender, because if there is no sender, then the recipient would be very sad, like Gabriel García Márquez's Colonel, whom no one wrote to. And if the sender doesn't have a recipient, then the sadness would be no less. To whom would he write? Fine, I think we're beginning to understand each other. So forget about legs, tables, paddles, and rafts, and concentrate on the sender and the recipient. *Ya?* Fine, there's no problem here, because the mystery has been cleared up: you are the recipient, and we are the senders. The only unknowns remaining are the two reasons that will explain why you are reading these lines. Great, I've already forgotten them. But I'll remember in just a second . . . Mmm . . . mmm . . . Oh, yes! Here they go:

It so happens that, as you most certainly already know (if not, you wouldn't be reading this letter), we *zapatudos* have decided to send a delegation to the Mexican capital. The purpose of the trip is to engage in dialogue with the legislators in order to achieve the constitutional recognition of indigenous rights and culture. Fine, it so happens, then, that we are like tables without legs, like rafts without paddles, like senders without recipients (and vice versa), like knights without horses, like_____ without _____ (you fill in the blanks. This is an interactive.com letter). In short, we need your financial help to carry out this trip, which, it is quite clear, has no other goal than peace with justice and dignity. And so there are the two reasons: We are writing you because we trust you, and because we know you will understand what we are so confusingly saying to you (I hope).

Don't worry, you can help with anything. We are accepting all the currencies of the world and the galaxies (they always come from honest people like you), and we will not speculate with the exchange rate.

What? All that talk just for that? Perhaps, but we didn't even know, for example, if this letter was going to reach you, because we don't even have anything for postage stamps. And just think how sad you would be if you were a recipient without a sender . . . Right? Good, and so we are putting our trust in you.

Vale. Salud, and, as no one has, of yet, said, *Recipients of the world, unite!* (or was it "senders"?).

From the mountains of the Mexican Southeast

SUBCOMANDANTE INSURGENTE MARCOS

Devils of the New Century

To the boys and girls of Guadalupe Tepeyac in Exile

"Miguel Kantun de Lerma, is Canek's friend. He writes him a letter and sends him his son, so as to make a man out of him.

Canek answers him, saying he will make his son an Indian."

—Ermilo Abreu Gómez, from
Canek: History and Legend of a Maya Hero

This is not a political text. It is about zapatista boys and girls, about those who were, about those who are, and about those who are to come. It is, therefore, a text of love . . . and war.

Children can make wars and loves, have meetings and misunderstandings. Unpredictable and unwitting magicians, children play and go about creating the mirror that the world of adults avoids and detests. They have the power to change their environment, and to turn, for example, an old frayed hammock into a modern airplane, into a *cayuco*,[1] into a car in order to go to San Cristóbal de Las Casas. A simple doodle, traced with the pencil, which La Mar[2] provides them with for these occasions, gives them the artillery for recounting a complicated history in which "last night" can encompass hours or months and "in a bit" could mean "the next century," in which (is anyone in doubt?) they are heroes and heroines. And they are, not just in their fictitious histories, but also, and above all, in the fact of their being indigenous boys and girls in the mountains of the Mexican Southeast.

Nine are the circles of Dante's inferno. Nine the prisons that confine indigenous children in Mexico: hunger, ignorance, illness, work, mistreatment, poverty, fear, forgetting, and death.

In the indigenous communities of Chiapas, childhood malnutrition reaches 80 percent. Seventy-two percent of the children do not even manage to complete the first year of primary education. And, in all indigenous homes, boys and girls, from the age of 4, must cut down and carry firewood in order to eat. To end those cycles, they must fight hard from the time they are children. They must fight fiercely. Sometimes they must make war, a war against forgetting.

I have said that this is a text about boys and girls who were. Since it is "ladies first" with horses and gentlemen, I will begin with this memory, which hopes not to be repeated.

I am talking about "Paticha." I have spoken of her before, and, through her, about all the neverborn of Mexico's cellar.

Much has been written, for better or worse, about the causes of the zapatista uprising. I am taking advantage of the opportunity here to propose another point of departure: the zapatista neverborn, that is, a good part of the zapatista children. It is the rare indigenous family in Mexico that does not lose three or four children before they reach the age of 5. Thousands in the mountains of the Mexican Southeast, tens of thousands in that attic abandoned by the reigning "modernity": the Indian peoples, the native inhabitants of these lands.

When she was less than 5 years old, Paticha died of a fever—a high temperature burned up her years and her dreams.

Who was responsible for her death? What conscience was enriched with her disappearance? What doubt was resolved? What fear overcome? What bravery flourished? What hand was armed? How many deaths like Paticha's made possible the war that began in 1994?

These questions are important, because the death of Paticha was a hidden death. I said before that she was not even considered to be deceased, since, as far as the powers were concerned, she was never born. And there were more who were neverborn, more like Paticha who died in the darkness of the night, in the forgetting.

Nonetheless, obscurities like her death are those which illuminated the imperfect night of this country, in 1994.

I.

And, speaking of fertile obscurities, there should be a scientific explanation for how a dark cloud can give way to the powerful glitter of a lightning flash. There are many ideological explanations, but even before a man realizes, in ceremonies, books, and colloquiums, the miracle of a night storm, obscurity has already created clarity, night has birthed day, and the fiercest fire has already become a fresh wind.

And so it is that this is an especially dark dawn. Nonetheless, to the surprise of the most brilliant meteorologists (or simply in order to contradict them), rays were streaming through the eastern horizon, dry branches of light falling from the luminous tree that the night conceals behind itself. The night is a black mirror in that way, a shadow breaking into yellow and orange. A mirror. The frame is formed by the four cardinal points of a horizon of up and down, trees and gray darkness. A mirror seen from the dark side of the mirror. The dark side of a mirror, warning of what is behind it, promising it . . .

All histories are peopled with shadows. In zapatista history, more than a few have been outlined by our light. We are full of silent footsteps that have, nonetheless, made the shouts possible. Many have kept silent so that the movement may go forward. Many vague faces have allowed other faces to be made clear. Someone said that zapatismo was successful because it knew how to weave nets. Yes, but behind ours are many weavers who have skillful hands, who have great ingenuity, who take prudent steps. And, while an incandescent and brief light is raised above every knot of the rebel net of the world's forgotten, they are still weaving new strokes and embraces in the shadows . . .

And speaking of weavers and of embraces, I tore myself away from La Mar's tepidness and freshness in bed and got up to take just a short walk, in this dawn in which February repeats its delirium and announces the arrival of the March hare. And just there, where the mountain is the land of the night of below, some fireflies were becoming excited by the humid warmth that announces a storm.

A small shadow was sobbing close to the hammock. I drew near until I was able to distinguish a little man, squat, mustachioed, and rather advanced both in years and in weight. Two beat-up wings made of red cardboard, a pair of small horns, and a tail that ended in an arrow point made him look like a devil.

Yes, a devil. A fairly ill-treated devil. A poor devil . . .

"*Poor devil* like hell!" the diminutive figure muttered.

I wasn't intimidated. Even though my head and legs were telling me to run far away from there, I am the man of the house (okay, of the hut, but I believe you understand me), and I should not be abandoning La Mar, who is the woman of the house. After so many Pedro Infante movies, I have been steeled to protect the house—since *Martín Corona* and *Here Comes Martín Corona*, I must check my impulse to take flight. Well, at least not without warning La Mar, who is, as I said previously, the woman of the house of which I am the man of the house.

And so I did not attempt any "strategic withdrawal," and, as I always do when seized by terror, I lit my pipe and started talking. I made some idle comments about the unsettled weather, and, seeing that there was no response, I ventured . . .

"Since you're listening to what I think . . ."

"You might as well be shouting," responded the little man. "And don't call me little man!" he screeched. "Luzbel, call me Luzbel," he hastened to interrupt my thoughts.

"Luzbel? That sounds like, like . . . Isn't that the angel who rebelled in pride against the Christian God, and as punishment they sent him to hell?" I said.

"That mess. But it wasn't like that. History, my unhappy mortal, is written by the victors, God, in this case. What really happened was a problem over salaries and work conditions. A union, no matter how angelic it might be, was not part of the divine plan, so God opted to invoke the exclusion clause. The mercenary scribes took it upon themselves to vilify our just fight, and so we went . . ." said Luzbel, getting comfortable and sitting down at the foot of a *huapac*.[3]

At that point I realized how small he actually was, but I didn't say anything. I suppose my silence encouraged him to continue talking, and that is what in effect happened, because Luzbel began recounting a history— fitting for a devil—of terrible horror and cruelty. His story seemed to be tragedy, comedy, or part of war.

II.

Luzbel remained silent for a bit. Except for the stars above and those below (the fireflies), nothing else was about in the outside night. I lit my pipe again. More to take advantage of the light from the lighter and to look at the figure of the little devil than out of a desire to smoke. Nine circles of smoke came out of the pipe. When the last of them had dispersed, he spoke.

The history Luzbel told me might wound the sensibilities of the good and of conscientious Christians, something that is not very advisable, especially during these times when the high clergy is struggling to turn back the clock of history. But, as I am not competing for indulgences—and I have already known the hell that the Powers impose on the poor—I have nothing to worry about. In any case, I have done my duty by warning the readers, and in reminding them that I am merely transcribing what Luzbel told me, to wit:

"The God of the rich and of the ledgers was very satisfied with the Free Trade Agreement, the steps toward the first world, economic globalization, and all that rubbish, which seemed more the product of hell than of the divine, even though we devils wouldn't be capable of such horrors.

"Anyway, what happened was that God had assigned, as he should, a guardian angel to care for each of the children of the Free Trade Agreement generation. There aren't many angels, and working as a guardian angel for children pays very poorly. But someone called Gabriel, a pro-management leader—an archangel, to be more specific—forced the wage scale in order to meet the quota. There were some protests, but not many. And so each child of the Free Trade Agreement would have his guardian angel.

"But it so happened that you, the zapatistas, decided to rise up in arms on that First of January in 1994 and change everything, even divine memory. Because it just so happened that God had not remembered about the indigenous children. It's not that he hadn't kept them in mind or that he was thinking of getting rid of them—he was simply unaware of their existence.

"The God of the rich is an employer like any other, but very old-school. And so he believed that, while neoliberalism was seeing to dispatching all zapatista children to another world, he would have to fulfill his divine duties and assign a guardian angel to every zapatista child.

"But because there were no longer any guardian angels available, he then began rehabilitating devils. To achieve this rehabilitation, he forced us to sign a humiliating commercial treaty that was damaging to hell's diabolical sovereignty. Hell had been having economic problems, and someone called Saint Peter had taken advantage of our difficulties in order to grant us financial credit that had, as one might imagine, a diabolical clause.

"Anyway, the fact was that God was able to have the infernal workforce at his disposal, under unfair conditions, and without it affecting the migration restrictions imposed on us devils if we cross the celestial border. Without our being aware of it, we were suddenly second-class employees, under orders from the one who had expelled us." Luzbel broke off, in what seemed like a sob. Then he continued . . .

"And so, from the extraterritoriality of his financial power, God put us to work as 'guardian angels' of those who had been forgotten in the first-world euphoria, the indigenous children. And now, instead of inciting good consciences to sin, perverting innocent souls, sponsoring business leaders, 'inspiring' the PAN governor of Querétaro, advising Bishop Onésimo Cepeda, or devising Fox's postelection campaign, now we are taking care of the children of the cellar, under miserable working conditions.

"So now we are 'guardian devils'!

"Really! At a miserable salary, God (who, one mustn't forget, is God of all creation, even of hell) is forcing us to guard zapatista children. And to think that there are still those who boast of divine goodness!"

III.

Luzbel was silent for a moment, and I took advantage of the pause to scribble a few words. And believe me, I was surprised myself. So much so that I immediately wrote Don Eduardo Galeano some lines, so that he could recount this in one of his books:

Date: The beginning of the third millennium

Don Galeano:

In neoliberal Mexico at the beginning of the twenty-first century, zapatista children are so poor that they do not even have guardian angels. Instead, they have devils with them, a little guardian devil.

During the stormy nights in the mountains of the Mexican Southeast, the children are praying: "Little Guardian Devil, sweet companion, do not abandon me, neither by night or by day," and so it goes . . .

Vale. Salud *and* nada de mate.

The Sup.

(End of letter to Galeano.)
Okay, I'm not going to drive the editorial staff crazy with any more dialogue punctuation, so I'll just recount what made this "guardian devil" unhappy.

IV.

It happened that it fell to Luzbel to be head of a squadron of "guardian devils." I don't know how many squadrons are necessary to guard all the zapatista children (who are a goodly number), but an infernal, horrific, diabolical job fell to Luzbel. He had to care for Beto, Heriberto, Ismita, El Andulio, Nabor, Pedrito, Toñita, Eva, Chelita, Chagüa, Mariya, Regina, Yeniperr, and, lastly—horror of horrors!—Olivio and Marcelo.

When it fell to him to be Beto's "guardian devil," Luzbel became desperate. It wasn't the hectic life of this child-soldier who with his slingshot challenged an armored vehicle—a Hummer with grenade launchers—as well as a "Black Hawk" helicopter of the NAFTA generation. Nor was it his tireless climbing up and down hills and ravines, looking for firewood for his house. No, what exasperated Luzbel (and made him ask for a custody change) were Beto's questions:

"How far away is the big city? Is it bigger than Ocosingo? How wide is the sea? What is so much water for? How do the people live who live in the sea? How big is the slingshot that can kill a helicopter? If a soldier's house and family are someplace else, why does he come to take away our houses from us and to persecute us? If the sea is as big as the sky, why don't we turn them upside down so that the government helicopters and planes will drown?"

Questions such as those were what motivated Luzbel's change in work. But it didn't go any better for him, because then they assigned him to care for Heriberto.

"It was terrible," Luzbel confessed. "That child hates school as if he were a secretary of public education, and the teachers as if he were a promanagement union leader. He prefers to play and to hunt for sweets and chocolate. You should see how you have to run after him when he hears a chocolate wrapper!"

After Heriberto, Luzbel went on to care for Ismita.

Luzbel recounted to me that one day Ismita had some trouble with Marikerr (that's what the girl is called, don't blame me), because he said she had broken a branch off Ismita's *nance* (fruit tree). "But how could she break it if she was so small and the tree so big?" Luzbel asked him. "She grabbed it and broke the branch," Ismita said and looked reprovingly at Marikerr, who was bent on a children's assault on the "Aguascalientes" store. The assault had been organized by Luzbel because, he said, "the children should prepare themselves for anything, even to govern." Ismita must be about 10 years old, but chronic malnutrition has granted him the stature of a 4-year-old child. Ismita compensates for his lack of physical height with moral greatness. He not only pardoned Marikerr for breaking the branch of his *nance*, he also offered her some soft drink and cookies he had gotten during the assault on the store.

"No one shares," Ismita told Luzbel when the latter had objected.

Generosity does not provoke the passion of hell, so Luzbel went to care for Andulio.

After walking a great distance, Luzbel reached the home of Andulio, he of the brilliant smile. We met Andulio during those terrible days of the 1995 persecution. May was a hot wind then, burning days and nights, and Andulio stayed up all night in a tree, trying to imitate a turkey with his song. He didn't approach us often, but we discovered he had accepted us when, one afternoon, he asked for a record player and, to the rhythm of a *corrido*, he began dancing. La Mar asked him then, in front of a poster, where the Sup was. Andulio hesitated and, a split second later, turned around and pointed to me. The Sup couldn't be in the poster and in the doorway at the same time, and so, as he pointed me out in the flesh, he repeated his philosophical materialism. I had forgotten to mention that Andulio was born without hands; a genetic malformation left stumps on the ends of his arms.

"That child may not have hands, but he does have a smile that's too angelic," Luzbel said, justifying a new change. And so he went to be with Nabor.

It wasn't any better with Nabor. With only three years behind him, Nabor nonetheless had a libido that would put Casanova to shame. Luzbel could do nothing but blush, and he immediately went to another community. And so he went to Guadalupe Tepeyac in Exile.

In this Tojolabal community, dislocated from their homes by the Mexican Federal Army, it fell to him to be "guardian angel"—excuse me, "guardian devil"—for Pedrito. Pedrito is a Guadalupe child born in exile. When the First Intercontinental Meeting for Humanity and against Neoliberalism opened, his mother gave birth to him. With three years behind him, Pedrito is friends with Lino, another Guadalupe child. Lino was born on February 9, 1995, and he was barely a few hours old when he was expelled from his home by soldiers of the Mexican Federal Army.

Returning to Pedrito, it so happens that he didn't want to go to school. I had already threatened to take his case to the community assembly, but no way. I warned him that if he didn't go, I was going to denounce him in a communiqué directed to the people of Mexico and to the peoples and governments of the world. Pedrito just looked at me, shrugged his shoulders, and said, "Send it—I don't even know how to read." La Mar defended him, saying that he was barely 3 years old, and Pedrito just stared at her, sighing, in love. But that is another history; we are now with Luzbel taking care of Pedrito.

It so happened that Pedrito decided to play horses. You are correct if you imagine that it fell to Luzbel to be the horse. And you are correct if you guess that Luzbel resigned.

"That child made the belt too tight," he said in justification.

V.

After Pedrito, Luzbel decided to switch to a more mild-mannered gender, and he devoted himself to caring for a zapatista girl, Toñita. Luzbel wasn't bothered by Toñita's tendency to look down on love, which "hurts a lot" (to my outrage, he characterized her tendency as "healthy"). Not by that, nor by having been dressed up like a doll by a Toñita who was determined to cut off his wings.

"You wouldn't have been the only one to have had them cut off," I said resentfully.

The guardian devil put up with all of that, but he could not tolerate that constant breaking and mending of teacups that is the life of zapatista girls.

And so Toñita's guardian devil resigned and went on to care for Eva. He didn't last long. When he was watching *School for Vagabonds* for the umpteenth time, he fell asleep, and Eva took the opportunity to embroider little flowers and "Viva the EZLN" on his wings. The shame forced Luzbel to immigrate.

After Eva came Chelita, a dark-haired girl of 6 or 7, with black eyes like stars. The same thing happened to Luzbel that happened to everyone: when Chelita looked at him, he was left frozen (not an adequate temperature for a devil). She made him fly through the skies (not an advisable direction, given the expulsion, et cetera), and she let out an "*¡Ave María Purísima!*" that was quite certainly too much. Luzbel felt as if they had ripped out his soul—excuse me, as if they had ripped off his wings—when they took him away from caring for Chelita and ordered him to be with Chagüa.

Chagüa, as her name indicates, is not called "Chagüa," but Rosaura, but no one calls her by her name. She must be about 8 years old. In a small gang of warlike children, the one who is the leader is not a boy, but a girl, Chagüa. She is the first and fastest in climbing trees to catch cicadas, she is the fiercest and most accurate in fights with stones and mud, she is the first to throw herself into the fray, and, up until now, no one has ever heard her ask for mercy. However, when she approaches us, something strange happens: Chagüa is a tender and sweet girl who embraces La Mar and asks her to tell her a story or to fix her hair, or she just hugs her and stays quiet, sighing from time to time.

Luzbel did not resign because of the confusion provoked by Chagüa's tender fury, but because he was hit on the head with a rock during an altercation, and the bump it created on his skull left him with a third horn that did not suit him at all. And so Luzbel went to care for another girl, Mariya.

Mariya must be about 7 years old, and in her village she is the one who has the best aim with a slingshot. We discovered this, we and the village, during one of our travels through those lands.

After walking for several hours, La Mar and I collapsed under the lintel of a hut. We had not even caught our breath when Húber, Saúl, Pichito, and an indeterminate number of children of equally indeterminate names arrived. All of them had brought their slingshots, and they asked to have a contest to see who had the best aim. Mariya was already sitting next to La Mar, and she didn't say anything. Without getting up, I organized the turns, and I indicated that they should set up a can ten steps away. Each and every one of them took a turn, and the can remained in place.

When I asked if everyone had had their turn, La Mar said, "Mariya hasn't."

To everyone's outrage, Mariya joined in and borrowed a slingshot.

A murmur of disapproval went through the group of boys (I wasn't among them, not because I wanted to be seen as a feminist, but because I didn't have the strength to get up and support my gender).

Mariya gave the boys a swift look of contempt, and that was enough to keep them quiet. A silence reigned, which had little to do with mockery and much with expectation.

Mariya drew the slingshot, closed one eye as mandated by slingshot manuals, and fired. The can leaped with a metallic crash.

Mariya and La Mar broke into cries of jubilation: "The women won!"

We boys were left shocked, contrite, and open-mouthed. "Don't worry," I told them in consolation, "We'll have the contest without Mariya next time." I don't think I convinced anyone.

Luzbel has been educated in the old school—that is, in his view, slingshots are not for girls. And so he had what we call a "crisis of macho conscience" when Mariya won in the rough and (formerly) masculine sport of firing at cans with a slingshot. And that is how Luzbel came to go elsewhere.

In other communities, Luzbel looked after Regina, a child of about 9 or 10 years of age who behaved as if she were 30. Mature and responsible, Regina is sister and mother to her little brothers and sisters, bodyguard of the insurgents, the best tortilla maker in the barrio, and a sun when she smiles. Despite his experience in infernal burnings, Luzbel resigned when he couldn't tolerate the scorching of his fingers when he turned the tortillas on the stove.

"It wasn't the burns," Luzbel told me, "but that I had to get up at 4 in the morning to make the fire, grind the maize, and make the tortillas. And that was just to start the day."

Lacking sleep, and with his fingers burned, Luzbel went to care for Yeniperr.

Yeniperr is an excellent example of the bird who conquers the machine. When the helicopters make low flights over the community, Yeniperr chases them with questions. In the face of such fierce projectiles, the warlike machines withdraw, and Yeniperr continues to flutter about amid lovebirds and hummingbirds. When Yeniperr flies, she often gets lost and has nothing to fear, unless Capirucho and Capirote are anywhere close by.

Luzbel lasted barely a few days with Yeniperr. According to what he told me, it wasn't the fear of government helicopters and planes that made him ask for a change in work.

"I've never been into this flying. That's why I'm a fallen angel," Luzbel said, rubbing his backside.

They should never have done it, but it so happened that they assigned Luzbel, owing to a lack of personnel, to care for two children: Olivio and Marcelo—that is, Capirucho and Capirote.

VI.

Olivio, or the self-styled "Sergeant Capirucho," has confessed to me that, when he is big, he is going to be "Sup." "And you, Sup, what are you going to be?" he asked me, knowing that the fulfillment of his aspirations would leave me without a job. "Me?" I asked, in order to gain time, "I'm going to be a horse, a child horse, and I'm going to go there, very far away," I said, pointing to an indefinite point on the horizon. "You can be sergeant," Olivio consoled me, while he discovered a little turtledove who was fluttering about, oblivious to Capirucho's hierarchical aspirations and to the fearsome slingshot hanging from his belt.

"Corporal Capirote," Marcelo answers when they ask him what he is called. Without any shame whatsoever, and perhaps making use of the military privilege of his rank, he went wherever he pleased and would start looking for sweets and chocolates, recounting incredible stories, or he would set about spying on the women while they were bathing.

Olivio and Marcelo, Capirucho and Capirote. These two boys play at confusing each other when they recite poetry. Four poems make up their repertoire, and they always devise ways to mix them up with each other. The result? It doesn't matter if, in the end, they get a piece of candy or a chocolate, if they can sketch "little marbles" or go hunting, always unsuccessfully, for rooks. Capirucho and Capirote believe that there is no better remedy for lack of love than a good rook to eat together.

These two dwarfs—excuse me, children—have overcharged batteries. They are about 7 years old, and they broaden their radius of activity every day. They pursue the *erello* (a species of salamander up to a meter in length) among thorns and *acahuales*,[4] but they don't get very close to it. They took Luzbel from one end of creation to the other, so that his wings were full of thorns and scratches; they filled his pockets with pebbles (for the slingshot); and they "fried his brain" with their constant blather. The nights were not enough to allow for Luzbel's recuperation, and he would have to follow behind them early in order to go with the boys to fish for snails, crabs, and shrimp; to go to the coffee fields; to be stung by ants, bees, or by any of the community's "wild" animals; to kick a deflated ball; to eat everything they found within their grasp and their height; and to listen to them recount exploits that had never occurred. But what depressed Luzbel the most was that they made him a target for practicing with the slingshot.

Luzbel is old now; his age goes back to the beginning of time. I am saying this not so you will pity him, but so you will understand him. I know Capirucho and Capirote, and I am certain that the work of caring for them would leave God himself (who, incidentally, is not young either) exhausted.

That is why Luzbel did not surprise me when he told me he was definitively resigning from taking care of zapatista boys and girls.

"I'd be better off going to Kosovo or Rwanda or anyplace else where the U.N. is carrying out its mission to promote wars," Luzbel said, sitting up. "There's bound to be more calm there."

And as he got ready to walk away, he added:

"Or the diocese of Ecatepec[5] or the upper echelons of Mexican business, which is turning into the same thing. There is corruption there, lies, outrages, theft, and all those evils more appropriate for orthodox devils such as myself."

I understand Luzbel's desperation and despair. I am certain he would rather not have tried to organize an angelic union if he had known that, in the course of time, he was going to have to follow after these children.

By the light of a firefly, I added a postscript to the letter to Eduardo Galeano:

> *P.S. Which Provides More Details*
> *Don Eduardo: In the indigenous mountains of Mexico, God is*
> *not alive. Nor the devil, not even if they pay him . . .*

It was almost dawn now, and so I said farewell to Luzbel and returned to La Mar.

VII.

The majority of the indigenous boys and girls of Guadalupe Tepeyac in Exile were born and raised away from their homes. There is another political party in the Mexican government, and these children continue to be held hostage (now by those self-styled "promoters of change") in order to force us to surrender. What has changed for these children? The history of their native town seems like a story to them, it is so far away in time and space that it seems to them to be a very long trip to return to it. Complicated and petty political calculations and stupid pride are what expelled them from their village and are what prevents them from returning to what belongs to them.

Not only in this nomadic village, but in all zapatista communities, boys and girls are growing up and becoming youngsters and adults in the midst of a war. But, contrary to what might be thought, the teachings they receive from their communities are not about hate or vengeance, nor are they about desperation or sadness. No, children in the mountains of the Mexican Southeast grow up learning that "hope" is a word that must be pronounced collectively and they learn to live with dignity and respect for difference. Perhaps one of the differences between these children and those from other areas is that these children learn, at a young age, to see tomorrow.

More and more boys and girls will continue to be born in the mountains of the Mexican Southeast. They will be zapatistas and, as such, they will not have guardian angels. We, "poor devils," will have to care for them until they are big. Big like us, the zapatistas, the smallest . . .

From the mountains of the Mexican Southeast

SUBCOMANDANTE INSURGENTE MARCOS

NOTES

1. A *cayuco* is a small boat, similar to a canoe.

2. *La Mar* has two meanings here. The word means "the ocean" in Spanish. La Mar is also the name of the woman with whom Marcos shared his hut and his bed.

3. A *huapac* is a tree native to Central America and southern Mexico. According to an EZLN communiqué dated January 3, 1998, branches from the *huapac* tree are used as long sticks for confronting the Mexican military and other forces of neoliberal repression. *Huapac* is also the name of a region in San Luis, Petén, Guatemala. This area was recently purchased by Petro Latina, a multinational company that is currently privitizing, extracting, and selling Latin American oil and gas resources.

4. An *acahual* is a species of sunflower found in abundance throughout Mexico.

5. Ecatepec is a municipality of the state of Mexico and the metropolitan zone of Mexico City, Mexico. Ecatepec is home to the Catholic cathedral and diocese.

On Indigenous Language

FEBRUARY 25, 2001, JUCHITÁN, OAXACA

Indigenous Brothers and Sisters of the Oaxaca Isthmus:
Brothers and Sisters of the Democratic Teaching Profession:
Student Brothers and Sisters:
Employee, Worker, and Campesino Brothers and Sisters:
The People of Juchitán:

Many years ago now—since that time the earth has insisted on making its procession around the sun almost eighteen times (when only a handful of men and women made up the EZLN, numbering no more than the fingers on our hands)—we had gone out hunting, impelled by hunger. Old Antonio was carrying his old *chimba*,[1] and he was walking attentively, looking at the ground, scanning the tracks in the earth and the sounds of the jungle.

As he explained it to me, we were trying to listen for the purring of the pheasant in season, the drumming of the *censo*'s teeth, the hoarse bellow of the *saraguato*,[2] or the thunderous rejoicing of the spider monkey.

To be honest (and I really should be honest, because I am speaking to you, my brothers), the one going hunting was Old Antonio. I was merely accompanying him with my first clumsy steps in the mountains of the Mexican Southeast. As far as my limited experience went, all the sounds were the same and meant nothing to me. The only sound I could absolutely identify was that of my stomach growling, and I understood its significance very well: hunger.

"A good hunter is not a good marksman, but a good listener," Old Antonio told me. "Everyone hears, but *listening* means discovering what every sound means."

I should say that at that moment the day had almost been vanquished by the night, and the limited horizon of the nearby hills was now beginning to be encroached on by harsh nocturnal bites.

And so we were seated at the base of a ceiba, "The Mother Tree," "The Support of the World," according to Old Antonio.

Perhaps because of that, the fire that lit Old Antonio's rolled cigarette and word illuminated far-off yesterdays. Old Antonio waited for me to light my pipe, and, taking the necessary memory from the common smoke, he recounted to me:

THE HISTORY OF THE FIRST LANGUAGE OF THESE LANDS

"The oldest of our old peoples tell that the first gods, not the very first, not those who birthed the world, but others, were a tad lazy.

"And it so happened that a goodly amount of the world had already been birthed by the very first gods, and the men and women of maize, the true ones, were already making the rest.

"And so these gods became lazy because they had no work and they wanted only to play and to dance. They were just fooling around, and they went about lifting up the women's skirts with their wind and tangling up the men's feet so they would fall down.

"Then the men and women of maize, the true ones, took courage, and they held an assembly in order to look into this problem.

"Since the men and women of maize were already set in their thinking that *he who governs, governs obeying,* they called these gods to the assembly.

"Because no matter how godlike the gods were, they still had to respect the agreements of the collective, which is what they then called *the agreement by everyone for the common good*.

"And so it came to pass that the gods arrived and they began making little jokes, and the assembly scolded them, and then these prankish gods remained quiet.

"When the women of maize spoke, they were very fierce, because the gods had been lifting their petticoats with their winds.

"When the men of maize spoke, they, too, were very fierce, because the gods had been moving around on the ground like snakes and tangling up their feet, so that they would fall down.

"And so in the assembly the men and women determined the crime of the gods, and they reached an agreement that the gods would have to clear the collective's field of rocks.

"And so the gods went to clear the rocks out of the field, yet they said, 'What? But we're gods, even though not the very first,' and they became seriously angry, and they picked up a large rock and went and smashed the house where the men and women of maize, the true ones, were guarding the first word, the one that sees behind and ahead if one knows how to listen to it.

"After this most unfortunate occurrence, the gods ran very far away, because they knew they had done a great wrong.

"Then the men and women of maize made their assembly to look into what they should do about this great wrong that had been done to them, because they knew that collectively they were indeed able to resolve great wrongs.

"And, without the first word, the men and women of maize would remain deaf to their history and blind to tomorrow, because the first word was the root of the past and the window to the path to come.

"Nonetheless, the assembly of the men and women of maize, the true ones, were not afraid, and they began seeking thoughts and they made them into words, and with them other thoughts and other words were born. That is why they say in Zapotec,[3] *Diidxá ribee diidxxá*—'Words produce words.'

"This is how they reached the agreement to guard their memory with great care and to make their word language. But they wondered what would happen if they forgot their language or if someone stole that memory from them, and then they also agreed to etch it in stone and to guard it well where their thoughts told them to do so. And some guarded the stone etched with memory in the mountain, and others gave it to the sea to guard.

"And now the men and women of maize were content.

"But it came to pass that those gods became lost, and, in exchange for finding their way, they recounted their mischief to the false god of hard excrement,[4] which is what money was called at that time.

"And then this false god visited evil on the land of the men and women of maize, the true ones, and he undertook to have the men and women of maize forget the very first word and thus remain deaf to their history, which was thereafter called 'forgetting,' and blind to their tomorrow, which is what they thereafter called 'being at a loss.'

"The false god knew that if the men and women of maize forgot their history and lost their way, their language would die, little by little, and, with it, the dignity it held.

"The false god of hard excrement—money—used, and uses still, much force and many traps. He did everything to destroy the language of our very first.

"But he always failed. And it happened that the men and women of maize, the very first, every so often would go to the mountain and to the sea to read what the stone etched with memory said.

"And so they resisted the attacks of the false gods of money, and that is why we indigenous have mountain and sea close to us.

"So that memory will not fail us, so that we shall not become lost, in order to have 'tomorrow.'"

Old Antonio ended his history when he threw the seventh cigarette made with his roller on the ground. I asked, "And what happened to those second-rate gods?"

Old Antonio berated me: "They were hardly second-rate. The ones now are second-rate: money and power.

"Well, it happens that nothing is known of them anymore, and so the indigenous always thought they might return to make their mischief.

"The women lengthened their petticoats and drew them together more at the hem so that the wind could not play with them.

"Men and women also walked slowly, attentive to the path they trod. That is why we indigenous walk looking down, but those who do not know this say that it's because we were defeated or because we are saddened by what we are. It is not true. We were never defeated: the proof is that we are here.

"Nor are we made sad by what we are.

"If we walk looking down, it is because we go watching our path carefully, in order not to trip, in order not to forget, and in order not to be at a loss."

Indigenous Brothers and Sisters of the Oaxaca Isthmus:
People of Juchitán:

The struggle for the recognition of indigenous rights and culture is also the struggle for respect for our language, for its safekeeping, for its greater glory.

Time and again, the false god of money has wanted to take our language away from us, because he knows that without it, we will no longer be ourselves, and then they will be able to take everything away from us.

When we say we demand the recognition of indigenous rights and culture, we are saying, among other things, that we demand the recognition of our language.

There are words in it that speak of the history we are, yes, but that also speak of tomorrow.

One must know how to listen to these words, and one must know how to brandish those words so that others might be born who will speak of a time yet to come.

Perhaps that is why the powerful do not want the constitutional recognition of our indigenous rights, because in that way they would have to recognize and respect our language, which is something they fear.

If we learn to listen, we would find in our language that for us, the indigenous, tomorrow means being as we are and being with everyone.

Long live indigenous language, and may those who walk and speak it live forever!

Democracy!
Liberty!
Justice!

From Juchitán, Oaxaca

CLANDESTINE REVOLUTIONARY INDIGENOUS COMMITTEE, GENERAL COMMAND OF THE ZAPATISTA ARMY OF NATIONAL LIBERATION

NOTES

1. The word *chimba* has various meanings throughout Latin America. Here, it is most likely being used in reference to a homemade firearm.

2. A *saraguato* is a variety of monkey that lives in the tropical jungles of the lowland region of southern Mexico. The saraguato's howl is so loud it can be heard more than five miles away.
3. Zapotec is an indigenous language, one of eleven spoken in the Mexican state of Oaxaca.
4. "The false god of hard excrement" sounds strange, but this is a direct translation. It is a reference to pre-Colombian mythology/religion in which evil gods, those that persecute humans, are named after diseases and human ailments. They represent sources of human pain, hardship, death. In this case, it is also a joke. Money = hard shit.

The Tree That Is the Mexican Nation

FEBRUARY 26, 2001, OAXACA, OAXACA

Indigenous Brothers and Sisters of Oaxaca:
Brothers and Sisters from Oaxacan Civil Society:
Brothers and Sisters from the Democratic Teaching Profession:
Student Brothers and Sisters:
Religious Brothers and Sisters:
Worker Brothers and Sisters:
Campesino Brothers and Sisters:
Employed Brothers and Sisters:
Brother and Sister Bank Debtors:
Neighborhood Brothers and Sisters:
Housewife Sisters:
Small and Middle-size Business-Owner Brothers and Sisters:
Professional Brothers and Sisters:
Artist and Intellectual Brothers and Sisters:
Mexican Brothers and Sisters Who Have Joined in on this March for
    Indigenous Dignity:
Brothers and Sisters from Other Countries Who Are Accompanying Us:

Through my voice speaks the voice of the Zapatista Army of National Liberation:

We wish to express our appreciation to the people of Oaxaca for having treated us as brothers in struggle ever since we entered the lands of this state.

From Tapanatepec to this capital city of Oaxaca, we have received welcome and support from the population, primarily from the indigenous.

The affection you have shown us—and which we believe we do not deserve—has moved us deeply.

We, the zapatistas, the smallest, those who live in the last corner of the Patria, have been made large by the strength Oaxaca has given us.

I hope that one day we shall be able to respond with even a small part of the devotion and care we have received.

We have learned a lot from you.

We have marveled at your organizational capacity, your fighting spirit, your sincere pride in the roots that give you color and name in these lands.

The Oaxacan indigenous make every indigenous, in any part of Mexico, feel proud of being indigenous.

Knowing you up close has done nothing but confirm our conviction that the national indigenous movement is enjoying, right now, one of its best moments.

We hope that what all we indigenous of Mexico seek will indeed now be possible and that the Indian peoples of these lands will have an important place here.

Thank you, people of Oaxaca!

The zapatistas salute you!

Brothers and Sisters:

For many days now, all Mexican indigenous and all honest men and women of Mexico have been listening to a multitude of stupid remarks about our indigenous selves and our March of Indigenous Dignity.

We all know whose voice speaks such idiocies.

We know because we have been hearing it for entire centuries.

It is the voice of the one who brought deception and lies to our lands.

It is the voice of the one who imposed death and misery as indigenous state policy.

It is the voice of the one who yesterday used the whip and the sword to conquer our land and who today uses modernization to do away with us.

It is the voice of stupidity.

It is the voice of ignorance.

It is the voice of arrogance.

It is the voice of the one who thinks he is superior to and stronger than us.

It is the voice of the one who cannot conceive of any way of living other than at the cost of our deaths.

It is the voice of the one who says that the indigenous peoples will make progress only when they cease being indigenous.

The one who uses that voice, who threatens and persecutes us, is so blindly stupid that he considers a region of the country to improve when the number of indigenous residing in it decreases.

Look at any government analysis and you will see that is how they classify the country.

In addition, they have the cynicism to declare: "This region has already improved because there is now a greater mestizo population than before, and there are fewer indigenous than before, or fewer people, that is, who speak an indigenous language."

And then we ask:

In the mind of the powerful, the country develops more as more indigenous disappear?

The development and modernization plans that the government praises, are they nothing more than plans to exterminate the indigenous?

Do they, the powerful, believe that they are deceiving us and that they are doing something new?

Because their ways of thinking and methods are not at all different from those with which they tried to exterminate us five centuries ago, a war of destruction and looting they called "civilization."

"Civilization" is what they have called the destruction of our society and our culture, the massacres of the indigenous, the seizure of our lands and wealth, the humiliation of and contempt for our culture, the mockery of our language, rejection of our clothing, disgust for our dark color, which is nothing other than the color of the earth.

Now the same war against us has taken another name, and it is called "modernization."

But the powerful forget that those who wanted to exterminate us no longer exist, and we are here.

We, the Indian peoples throughout Mexico, are living—no, we are *surviving*—the most shocking conditions of poverty.

The powerful say, "If they are in poverty, it is because the indigenous are lazy; they run away from work and waste what little they have."

"Lazy," they say to those who raised buildings, cities, great works, entire societies, which were the marvel of the whole world before they were destroyed.

They say we run away from work and yet few, very few, are the communities in which the voluntary work of the collective is added to each individual's work.

They say we waste what little we have, but they have been the ones who have looted our riches; who have made the water filthy with the fecal waste of money; who have destroyed the forests to traffic in wood; who used up the minerals of our mountains; who imposed crops that wore down and damaged the land; who promoted the planting, trafficking, and use of drugs; who fattened themselves with our blood-made work.

They are, in short, the ones who have destroyed our house with their ambition and force.

And now they blame us for not having a good house.

And so we would like to ask those powerful ones:

How many rich and powerful indigenous are there in this country?

How many indigenous are owners of industries that contaminate the water and damage the environment?

How many indigenous have enriched themselves with the covert and brazen destruction of trees?

How many indigenous-owned mines?

How many indigenous have agro-industries?

How many indigenous are leaders of drug cartels?

How many indigenous have made themselves powerful by exploiting other indigenous?

How many indigenous have devoted themselves to persecuting, torturing, imprisoning, corrupting, deceiving, and assassinating other indigenous?

No, it has not been we who have destroyed our house.

It has been them, the man-eaters, those with two faces and sticky fingers, the fathers of the lies.

Before they arrived, dealing out death and destruction, the wealth of the earth was not lusted after.

Because the wealth of the earth was the wealth of those who inhabited it, and the one who stole it was stealing only from himself.

And that stupidity of stealing the wealth of the earth is what they are offering us as "modernity"?

And then they call us, the indigenous, "ignorant."

Did we not care for the land before they arrived?

Did we not care for our mother?

Did they not turn her into a prostitute, young and carefree before, and today dried-up and old?

Did we invent the methods of overexploitation of natural resources?

Are we the ignorant ones?

Does being wise mean doing everything possible to destroy the only house one has?

Up until now, no one has discovered another habitable planet, so this is the only one we have.

Perhaps words have changed quite a bit.

For us, the one who seeks his brothers' and his own ruin is stupid and ignorant.

For us, the one who seeks his own progress, and that of others, is wise and intelligent.

But they, nonetheless, keep us away from technical and scientific knowledge.

Why?

Only because our color is the color of the earth?

Or because our indigenous way of thinking would lead us to using that science and that technology to care for the earth and to improve oneself in the only way possible—that is, with the peoples we are?

Because our sense of community collides with their individualist sentiment?

Because it is easier to deceive, loot, and defeat one person, who is alone, than the many who are united collectively?

The powerful call us "ignorant" and say that our beliefs concerning work and collective benefit are the products of foreign, communist, and subversive ideas.

Perhaps they are unaware that collective work and benefit already existed in these lands long before the foreigner "discovered" us.

The powerful call us "lazy" and say that our hands are good only for making crafts.

Perhaps they are unaware that, since before their long war against us, we have been making things they could not even imagine.

So great are, and were, our works.

The powerful do not think, but they have money to buy someone to think for them.

And then those purchased thoughts say: "The indigenous want to return to the past. They want to exchange the tractor for the hoe, scientific knowledge for magic, paid work for slavery, to promote the buying and selling of women, to exchange free elections for *caciquismo*."[1]

No, we do not want to return to the past.

We lived in the past.

We have hoes and not tractors.

We don't even have schools or universities to be shut down, strangled by their budgets or by the Federal Preventive Police.

Our women are fighting for their gender rights, and not just now.

We have slavery, and the powerful are the masters.

We do not want to return to the past.

But nor do we want to continue living and dying in it.

We want science and technology, not in order to kill the earth and good thinking, but to make it better and richer.

We want to free ourselves from the slavery that the powerful subject us to, but not in order to make ourselves equal to him, to be stupid and evil.

We want to live in the present and to build a future with everyone.

What we do *not* want is to cease being indigenous.

We are proud of being so.

We are proud of our language.

We are proud of our culture.

We are proud of our clothing.

We are proud of our struggle as women and as indigenous and as poor.

Proud of our methods of governing ourselves.

Proud of our methods of working.

Proud, in short, of being the color of the earth.

That is why we want indigenous autonomy.

Not in order to separate ourselves from the country and to add one more poor country to the ranks of those that already exist in abundance.

Not in order to return to a past that we have not even been able to leave.

We want it in order to care for the earth with wisdom.

In order to make it rich and prosperous for us and for the entire country.

In order to avoid their looting it and destroying it and killing it.

In order to be able to work individually or collectively, but always taking care that one person does not profit to the detriment of others.

We want indigenous autonomy.

Not in order to create fundamentalist despots.

Not in order to replace the color of the earth with the color that is now humiliating us.

We want it so that the majority is valued all the time, and not just every once in a while.

So that the *one who governs, governs obeying.*

So that governing is a responsibility for the collective, and not a means of enriching oneself at the cost of the governed . . .

So that political and economic success no longer subjugate he who is different and no longer force him to cease being what he is.

Not so that everyone will be like us.

But, rather, to be ourselves, respecting and being respected by the other who is different from us.

Those of us who are the color of this Mexican earth want indigenous autonomy, and we are going to achieve it.

No longer will anyone have any plans or programs that do not take us into account.

No Plan Puebla-Panama nor Trans-Isthmus Megaproject, nor anything that means the selling or destruction of the house of the indigenous, which—it must not be forgotten—is part of the house of all Mexicans.

No longer will the color of one's skin, or the way of dress, or the language with which one clothes words, or the way one governs, or the relationship with land be a reason for persecution, contempt, or marginalization.

We want indigenous autonomy because it is the only visible means of preventing this country from ending up in pieces and squandered.

Because it is the only visible means for saving Mexico from those who are proposing to finish it off as a nation and who are trying to turn it into a high plateau of nostalgia of what was and what could have been.

For Mexico—that is why we want indigenous autonomy.

Brothers and Sisters:

The oldest elders of these Oaxacan lands tell that the first man was born from a tree. The first man grew, and he took good care of the tree that was his mother and father. Then one day he realized the tree was head-down, and he worked to put it where its roots should be, and thus the tree grew and never had to dry up and never had to die.

We are all part of the tree that is the Mexican nation.

But some of us are leaves, others flowers, others trunk, others branches, others fruit, and others root, which nurtures and provides a foundation.

We are different, then, but we have one single life.

Tomorrow is possible only if it is inclusive.

But this country is upside-down. It has been determined, for almost 200 years, to destroy its roots. How will it be nurtured and have a foundation if it destroys its roots?

The entire country must be turned right-side up, so that it can grow and never dry up and never die.

And so, if anyone asks what this March of Indigenous Dignity, the March of the Color of the Earth, wants, here is the answer:

To turn the entire country right-side up so that it will finally be the tree where all of us who are different will have a common tomorrow as a nation, which is also the only possible tomorrow.

A tomorrow when all Mexicans, including the indigenous, will have . . .

Democracy!
Liberty!
Justice!

Salud, Mixtec Brothers and Sisters!
Salud, Cuicatec Brothers and Sisters!
Salud, Zapotec Brothers and Sisters!
Salud, Triqui Brothers and Sisters!
Salud, Chocholtec Brothers and Sisters!
Salud, Mazatec Brothers and Sisters!
Salud, Mixe Brothers and Sisters!
Salud, Chinantec Brothers and Sisters!
Salud, Huave Brothers and Sisters!
Salud, Zoque Brothers and Sisters!

Salud, Chontal Brothers and Sisters!
Salud, Tacuate Brothers and Sisters!
Salud, Nahua Brothers and Sisters!
Salud, Ixcatec Brothers and Sisters!
Salud, Amuzgo Brothers and Sisters!
Salud, Chatino Brothers and Sisters!
Salud, Black Brothers and Sisters!
Salud, Oaxacan Brothers and Sisters!

From the dignified indigenous lands of Oaxaca

CLANDESTINE REVOLUTIONARY INDIGENOUS COMMITTEE, GENERAL COMMAND OF THE
ZAPATISTA ARMY OF NATIONAL LIBERATION

We, the Indigenous, Are the Guardians of History

FEBRUARY 27, 2001, TEHUACA (TEHUACÁN), PUEBLA

Indigenous Náhuatl, Popoloc, Mixtec, Totonac, and Mazatec Brothers and Sisters Who Are Gathered Today in Tehuaca (Tehuacán), Puebla:

Brothers and Sisters of Tehuacán Civil Society:

We want to thank all of you for the honor you are extending us by receiving us on your lands.

We, the zapatistas, know the heroic role that the indigenous of these lands have played throughout the history of Mexico, and that is why we are all now trying to understand our history as indigenous. And that is why we have to search in our memory.

The indigenous of our lands tell that, a very long time ago, men were not men, but rather birds of many colors, of varied songs and of high flights.

And these birds did many things.

For example, in its beginning, the world was gray, and these birds touched the things in the world and gifted them with color.

There were others, for example, who let loose their song wherever they went. They were so beautiful that they turned into other birds and flew from one place to the other, singing songs that birthed new songs. In its beginning, the world was mute, and these birds gifted it with music.

And there were some others who made trails and walked them over and over, so they would become paths, and in that way no one would lose the route or destination. Because in its beginning, the world had neither route nor destination in its flight.

And other birds were born that broke the silences and gave sound and language to the world. Because in its beginning, the world had neither sounds nor silences; there was only noise.

With the world painted, the paths drawn, the silences and sounds set, the birds made themselves into men so the thousand colors with which the world had been painted could be seen, so the paths could be trod, and so the silences could be heard and the sounds and words could be thought, felt, spoken, and lived.

Because our most ancient say that words are sounds that are lived, not the noise that fills.

Brothers and Sisters:

We are indigenous, and many people ask who the indigenous are.

We, the indigenous, are the guardians of history.

In our memory we guard all colors, all routes, all words, and all silences.

We live so that memory might live and, living, not be lost.

We, the indigenous, are those who are grounded in the color of the earth and who paint the first colors of the world's multitude.

We, the indigenous, are those who signal the time from which we came, our past living today so that it will not be lost and so we will not be lost.

We are also those who note the tomorrow that is to come. We use all the colors to draw attention to the common destiny of all.

We, the indigenous, are those who make and unmake the silence with words that look toward both sides. That alone is what history is.

And if we were high-flying birds of many colors before, now we indigenous guard that memory so that human beings might once again be the great color that all colors contain, the singers of all sounds, and those of many and high flights.

And if someone asks who we indigenous in Mexico are, all of us shall respond:

We, the indigenous, are both those who walk the path and who are the path itself. We are those who are walking today so that Mexico shall not become lost, and so that it can then become, with everyone and in enough time, the nation of all colors, the one of multiple songs, the one of high flights.

Thank you, Brothers and Sisters of Tehuacán!
Long live the Mexican indigenous!

Long live all Mexicans!

From Tehuacán, Puebla

CLANDESTINE REVOLUTIONARY INDIGENOUS COMMITTEE, GENERAL COMMAND OF THE ZAPATISTA ARMY OF NATIONAL LIBERATION

All That Remains Is to Choose

Indigenous Brothers and Sisters Gathered Today in Puebla de los Angeles,
    Puebla:
Brothers and Sisters of Pueblan Civil Society:
Worker and Campesino Brothers and Sisters:
Brothers and Sisters from the Barzón:
Town of Puebla:

Through my voice speaks the voice of the Zapatista Army of National Liberation.

We wish to say that it is an honor for us, the zapatistas, to be able to set foot on the dignified soil of Puebla.

Because flowering from Puebla's soil is the wise struggle of the indigenous, of workers, of campesinos, of teachers, of students, of housewives, of neighbors, of honest religious men and women, of professional persons, of the employed, of small- and midsize-business owners, of debtors, of committed artists and intellectuals, of homosexuals and lesbians, of women, and of old ones, youth, and children.

So much wisdom and so much dignity will undoubtedly make us, the zapatistas, better.

That is why we have come to Puebla—to learn from you.

Thank you for allowing us to be students of the great lesson you give those who walk this land during these times.

Thank you, Puebla!

We wish to pay our regards to the memory of two people from Puebla who died some time ago in order to give voice to those of us who had no voice—Julieta Glockner and Francisco Cabrera Huerta.

Brothers and Sisters:

We have reached the gates of the Valley of Mexico.

From here forward, our march, the March of Indigenous Dignity, the March of the Color of the Earth, will begin to make a circle around the valley where the powers reside.

This circle will extend from these Pueblan lands, tracing their arch of dignity by the states of Tlaxcala, Hidalgo, Querétaro, Guanajuato, Michoacán, and the state of Mexico, and it will be closed in the lands of our general Emiliano Zapata, in the state of Morelos.

With the circle complete, we shall make our entrance into Mexico City.

The final circle of the March of Indigenous Dignity begins, then, in Puebla.

That is why we have chosen, at the beginning of this final circle, to speak a word that looks very far ahead.

A word that might not, perhaps, find its true meaning immediately.

A word that requires time and wind in order to find its place in the heart of everything that we are.

A word that speaks tomorrow.

A word that comes from very far back and, because of that, walks very far ahead of us.

A word that is greater than us and that, nonetheless, must be spoken.

A word that is spoken only together, that demands that everyone live it in order for it to be able to be pronounced.

"Dignity" is how this word speaks.

And dignity is a bridge.

It needs two sides that, being different, distinct and distant, are made one by the bridge, without ceasing to be different and distinct, but ceasing, then, to be distant.

When the bridge of dignity is extended, the *We* that we are speaks, and the *Other* that we are not speaks.

The One and the Other are on the bridge that is dignity.

And the One is not more or better than the Other, nor is the Other more or better than the One.

Dignity demands that we be *We*.

But dignity is not only us being Ourselves.

The Other is necessary for there to be dignity.

Because we are always Ourselves in relation to the Other.

And the other is Other in relation to ourselves.

Dignity is, therefore, a looking.

A looking at Ourselves, who are also looking at the Other looking at themselves and looking at us.

Dignity is, therefore, recognition and respect.

Recognition of what we are and respect for that which we are, yes, but also recognition of what the Other is and respect for what the Other is.

Dignity is, therefore, bridge and looking and recognition and respect.

Therefore, dignity is tomorrow.

But tomorrow cannot be if it is not for everyone, for those who are *We* and for those who are *Other.*

Dignity is, therefore, a house that includes the Other and Ourselves.

Dignity is, therefore, a house with one single floor, where we and the other have our own places—which is what life is—and nothing else, but the same house.

Therefore, dignity should be the world, *a world where many worlds fit.*

Dignity, therefore, does not yet exist.

Therefore, dignity is yet to come.

Dignity, therefore, is struggling so that dignity might finally be the world.

A world where all worlds fit.

Therefore, dignity is, and it is to come.

It is the path to travel.

Dignity is tomorrow.

Brothers and Sisters:

When we speak of indigenous dignity, we are speaking of what we are as indigenous, and of what the other is who is not like us.

Indigenous dignity is not dominating the other who is not indigenous, subjecting him, destroying him, humiliating him, ignoring him, forgetting him.

Indigenous dignity is a bridge that needs the other side to extend itself to, an other in order to look at him and to be looked at.

When we speak of the March of Indigenous Dignity, we are speaking of the indigenous who see ourselves as indigenous, without shame, without embarrassment, without sadness, without the death of what we are.

When we speak of the March of Indigenous Dignity, we are also speaking of the indigenous, whom we are, being looked at, which is to say respected by, the nonindigenous.

When we speak of the March of Indigenous Dignity, we are also speaking of the indigenous, whom we are, seeing and looking at the nonindigenous, which is to say we are respecting them.

The March of Indigenous Dignity cannot be carried out just by the indigenous.

The March of Indigenous Dignity must be the march of the indigenous and the nonindigenous.

Only in that way shall we be able to build the house, which is what they used to call the world, where all of us, who are equal because we are different, fit.

Brothers and Sisters:

The most ancient indigenous tell many stories about the world's past.

One of them tells us that, in the beginning, everything in the world was immersed in darkness and obscurity and silence and sadness.

The people of that time had already become accustomed to living in that way.

But then the time arrived when time began to walk, and the sun and music were born.

In those times, the sun would sometimes cover itself so it would not get cold, and, since the sun's covers had many holes, pieces of light pierced through.

Our earliest forebears called it "day" when the sun went about undressed, and "night" when the sun was protected from the cold by the many-holed covers.

"Stars" are what they called the many holes that pierced the night.

Along with the day and night, music arrived, and with it, joy.

When that happened, our forebears also recount how there were people who were afraid, and who set about digging deep holes or surrounding themselves with large rocks.

They did that so their eyes, accustomed to the dark and to the obscurity, would not be hurt by the light.

They did that so their ears, accustomed to the noise of sadness, would not be hurt by the joy of music.

Our earliest forebears also tell how one of the people, hidden in her hole, finally died of sadness, and how another died when the great rocks of arrogance fell on top of her, instead of protecting her.

There were, however, also those who learned to see and to listen, not to the new, because it was already there, but to the good.

Because the world teaches that things are not good or bad in themselves, but rather, when we touch them, we make them either good or bad.

The new man is, in reality, the same old man, but he is made good through touching things with dignity, with respect.

Brothers and Sisters:

The March of Indigenous Dignity has caused some to set about digging deep holes or to trying to protect themselves by closing themselves off, surrounded by large rocks.

The fact is they are accustomed to not looking at the other who we are.

And, therefore, when we make ourselves light from the shadow we are, we hurt their eyes, and our word is music that wounds their ears.

But there are those who are learning to see the good that is this march.

They are learning, and we are learning, to look and to look at ourselves, to speak and to listen, to speak to ourselves and to listen to ourselves.

They are learning, and we are learning, then, to be dignified.

And so all that remains is to choose: Either we learn together to be dignified, or we shall die and be outraged alone.

Our most sincere condolences to those who choose not to look at us and not to listen to us.

Long life to those of us who, all together, are learning to live.

Because to live without dignity is to be quite dead.

Salud to ourselves and to the other!

Salud, Puebla!

Democracy!
Liberty!
Justice!

From Puebla de los Angeles, Puebla

CLANDESTINE REVOLUTIONARY INDIGENOUS COMMITTEE, GENERAL COMMAND OF THE ZAPATISTA ARMY OF NATIONAL LIBERATION

NOTE

1. *Caciqiusmo* originates from the word *cacique*, meaning a local political boss. Some of the first *caciques* were indigenous chiefs purchased by colonial authorities to implement Spanish hegemony. Over time, *caciques* gained a reputation for corruption, for being tools of colonialism. *Caciquismo* also refers to the political effects of ninteenth-century Bourbon Restoration, a conservative reactionary movement and resurgence of Roman Catholic hegemony. Modern-day *caciques* work in favor of the power of political parties and multinational corporations.

It Is the Hour of the Word

Brothers and Sisters of the National Indigenous Congress:
Brothers and Sisters of National Civil Society:
Brothers and Sisters of International Civil Society:

Through my voice speaks the voice of the Zapatista Army of National Liberation.

When the seventh month of last year came to pass, the rains were beginning to prevail in the mountains of the Mexican Southeast. We then went to speak with our foremost ones, and we said:

"The one who said he was eternal and fixed has fallen. He was brought down by the brother, the sister, the one who has a name and a face but, being small, seems to be without a name and a face, the one who is like us, the one who is the color of the earth and all colors, the one who is below, the one who, like us, is denied tomorrow.

"In the place of the one who fell is one who seems to be nothing but the same. He talks a lot and says that everything has changed. But our debt is still unpaid, since the very first of these lands and this history are still an unresolved matter, a closed issue to the ones who are the government, both old and new.

"We see brothers and sisters from other lands, of varied languages, their ears attuned, their word generous and friendly. Their heart is great today, although the one who hears little and speaks a lot tries to make it small.

"Thus we are asking you, Brother and Sister Chiefs, what we who are governed by you should do."

"It is fine," said our main ones. "Let us go question our elders. You wait here and, as always, sharpen the machete and the word—which is to say, sharpen hope."

We did not wait long, because the foremost ones returned soon. They returned and looked to see if the edges of the machetes were good, and then they gave the word:

"We have now spoken with our eldest ones, and they gifted us with a word that says what and how and where and why.

"Then, open your hearts, *guerreros*, zapatista women and men, our Votán[1] Zapata, guardian and heart of our people."

Our eldest ones said to us:

"It is the hour of the word. So then, put the machete away, and continue to hone hope. Seven times around the mountain, seven the river that runs down it. It speaks with seven of our deaths. Seven times it makes a ship of the sea. Seven times it closes your hut. Seven times it dresses the color of the earth and seven times reveals the word. Because seven is coming now, and seven is the *caracol*[2] for the one who feels it strongly. Because now the spiral is coming which can be a path within and without, a route and a hope.

"With that done, prepare your feet which we gave you, and open your attentive eyes and your ears. Become our word once again. You will no longer be *you*, now you are *us*. Do not be upset by everything the one who speaks a lot says. It is merely noise, rude music. Nothing will be given to you that is not fought for by us. Nothing will be presented to us that we do not take hold of. Nothing that we do not struggle for will live with us. And so walk the path, walk the land of the other who is, like us, from the land that is, like us, all the colors of the earth.

"Walk, walk and speak. Take our face now. Take color and the word from the earth. Take our voice now. Go with our gaze. Make yourselves our ear in order to listen to the word from the other. You shall no longer be you, now you are us.

"Go down from the mountain and seek the color of the earth that is in this world. Walk for seven days, and raise the color from the earth. Seek the other colors that speak with the one of the earth. Learn to speak to the heart, which walks in the other. Be small in front of the weak and, along with him, you shall become great. Be large in front of the powerful, and do not tolerate our being humiliated in silence, which shall increase in your journey.

"With the humble, be humble. With the arrogant, do not tolerate anything that smacks of mockery or dishonesty. Do not forget your mission. And always keep your distance from that which pushes you away. Speak, thus, to the *we* who are the collective color and which is throughout Mexico. Make room for all those colors that coexist with the color of the earth.

"Forget about borders if the word is sister to the other. Be suspicious of those who speak a lot, and listen attentively to those who wisely remain silent. Call the great collective, which the nation demands, to be with us. Join dreams and sorrows. Walking, join tomorrows. Become a great echo of those who, in Indian lands, are silent.

"Do not be silent concerning any pain, no matter how distant; make it yours and speak. Tell the other he is brother and she is sister. Seek a place for the color of earth and hope to bear fruit. See the house of the Purépecha,[3] older brother and great sister nobility. Use the word with respect with him.

"Greet those who govern those lands obeying. Give our embrace to all those peoples who give pride to the color of the earth, and ask him respectfully for permission to speak. If there is no permission, lower your head and be silent. If there is permission, lower your head and speak.

"Speak to your first heart. Ask for shelter and hospitality there. There you will find support and the other who is us in color and in tomorrow.

"Arrive, then, on the seventh day, arrive and seek from the color of the earth the mutual dignity that has arisen. Join sorrows and hopes seven times. Listen seven times to what the word says of he who is the color of the earth and hope.

"If necessary, seven times seven shout and seven times seven remain silent. Open your heart then and, with it open, listen to other words. Then, let the word speak of those who are us, in the color of the earth that we are. Do what we tell you—one part speaks and the other is silent—so that it can be said in the land that grows upward, which they call city.

"Tell them, then, who we are, who are speaking through your mouth. With that done, let the word, which is to come, follow. The word that is tomorrow. That which seeks a place for those who have the color of the earth, which is hope.

"Call on all to struggle for that which belongs to everyone and harms no one. A dignified place for those of us who are the color of the earth, hope."

Brothers and Sisters:

We are indigenous, and we represent the Zapatista Army of National Liberation, which rose up in arms against the supreme government seven years ago and which holds high its banners of democracy, liberty, and justice for all Mexicans.

We came from a race of *guerrero*[4] indigenous. The blood that runs through us is from the ancient Mayans. It is that which gives us life and which arms us. We are *guerreros.*

We are the last of a generation of men and women who have been collectively entrusted with being guardians and heart of our peoples.

As *guerreros*, we are beings of the sword and the word. With both, we must safeguard the memory which our peoples are and which allows them to resist and to aspire to a better tomorrow.

As *guerreros*, we were prepared in the sciences and the arts, in honor and war, in sorrow and hope, in silence and the word.

We are guardians; we do not take anything away from anyone, nor do we permit anyone to take anything away from us. If they shout, we shout. We respond softly to those who speak softly to us. If they attack us, we defend ourselves. And those who insult or threaten us receive our contempt, and we wield the word like a sword.

As *guerreros*, we are as those who order us, those whom we serve with honor, for whom we give life or death, who give us a face and who name us, those who told us to come here, those who are our strength, even though they still speak in the shadows.

We are those who are commanded by all the colors that are in the color of the earth. We are the smallest. They call us zapatistas. We are asking for a place among you, for us *guerreros*, a space for the ear and the word.

Salud, Indigenous Brothers and Sisters!
Salud, Purépecha Brothers and Sisters!
Salud, Mexican Brothers and Sisters!
Salud, Brothers and Sisters of All Colors!

May the color of the earth, which we are, live forever!

Democracy!
Liberty!
Justice!

From the Purépecha community of Nurio, Michoacán

CLANDESTINE REVOLUTIONARY INDIGENOUS COMMITTEE, GENERAL COMMAND OF THE ZAPATISTA ARMY OF NATIONAL LIBERATION

NOTES

1. Votán is a principal deity within Mayan culture and religion. Some historical records identify him as an ancient leader and holy man. Votán also represents the third day of the Mayan Tzeltal Calendar and corresponds to "the heart of the people." Subcomandante Marcos first references Votán Zapata in a communiqué dated April 10, 1994. In another communiqué, dated December 1994, Subcomandante Marcos relates Old Antonio's history of the Mexican Revolution, which unites Mayan deities—Ik'al and Votán—together with the historical revolutionary Emiliano Zapata. In this story, we are introduced to the concept of *caminar preguntando*, to "walk questioning."

2. *Caracol* is the Spanish word for "conch" or "spiral-shaped shell." The *Caracoles* are also zapatista community centers, where public services are provided, committees and cooperatives are centered, and contact with international civil society is mediated.

3. The Purépecha are an indigenous people from the northwestern region of the Mexican state of Michoacán.

4. *Guerrero* means "warrior" in Spanish.

To the Indigenous National Congress

People of Nurio:
Purépecha Brothers and Sisters:
Brothers and Sisters of the National Indigenous Congress:
Brothers and Sisters from National Civil Society:
Brothers and Sisters from International Civil Society:

Through my voice speaks the voice of the Zapatista Army of National Liberation.

The history that gathers us together today is not new.

The grievances that convoke us are not new.

Our struggle is not new.

Neither sorrows nor combat have time or owner.

We are born to them, and they are everyone's.

Sorrow unites us and makes us one, even though we are many.

We are these sorrows:

Amuzgo Brother, Sister:

They mock our clothing, our customs, our culture, everything that makes us ourselves to ourselves. They turn identity into something shameful.

Cora Brother, Sister.

They persecute our history and persecute us. Many times persecuted, we are indigenous so the one who persecutes might have meaning.

Cuicateco Brother, Sister.

They stifle us with their lies. They lie and portray us as an image of apathy and discouragement. They lie and portray us as an image of resignation and immobility.

Chiapa Brother, Sister.

They tamper with our name. They call us another way, ignoring our history, and they force us to call ourselves as they call us, and not as we ourselves call us.

Chinanteco Brother, Sister.

Our homes are lacking in all services. We live in poverty, we die in poverty, and in poverty our children are born and grow up. Our houses are coffins where our families are crowded together. We do not have potable water, we do not have electricity, we do not have sewage systems, we do not have construction materials.

Chocholteco Brother, Sister.

Our communities are crowded together, out of sight. They deny our existence, and, since they cannot do away with us, they then conceal us from themselves and from others.

Chol Brother, Sister.

They wrench us from our homes with poverty and force us to travel far away from our own, so that our arms might serve the powerful.

Chontal Brother, Sister.

They make war on us in many ways. Sometimes with bullets, sometimes with deceit, sometimes with poverty, sometimes with jails. Always with *forgetting.*

Guarijío Brother, Sister.

Today, memory is a crime. We are memory. We are indigenous. We are criminals. Our blood fills jails and cemeteries. This is the sentence: prison and a coffin for memory.

Huasteco Brother, Sister.

We live fewer years than they do, we become ill more than they do, twice the number of our children die compared to theirs, and we have more accidents than they do. We have more death. But we have fewer hospitals, we have fewer doctors, we have fewer nurses, we have fewer medicines, and we have less life.

Huave Brother, Sister.

Our work is poorly paid. Coyotes and *cacique* ally with each other in order to steal from us with their pricing. Long and painful working days are converted into just a few coins that are not enough for anything.

Kikapú Brother, Sister.

We work with work in order to have work so they will give us work and thus be able to work our work.

Kukapá Brother, Sister.

The music of our words is noise to their ears, and they would have their noise become music to our ears.

Mame Brother, Sister.

Alcohol is poison for our blood, and the price we pay for the poison only serves to fatten the powerful. We ask for food and we get alcohol, which corrupts our joy and ends up saddening our hearts.

Náhuatl Brother, Sister.

If we suffer injustices and unfairness and we protest, we are crushed. If we demand our rights, we are crushed. If we speak, we are crushed. If we organize, we are crushed. If we resist, we are crushed. Repression is always the response we receive. We never receive the attentive ear, the sincere word, sisterly generosity. Always threats, jail, and death.

Ñahñu Brother, Sister.

To the powerful, our color represents weakness, backwardness, ignorance, malevolent resentment, bad jokes, and a contemptuous gesture.

O'odham Brother, Sister.

They want to purchase our dignity, the only thing left without a price. If they cannot do so, then they persecute it, they imprison it, they kill it.

Pame Brother, Sister.

They take our lands in order to sow and reap the death that is made candy in veins and lungs. They take the profits; we are the flesh for the jails.

Popoluca Brother, Sister.

Even though we, the indigenous, work very hard, we do not make progress. And the one who does not work makes progress at the price of our poverty. We work and we reap poverty; the rich do not work and are rewarded with more riches.

Purépecha Brother, Sister.

Our language is persecuted. They fear it for what it says and denounces.

We live in a corner that they force us into. Less and less are the air, ground, and sky left for us.

Matlatzinca Brother, Sister.

History is clear: We contribute the deaths, the blood, the pain, our homes and devastated countryside, our dead people dying mortal deaths.

Maya Brother, Sister.

We have no teachers because we have no schools, and we have no schools because we have no teachers. Government educational programs consist in teaching ignorance to our people.

Mazahua Brother, Sister.

They contaminate the water and turn it into merchandise; they steal it, and they sell it. They leave the land without sustenance so that it will die of thirst.

Mayo Brother, Sister.

They make us confront each other. They sow discord between us and put the death of the brother in the hand of the brother.

Mazateco Brother, Sister.

Our food is meager and poor. We know of meat, milk, and eggs by name, but they are always lacking on our tables. The only things that abound on our tables are our childrens', and our own, hungry mouths.

Mixe Brother, Sister.

As women, we are thrice slain. Slain as poor persons. Slain as indigenous. Slain as women. They kill us three times.

Mixteco Brother, Sister.

They fear it because it allows past history to be seen. They fear it because today it rebels. They fear it because it announces a tomorrow. They fear our language, and that is why they persecute and kill it.

Rarámuri Brother, Sister.

What matters to the powerful in these lands is not us, but rather the resources that are within it. And so the tree is killed in order to make wood, and the wood is used to make money for the powerful, but for us, it makes only adversity.

Tenek Brother, Sister.

We are a decorative object, a bright and colorful adornment, forgotten in a corner of society. We are a picture, a photograph, a weaving, a craft, but never a human being.

Tlahuica Brother, Sister.

Our children grow up educated in fear. They fear growing up, they fear being Indians, they fear the other who is not Indian, they fear being children.

Tlapaneco Brother, Sister.

They do not want to give us any space other than that of the museums of ancient, past things, which will be left behind in an already distant yesterday.

Tojolabal Brother, Sister.

Our towns are filled with armies that are occupying our lands, destroying our forests, polluting our waters, profaning our churches, dismantling our homes, introducing drugs, alcohol, and prostitution. They pursue us with hunting dogs, planes, helicopters, war tanks, and thousands of soldiers.

Totonaco Brother, Sister.

For us, justice is a cruel and shameless joke or a mausoleum or bars or disappearing. Being indigenous is a punishable crime, a crime not written in any legal code but that exists in the minds of the police and the judges.

Triqui Brother, Sister.

Humiliation is the future they offer us. In it, we will always have to lower our heads in front of the powerful, be the butt of jokes and contempt, and be inferior, forgettable.

Tzeltal Brother, Sister.

Our good lands are being occupied by the rich, and they throw us onto stony ground where the land can barely squeeze a sigh.

Tzotzil Brother, Sister.

They finance, organize, arm, and train paramilitary groups in order to kill us. And then they present the killings as if they were fights between campesinos, as "intercommunity conflicts," as if the hand that killed was dark and not as it actually is, the color of money.

Wixaritari-Huichol Brother and Sister.

They steal our lands from us, and the powerful conceal their theft behind laws made to serve them and to hurt us. Thanks to the law, the powerful have turned our lives and our history into a crime.

Yaqui Brother and Sister.

The power above tries to buy our consciences, to corrupt us in order to turn us into slaves, into servile animals to conceal justice behind the lie.

Zapotec Brother and Sister.

The economic policies of the powerful force us to abandon our land and to immigrate to the United States. Besides leaving behind our families, our history, our culture, our home, our land, our friendships, our people, we must then confront the armed racism of the border police and the fascist ranchers. Death forces us to leave our land, and, by leaving, we must confront death.

Zoque Brother and Sister.

They corner us so we will betray the blood that gives us life, so we will serve the powerful in his dirty work of erasing the color of the earth.

Brothers and Sisters of the Indian peoples that we are today:

We are nothing to the powerful but a figure in their accounts. We are a bothersome number. One number in the balance sheet. They measure us in order to disappear us. To measure their time and cost. They measure us in order to exploit us. To measure their time and profit. They measure us in order to control us. In order to measure their time and expense.

Brother, Sister . . .

Amuzgo, Cora, Cuicateco, Chiapa, Chinanteco, Chocholteco, Chol, Chontal, Guarijío, Huasteco, Huave, Kikapú, Kukapá, Mame, Matlatzinca, Maya Yucateco, Mayo, Mazahua, Mazateco, Mixe, Mixteco, Náhuatl, Ñahñu, O'odham, Pame, Popoluca, Purépecha, Rarámuri, Tenek, Tlahuica, Tojolabal, Totonaco, Triqui, Tzeltal, Tzotzil, Wixaritari-Huichol, Yaqui, Zapotec, Zoque.

Brothers and Sisters:

Today they want to make us fashionable. Today they want to make us entertainment, passing news. Today they want to make us short-lived and transitory again, fleeting, disposable, dispensable, forgettable.

When has history been fashionable?

When has memory been up for sale?

When have the roots been a transient shop window?

When is the past momentary?

When is wisdom dissoluble and transitory?

When is firmness fleeting?

When are the foundations disposable?

When can tomorrow be dispensed with?

When can it be forgotten that they exist because we exist?

Forty of us Indian peoples, of the fifty-seven in Mexico, have been received in the house of Purépecha.

It was in Nurio, Michoacán. So it was recorded by our scribes.

We were reunited by sorrow and hope.

Sorrow and hope will make us walk once again, like yesterday, like always.

But now we do not go alone.

Not apart from ourselves.

Not apart from the others.

Now we will march once more. But the seven days that will carry us to the land that grows upward, to the one that makes laws, shall tremble with all the indigenous that we are.

Though we have been united by sorrow, though hope unites us, nothing shall have meaning if we are not united by tomorrow.

Democracy!
Liberty!
Justice!

From the Purépecha community of Nurio, Michoacán

CLANDESTINE REVOLUTIONARY INDIGENOUS COMMITTEE, GENERAL COMMAND OF THE ZAPATISTA ARMY OF NATIONAL LIBERATION

Mexico City: We Have Arrived, We Are Here

MARCH 11, 2001, ZÓCALO IN MEXICO CITY

Mexico City:
We have arrived.
We are here.
We are the National Indigenous Congress and zapatistas who are,
together, greeting you.

It is not accidental that the grandstand where we meet is located where it is. It is because, from the very beginning, the government has been at our backs.[1]

Sometimes with artillery helicopters, sometimes with paramilitaries, sometimes with bomber planes, sometimes with war tanks, sometimes with soldiers, sometimes with the police, sometimes with offers for the buying and selling of consciences, sometimes with offers for surrender, sometimes with lies, sometimes with strident statements, sometimes with forgetting, sometimes with expectant silences. Sometimes, like today, with impotent silences.

That is why the government never sees us, why it does not listen to us.

If they quickened their pace a bit, they might catch up with us.

They could see us then, and listen to us.

They could understand the long and firm perspective of the one who is persecuted and who, nonetheless, is not worried, because he knows that it is the steps that follow which require attention and determination.

Brother, Sister:

Indigenous, worker, campesino, teacher, student, neighbor, housewife, driver, fisherman, taxi driver, stevedore, office worker, street vendor, brother, unemployed, media worker, professional worker, religious person, homosexual, lesbian, transsexual, artist, intellectual, militant, activist, sailor, soldier, sportsman, legislator, bureaucrat, man, woman, child, young person, old one.

Brother, Sister of the National Indigenous Congress, rainbow of the best of the Indian peoples of Mexico:

We should not have been here.

(After hearing this, I'm sure that the one I have turned my back to is applauding like crazy for the first time. So I'm going to repeat it . . .)

We should not have been here.

The ones who should have been here are the zapatista indigenous communities, their seven years of struggle and resistance, their ear and their looking.

The zapatista people. The men, children, women, and old ones, support bases of the Zapatista Army of National Liberation, who are the feet that walk us, the voice that speaks us, the looking that makes us visible, the ear that makes us heard.

The ones who should have been here are the insurgent women and men, their persistent shadow, their silent strength, their memory risen.

The insurgent women and men. The women and men who make up the regular troops of the EZLN and who are guardian and heart of our peoples.

It is they who deserve to see you and to listen to you and to speak with you.

We should not have been here.

And nonetheless, we are.

And we are next to them, the men and women who people the Indian peoples of all Mexico.

The Indian peoples, our very first, the very first inhabitants, the first talkers, the first listeners.

Those who, being first, are the last to appear and to perish . . .

Indigenous Brother, Sister.

Tenek.
    We come from very far away.
Tlahuica.
    We walk time.
Tlapaneco.
    We walk the land.
Tojolabal.
    We are the bow and the arrow.
Totonaco.
    Wind walked.
Triqui.
    We are the blood and the heart.
Tzeltal.
    The *guerrero* and the guardian.
Tzotzil.
    The embrace of the compañero.
Wixaritari.
    They assume us to be defeated.
Yaqui.
    Mute.
Zapotec.
    Silenced.

Zoque.

We have much time in our hands.

Maya.

We came here to give ourselves name.

Kumiai.

We came here to say "we are."

Mayo.

We came here to be gazed upon.

Mazahua.

Here to see ourselves being looked upon.

Mazateco.

Our name is spoken here for our journey.

Mixe.

This is what we are:

The one who flourishes amid hills.

The one who sings.

The one who guards and nurtures the ancient word.

The one who speaks.

The one who is of maize.

The one who resides in the mountain.

The one who walks the land.

The one who shares the idea.

The true we.

The true man.

The ancestor.

The *señor* of the network.

The one who respects history.

The one who is of a people of humble custom.

The one who speaks flowers.

The one who is rain.

The one who has knowledge to govern.

The hunter of arrows.

The one who is sand.

The one who is river.

The one who is desert.

The one who is the sea.
The different one.
The one who is person.
The swift walker.
The one who is good.
The one who is mountain.
The one who is painted in color.
The one who speaks right word.
The one who has three hearts.
The one who is father and older brother.
The one who walks the night.
The one who works.
The man who is man.
The one who walks from the clouds.
The one who has word.
The one who shares the blood and the idea.
The son of the sun.
The one who goes from one side to the other.
The one who walks the fog.
The one who is mysterious.
The one who works the word.
The one who governs in the mountain.
The one who is brother, sister.

Amuzgo.

Our name says all of this.

Cora.

And it says more.

Cuicateco.

But it is hardly heard.

Chinanteco.

Another name covers our name.

Chocholteco.

We came here to be ourselves with those we are.

Chol.

We are the mirror for seeing ourselves and for being ourselves.

Chontal.

    We who are the color of the earth.

Guarijío.

    Here, no longer shame for the color of our skin.

Huasteco.

    Language.

Huave.

    Clothing.

Kikapú.

    Dance.

Kukapá.

    Song.

Mame.

    Size.

Matlatzinca.

    History.

Mixteco.

    Here, no longer embarrassment.

Náhuatl.

    Here, the pride of being the color we are—
        the color of the earth.

Ñahñu.

    Here, the dignity that is seeing ourselves being seen being
        the color that we are—
        the color of the earth.

O'odham.

    Here, the voice that births us and inspires us.

Pame.

    Here, the silence no longer.

Popoluca.

    Here, the shout.

Purépecha.

    Here, the place that was concealed.

Rarámuri.

    Here, the dark light, the time, and the feeling.

Indigenous Brother, Sister:
Nonindigenous Brother, Sister:

We are here to say "we are here." And when we say "here we are," we are also naming the other.

Brother, Sister, who is Mexican and who is not Mexican.

With you we say "here we are" and we are with you.

Brother, Sister, indigenous and nonindigenous.

We are a mirror.

We are here to see each other and to show each other, so you may look upon us, so you may look at yourself, so that the other looks in our looking.

We are here and we are a mirror.

Not reality, but merely its reflection.

Not the light, but merely a glimmer.

Not the path, but merely a few steps.

Not the guide, but merely one of the many routes that lead to tomorrow.

Brother, Sister, Mexico City:

When we say "we are," we are also saying "we are not" and "we shall not be."

That is why it is good for those who, up above, are money and the ones who peddle it to take note of the word, to listen to it carefully, and to look with care at what they do not want to see.

We are not those who aspire to make themselves powerful and then impose the way and the word. We will not be.

We are not those who put a price on their own or another's dignity and convert the struggle into a market, where politics is the business of sellers who are fighting not about programs, but for clients. We will not be.

We are not those who are expecting pardons and handouts from the one who feigns to help, when he is in reality buying, and who does not pardon but humiliates the one who, by merely existing, is a defiance and challenge and claim and demand. We will not be.

We are not those who wait, naively, for justice to come from above, when it comes only from below. The liberty that can be achieved only with everyone. The democracy that is the ground for all and is fought for all the time. We will not be.

We are not the passing fashion that, made into a ballad, is filed in the calendar of defeats that this country flaunts with such nostalgia. We will not be.

We are not the cunning calculation that falsifies the word and conceals a new fakery within it. We are not the simulated peace longing for eternal war. We are not those who say "three," and then "two" or "four" or "all" or "nothing." We will not be.

We are, and we shall be, one more in the March.

Of Indigenous Dignity.

The color of the earth.

That which unveils and reveals the many Mexicos that hide and suffer under Mexico.

We are not their spokesperson.

We are one voice among all those voices.

An echo that dignity repeats among all the voices.

We join with them; we multiply with them.

We will continue being *echo*. We are, and we shall be, *voice*.

We are *reflection* and *shout*.

We shall always be.

We can be with or without face, armed with fire or without, but we are zapatistas, we are and we shall always be.

Ninety years ago, the powerful asked the one from below, the one called Zapata:

"With what permission, *señores*?"

And those from below responded, and we respond:

"With ours."

And with our permission, for exactly ninety years, we have been shouting, and they call us "rebels."

And today we repeat it: *We are rebels*.

Rebels we shall be.

But we want to be so with everyone we are.

Without war as house and path.

Because so speaks the color of the earth: The struggle has many paths, and it has but one destiny: to be color with all the colors that clothe the earth.

Brother, Sister:

Up there they say that this is the end of an earthquake. That everything will pass except their being above us.

Up there they say that you are here to watch in morbid fascination, to hear, without listening to anything. They say that we are few, that we are weak. That we are nothing more than a photograph, an anecdote, a spectacle, a perishable product whose expiration date is close at hand.

Up there they say that you will leave us alone. That we shall return to the land in which we are alone and empty.

Up there they say that forgetting is defeat, and they want to wait for you to forget and to fail and to be defeated.

They know up there, but they do not want to say it: *There will be no more forgetting, and defeat shall not be the crown for the color of the earth.*

But they do not want to say so, because saying it is recognizing it, and recognizing it is seeing that everything has changed and continues to change.

This movement is yours, and because it is yours, it is ours.

Now, and it is what they fear, there is no longer the "you" and the "we," because now we are all the color we are, of the earth.

It is the hour for Fox[2] and the one he serves to listen and to listen to us.

It is the hour for Fox and the one who commands him to see us.

Our word speaks one single thing.

Our looking looks at one single thing.

The constitutional recognition of Indigenous Rights and Culture.

A dignified place for the color of the earth.

It is the hour in which this country ceases to be a disgrace, clothed only in the color of money.

It is the hour of the Indian peoples, of the color of the earth, of all the colors that we are below, the colors we are in spite of the color of money.

We are rebels because the land is rebel if someone is selling and buying it, as if the land did not exist, as if the color we are did not exist.

Mexico City:

We are here. We are here as the rebellious color of the earth that shouts:

Democracy!
Liberty!
Justice!

Mexico:

We did not come to tell you what to do, nor to guide you along any path. We came to humbly, respectfully, ask you to help us to not allow another day to dawn without this flag having an honorable place for us who are the color of the earth.

From the Zócalo in Mexico City

CLANDESTINE REVOLUTIONARY INDIGENOUS COMMITTEE, GENERAL COMMAND OF THE ZAPATISTA ARMY OF NATIONAL LIBERATION

NOTES

1. The speaking platform was erected in front of the presidential palace, so that when the EZLN gave their speeches, they literally had their backs to the government.
2. Vicente Fox Quesada was president of Mexico from 2000 to 2006. He is a member of the National Action Party (PAN). His election marked the end of the Institutional Revolutionary Party's seventy-one years of political domination.

Paths of Dignity: Indigenous Rights, Memory, and Cultural Heritage

Text presented by Subcomandante Insurgente Marcos at the "Paths of Dignity: Indigenous Rights, Memory, and Cultural Heritage" intercultural meeting, held on March 12, 2001, in the Olympic Village Sports Center, organized by the National School of Anthropology and History (ENAH), and with the participation of José Saramago, Alain Touraine, Manuel Vázquez Montalbán, Bernard Cassen, Carlos Monsiváis, Elena Poniatowska, Carlos Montemayor, and Pablo González Casanova.

A good noontime to all:

We'd like to express our appreciation to the National School of Anthropology and History for giving us the opportunity to say our word alongside these people who, in addition to giving light to words, are also human beings accompanying a struggle written solely by humanity's greatest.

Starting this talk isn't easy.

And it's not just because these luminaries who are with us shine so brightly they leave barely any dark places, favored haunts of the shadows that we are. It's also because an impertinent beetle wouldn't let me prepare anything calm and sensible, interrupting me with all sorts of absurd, incomprehensible stuff.

Maybe you've heard of him before: the self-styled Don Durito of the Lacandona, with his self-appointed mission, as he puts it, to right wrongs and succor the poor and weak? For some reason beyond my comprehension, Durito has deemed that I, too, am of the poor and weak and that my whole life is an injustice.

You know, what's been keeping me awake all these days isn't the volume of Fox's contradictions or the death threats so generously extended to us by the PAN. No, it's Durito, who keeps insisting that the bus is not a bus but a ship, and that the march can't be marching but is sailing because it is buoyed by the sea.

By what little I can make out, Durito's going to the rock concert that's happening today in the Zócalo, where, we are told, Joaquín Sabina, Maldita Vecindad, Santa Sabina, and Panteón Rococó will be participating, as well as a good number of young people.

But like everything else on this march, that's a story to come.

In the world of culture and the arts, zapatismo has found generous ears and echoes that speak their dignity. In music—especially rock—and in the visual and dramatic arts, in literature and in science, we find good people, human beings, following their own paths of dignity. So we'd like to take advantage of this event to give our regards to all those men and women who fight for humanity through cultural work.

To speak like zapatistas about the paths of dignity, we will tell a story called:

THE OTHER PLAYER

In their solemn corner, the players
control the slow pieces. The board
holds them until dawn in its strict
field where two colors despise each other.
[...]

When the players are gone,
when time's consumed them,
the rite itself has not stopped.
[...]

> The player, too, is a prisoner
> (sentenced by Omar) on another board
> of black nights and white days.
> God moves the player, and he the piece.
> What God behind God opens the play
> of dust and time and dream and suffering?

—JORGE LUIS BORGES, FROM "CHESS"

Here's the story:

A group of players is engrossed in an important professional chess match. An indigenous man approaches, observes it, and asks them what they are playing. No one answers him. The man goes closer to the board and considers the positions of the chessmen, the stern, grim faces of the players, the air of anticipation in the gathering around them. He repeats his question. One player takes the trouble to answer: "It's something you could never understand. It's a game for people of substance and learning."

The indigenous man keeps quiet but also keeps watching the board and the opponents' moves. After a while, he ventures another question: "Why do you keep playing when you already know who's going to win?"

The same player who answered before tells him: "You'd never understand. This is for masters. It's beyond your mental reach."

The indigenous man says nothing. He looks some more, and then he leaves. A little while later, he comes back, carrying something with him. With no more words, he goes up to the game table and sets an old mud-covered boot in the middle of the board. The players, taken aback, angrily stare at him. With a cunning smile, the indigenous man asks: "Check?"

End of story.

Samuel Taylor Coleridge, the English poet of the cusp of the eighteenth and nineteenth centuries, wrote: "If a man were to cross through Paradise in a dream, and they gave him a flower as proof that he had been there, and if, upon awakening, he were to find that flower in his hand . . . what then?"

In this March of Indigenous Dignity, we zapatistas have seen a part of the map of the national tragedy that is not broadcast on primetime radio or television news programs. Any of those present here might argue that what we saw has no merit whatsoever, and that a march wasn't necessary in order to realize that the *Mexico of below* is the majority, in numbers and in poverty.

But I did not come to talk to you about poverty rates, about constant repression, or about deceptions.

During this march, the zapatistas have also seen part of rebel Mexico, and this seeing themselves and seeing others is nothing other than dignity. The *Mexico of below*, especially the indigenous, speaks to us of a history of struggle and resistance that comes from afar and that beats everywhere in the present. It is a history that looks forward.

From the mountains of the Mexican Southeast to the Zócalo of Mexico City, the zapatistas have crossed a territory of rebellion that has given us a flower of dark dignity as proof that we were there. We have reached the center of power, and we find that we have that flower in our hands, and the question, as in Coleridge, is "What then?"

Contrary to what the columnists of the political class might suppose, the question does not refer to what follows, but rather to what that dark flower means. And above all, to what it will mean in the future.

I know that in these times of modernity, when intellectual quotients are replaced by bank accounts, poetry by advertising spots, and science by verbal diarrhea, speaking of dreams can sound only anachronistic.

Nonetheless, the struggle of the Indian peoples for their dignity is fundamentally a dream—indeed, a very otherly dream.

The indigenous struggle in Mexico is a dream that not only dreams the tomorrow that includes the color of the earth, it is also, and above all, a dream that fights to hasten the possibility of that tomorrow.

We Indian peoples have reappeared precisely when what they have denied us has seemed strongest and most solid. And our dream has already foretold that the monuments neoliberalism is erecting to itself are nothing but future ruins.

The power wants to ensnare the indigenous struggle in nostalgia, chest beating, and the "boom" in folk crafts. It wants to fence the Indian struggle within the framework of the past, using fashionable marketing language like "The past reaches out to us with its unpaid accounts." As if settling these accounts would be the effective solvent for wiping out that past, and then the "today, today, today" that Fox used as an election platform and uses as a government program could reign without any problems. The same "today" that neoliberalism has converted into a new religious faith.

If we warn that they are trying to make the indigenous movement fashionable, we are not referring only to the public-relations efforts that are trying to contain it.

After all, fashion is nothing more than a return to a past whose final horizon is the present, the today, right now, the fleeting moment.

In the struggle for dignity, there is an apparent turn to the past, but—and this is fundamental—the final horizon is the future.

❧   ❧   ❧

Mexico's indigenous struggle has not come to turn back the clock. It is not about returning to the past and declaiming, in an emotional and inspired voice, that "all previous times were better." I believe they would have tolerated, and even applauded, that.

No, we Indian peoples have come in order to wind the clock and to thus ensure that the inclusive, tolerant, and plural tomorrow—which is, incidentally, the only tomorrow possible—will arrive.

In order to do that, in order for our march to make the clock of humanity march, we Indian peoples have resorted to the art of reading what has not yet been written. Because that is the dream that animates us as indigenous, as Mexicans, and, above all, as human beings. With our struggle, we are reading the future which has already been sown yesterday, which is being cultivated today, and which can be reaped only if one fights—if, that is, one dreams.

To the skepticism made state doctrine, to neoliberal indifference, to the cynical realism of globalization, we Indian peoples have countered with memory, the word, and the dream.

By throwing ourselves into this fight with everything we've got, the Mexican indigenous, as individuals and as a collective, have operated with a universally human impulse, that of *rebellion*. It has made us a thousand times better than before, and it has turned us into a historic force, not for its significance in terms of books or monuments, but for its ability to make history, in lower case. The key to the story of "The Other Player" isn't that the old mud-filled boot interrupts and subverts the *señores*-of-power's chess game . . . The key is the smile the indigenous smiles because he knows something. He knows that the other player, which is himself, is missing, and that the other player—which is not himself, but is still other—is also missing. But most of all, he knows that the fight is not over and that we haven't lost. He knows that it has barely begun. And he does not know because he *knows*, but rather because he *dreams*.

In short, we indigenous aren't part of yesterday. We're part of tomorrow.

And boots, culture, and tomorrows remind us of something we wrote some time ago, looking back and dreaming ahead:

"A boot is a boot that has lost its way and that's looking for what all boots long for, a bare foot."

And that's why it occurs to me that in the morning that we dream, there'll be no boots or jeans or soldiers, but there will be bare feet, which is how feet should be when morning's just beginning.

Thank you.

From the National School of Anthropology and History

SUBCOMANDANTE INSURGENTE MARCOS

P.S. I know it might be disconcerting to some that, in speaking of culture from the indigenous point of view, I turn to other voices, in this case Borges and Coleridge, but that is how I remind myself, and remind you, that culture is a bridge for everyone, above calendars and borders, and, as such, must be defended. And so we say, and say to ourselves, *no* to cultural hegemony, *no* to cultural homogeneity, and *no* to any form of hegemony and homogeneity.

To the Boys and Girls of the Isidro Favela Neighborhood

MARCH 18, 2001

To the Boys and Girls of the Isidro Favela Neighborhood:

Through my voice the voice of the Zapatista Army of National Liberation is *not* speaking.

Yes, you heard the "is *not* speaking" correctly, and it so happens that I was gazing at the walls in the room where we were staying yesterday, and I was looking for an idea or something that would wind me up to say a few words that would simultaneously be analysis, reflection, gratitude, invitation, et cetera, or something that's at least as good or even better than one of those games where everybody participates and there's joy and songs and dances . . .

That's what I was up to, when the lights went out. The most incomplete darkness reigned around me. And I say "incomplete" because almost immediately there appeared, under the doorjamb, a kind of miniaturized Christmas tree, laboriously moving. I checked the calendar, and it told me "This is the month of March; there are no little Christmas trees in March."

Panic overtook me. But I pulled myself together, since, given that stuff about us zapatistas being very brave, it wouldn't look good if I were to panic. So you guys better not go around saying I'm afraid of the dark. Of course, we children are, in fact, afraid of the dark, which is why we zapatistas are fighting so that all us children can have light, but okay, that's another story.

I'm telling you that, from under my door, something appeared that looked like a little Christmas tree, advancing toward me. When it got close, I realized it wasn't a little Christmas tree, but one of those strings of colored lights that was being dragged by something that looked like a little dented car or a little deflated ball or . . .

"Little dented car your *abuelo*, and little deflated ball your *abuela!*"[1] screamed that thing that looked like a little deflated ball or a little dented car. I happen to like my *abuelita* very much, so I turned on the lights in order to give . . . whatever it was! . . . its just deserts.

When I turned on the lights, surprise!—I discovered that it was nothing more and nothing less than a cantankerous beetle who calls himself "Don Durito of the Lacandona," although his real name is Nebuchadnezzar. He allows his friends to call him "Durito."

"Excuse me, Durito," I said to him. "But I didn't expect to see you here. Why are you dragging that string of Christmas lights? Don't you know we're just barely into March?"

"Of course I know! If you really were a zapatista, then you'd know that we zapatistas are fighting so that children can have Christmas whenever they want, whether in March or July, or a Christmas for every month of the year—"

"Okay, okay. Why are you bringing those Christmas lights?"

"Because I've come in disguise."

"And what are you disguised as?"

"As a patrol car."

"As a patrol car?"

"Yes, I'm in charge of looking after security for the zapatista delegation, and I disguised myself as a patrol car so no one would realize that I am the great, the incomparable, the supreme Don Durito of the Lacandona! Completely digitized, guaranteed, and with batteries included!"

"Digitized, guaranteed, and with batteries included?" I asked.

Durito answered, "Yes, I'm into business excellence now." And he continued:

"And tell me, dented carrot nose, what are you doing?"

"A message or greeting to the children of the neighborhood where we are, in order to thank them for having us."

"Fine—step aside. This is a job for the unbreakable Durito. I'm going to dictate a story to you. You'll read it to them, and it's going to be the delight of the small and the large."

I tried to protest. "But Durito—"

"It's not negotiable! Write this:

"THE STORY OF THE LITTLE DENTED CAR"

"Once upon a time there was a little wind-up car that no longer had a cord. Or, it did have one, but no one wound it up. And no one wound it up because it was an old little car, completely dented. It was missing a tire, and when it did work, it just went round and round.

The children didn't pay it much attention because they were into Transformers and Pokémon and Knights of the Zodiac and other things.

And so the little dented wind-up car didn't have anyone to wind it up. And then the lights went out in the great city, because the one who governed had privatized the electricity industry and the rich had taken all the light to other countries, and the Transformers and Pokémons and Knights of the Zodiac wouldn't run anymore. And then the little dented car said: "I have a cord, but I don't have anyone to wind me up."

And a little boy heard him and wound him up, and the little car began turning round and round, and the little boy said, "And now?"

"Not like that," said the little car. "Turn me upside down."

The child did so, and he asked, "What now?"

"Put a rubber band on the motor there." And the little boy did.

The little car said: "Now pull my cord, and you will see that light is going to be generated," and yes, the little boy did, and there was light once again. And this was repeated in all the homes where they had a little dented wind-up car, and where they didn't, they continued without light. And in the end the little car said: "That's exactly how you have to do things. Turn things upside down so that the world will have light once again. *Tan-tan.*"[2]

Moral: Better that the electricity industry not be allowed to be privatized, because what if everyone doesn't have a little dented wind-up car?

From the Isidro Favela Neighborhood
Don Durito of the Lacandona (batteries included), Mexico, March of 2001

"Durito!" I protested.

"What?!"

"No one's going to like that story!"

"Why not? It's lovely, it's substantial, it doesn't need batteries, and it's unbreakable. And I'm leaving now, because there goes Fernández de Cevallos, and I brought a razor along with me."

And so this is the story, boys and girls of the Isidro Favela neighborhood. I hope you have enjoyed it and that you understand now that the voice of the EZLN is not speaking through my voice, but, in this case, the voice is speaking of a beetle by the name of "Don Durito of the

Lacandona," who, he says, is devoted to helping the poor and challenging the powerful.

Vale. Salud, and, if you see him around here, tell him to give me back
the tobacco he took without letting me know.

THE SUP, SNEEZING

NOTES

1. *Abuelo* means grandfather and *abuela* means grandmother in Spanish. Talking about someone's grandmother in most languages is insulting.
2. *Tan-tan* is an exclamation of accomplishment, similar to "ta-dah."

The Hand That Dreams
When It Writes

*Brothers and Sisters of the Autonomous Metropolitan University (UAM)–
Azcapotzalco:*
Brothers and Sisters of the Neighborhoods of Northwest Mexico City:

You must all excuse me, but I have not managed to prepare anything
special for this event. I have therefore had to resort to the advice of a
specialist in issues of this area who says that he worked in what was
once a refinery, located near here.

Since you are, most certainly, very knowledgeable about the history of
the lands you walk, you will already know that I am referring to Durito,
known (he says) at that time as "Heavy Metal Durito," and not exactly
because of his spectacular abilities, but because he was buying and selling barrels from the refinery and reselling them as archeological pieces
to Coparmex leaders, who, as everyone knows, are very knowledgeable
about history and have always been concerned about the preservation
of historical heritage.

"It was really easy," Durito tells me. "They only had to see that the pieces
were oxidized and rusted to be convinced that they belonged to an
ancient civilization."

Durito studied at the UAM, and he was a professor there, and he had to
engage in these things in order to pay for his tuition and cover his salary.

Durito became bored quickly because, he said, there was nothing admirable about conning imbeciles, and he thought it would be better to fight for the helpless. And so he became a university worker, and he went to refineries, which required his modest efforts and his precocious business initiative.

Durito, as everyone already knows (and if you don't know, you're spending your tuition to no avail), embraced the noble profession of knight errantry, and he learned a million and one arts, as well as a wealth of knowledge that would put the *Encyclopaedia Britannica* and all its cybernetic links to shame, reducing it to the category of school dictionary with the brand name "The Crumbs S.A. de C.V. de R.L.," whose motto is "The street vendor closest to your wallet."

And so, I then asked Durito if he knew why the "hard-liners" in the Congress didn't want to engage in dialogue with the zapatistas. And here is what he told me:

"My dear and flu-ridden peanut-nose—"

"It's not flu, it's *imecas*,"[1] I interrupted him.

"So be it," Durito conceded. "Don't think those scoundrels are refusing you the ear and the word because of that ghastly mask, since it's common knowledge that you'd be even more ghastly without it . . ."

Durito paused so that all of you could start shouting that marvelous slogan that reconciles us with ourselves; it goes: *You are not ugly, you are not ugly!*

Since the slogan was just a slogan, and reality is reality and nothing more, Durito continued:

"You must find the reason yourself in what I am going to tell you . . .

The professional politician is accustomed to confronting life as if it were a pencil, of the kind that almost no one uses any more, with lead on one end and an eraser on the other. Making politics has come to be like that, like a continuous writing and erasing . . . They try to rectify errors with the eraser, to start each page over again, to embellish the letters, to hone the word, to decorate the world. The politician always tries hard to improve his penmanship, and he makes power a magnificent pencil sharpener with which he hones his words and tries to turn them into something elegant and seductive. He astonishes many, and some applaud him. But a pencil sharpener, as every student knows, in addition to sharpening the pencil, also uses it up and makes it smaller. Soon it is so small that it becomes useless, and it ends up, like everything the politician hones, in the wastebasket.

"Another pencil then takes its place, and the writing of politics begins again. The intellectuals of dead letters call this 'democratic change.' But the power is always ready to offer another pencil sharpener, and there will always be a wastebasket for the sharpened pencils of politics.

"The history of those who are powerful in politics does nothing but repeat itself. The words are the same; only the drawing of the letters changes—their slant, their flourishes, their size. But the words do not change, and ergo, neither do the worlds.

"The problem, then, is not the beauty of the letters, but that words announce the worlds that, after being left behind, give birth to other words, and so on.

"For example, at times a pencil is not even necessary. At times it is enough for a hand to trace a name on the sea or the sand. A world in which there are two: the one who is named, and the one who has in his hand the point that creates the mutual tomorrow.

"Did you understand?" Durito asked me.

"Sure," I responded. "It's better to use an automatic pencil, the refillable kind."

"Good heavens! What strange and perverse wizard has cursed me by making you my assistant? In truth, I have never known a companion so long of nose and so short of wit. Automatic pencil, my foot! Think, blockhead!"

"A quill pen, then?" I suggested timidly.

Durito exploded: "It's too much! I'm losing the best years of my life trying to educate a scoundrel like you! To the devil with quill pens, as well! And let's go, because we have to go to Azcapotzalco, and then to Iztapalapa, and afterward to Xochimilco, where they had the idea of dividing up this university so that it would be easier to control it. And, you see now, divided and everything, zapatista it is, and zapatista it will be."

"Let's go, then," I said, resignedly. But without Durito noticing, I threw away the indelible ink marker with which I wrote in one of the bathrooms, "UAM–Azcapotzalco has two 'Z's,' so that even if they want to abbreviate it, it will always be zapatista."

Vale. Salud, and don't think I didn't understand. The issue is not about what you write with, but the hand that dreams when it writes. And that is what the pencil is afraid of, to realize that it is not necessary.

From the Azcapotzalco Unit of the Autonomous Metropolitan University

CLANDESTINE REVOLUTIONARY INDIGENOUS COMMITTEE, GENERAL COMMAND OF THE ZAPATISTA ARMY OF NATIONAL LIBERATION

NOTE

1. The Metropolitan Index of the Quality of Air (IMECA) is a unit of measure used to determine levels of pollution and contamination in urban areas.

For Each Book, for Each Flight, There Is a Silence

MARCH 20, 2001, IZTAPALAPA UNIT OF THE
AUTONOMOUS METROPOLITAN UNIVERSITY

Brothers and Sisters of the Iztapalapa UAM:
Students, Teachers, and Workers of the SITUAM:
Brothers and Sisters of the Neighborhoods of East Mexico City:

We would like to thank everyone for the time and the space they have opened for our word. If we are taking pencils, erasers, and pencil sharpeners to the UAM–Azcapotzalco, we are bringing books, libraries, and silences to the UAM–Iztapalapa.

Books, as everyone knows, are misunderstood beings. The Indian peoples are also misunderstood, but the similarities do not end there. Books are also persecuted, as are we, and they have their own jails, with cruel cells disguised as shelves, and their legal proceedings can be read in the card files, organized, absurdly, in alphabetical order, ignoring the fact that books can be classified by their flights. There are those of timid and stuttering flight, which, instead of flying, barely make a few little leaps. There are those of florid flight, which trace joyful lines when their page-wings are unfurled. There are the dilettantes, which in addition to going about the branches, flit from one tree to the other, without deciding or committing themselves to anything or anyone. There are those of impotent flight whose weight keeps them from moving at all, let alone from trying to fly. There are those of volatile flight, who barely begin a giddy flapping before dissipating. There are those of long and decided flight, who know from the beginning where they are going, and they fly there with determination. There are those of unpredictable flight, who do not reveal their nature until they are open. There are those of nostalgic flight, who look backward and stumble in the present. And there are those that look all around in order to thus know where they are and where they are heading.

As everyone knows, there are also many kinds of silences. There are silences indifferent to everything that takes place around them. There are silences that are cynical toward another's pain. There are those that are complicit with crime and unfairness. There are those that are impotent in the face of those who commit outrages. There are those that are arrogant, who humiliate with the word denied. There are those fertile for dream. And there are those that are subversive and rebellious.

For each book—which is to say, for each flight—there is a silence. Not infrequently, however, misunderstandings reign, and then the prison closes over both: containing the flight and the silence.

But other times there is a meeting, and silence flies flight, and flight silences silence. And then miraculous things take place: lights leap forth that illuminate corners whose existence we ignored. Thoughts are born that no word can contain. Paths are opened for those with no feet. Or, as with us, keys are created for doors that are yet unmade.

A silence may most certainly meet with a book, and, upon meeting, free the flight that encloses and lift the flight upward and break the silence.

We should not be surprised or frightened if there are libraries and books, jails and silences and flights.

We should be surprised or frightened if there is nowhere a silence poised to be broken to thus free the flight that the word promises. We should be surprised or frightened if someone believes they are free if they stay far away from books and libraries, who believes they are free if they are silent alone and if they speak alone.

Iztapalapa:

Just as there is a book in a library waiting for the silence to free it, we have not just one but many flights in ourselves that are waiting to be liberated, as flights are in fact liberated with a fighting word: *dignity*.

From the Iztapalapa Unit, Autonomous Metropolitan University

CLANDESTINE REVOLUTIONARY INDIGENOUS COMMITTEE, GENERAL COMMAND OF THE ZAPATISTA ARMY OF NATIONAL LIBERATION

Flags, Glue, and Hands

Brothers and Sisters of the UAM–Xochimilco:
Students, Teachers, and Workers of the SITUAM:
Brothers and Sisters from the Neighborhoods of Mexico City:

Thank you for waiting for us, for receiving us, and for listening to us.

Here, at the UAM–Xochimilco, we would like to thank the entire community of the Autonomous Metropolitan University, above and beyond the divisions that they paradoxically call "units."

It is not the first time that the UAM community has opened its ears and heart to the zapatistas. Since the First of January in 1994, we have known of your unselfish and unconditional support for the struggle of the zapatista peoples.

We would especially like to express our gratitude to the SITUAM, for the support they have lent throughout this time.

We took pencils, erasers, and pencil sharpeners to the UAM–Azcapotzalco. For the UAM–Iztapalapa, it was books, libraries, and silences. For the UAM–Xochimilco, we have come to deliver flags, glue, and hands.

And in order to do so, we have invited a genius of modern communication, a sublime artist, the unreachable dream of the "headhunters," the greatest exponent of knight errantry, the most pompous of beetles—

"Stop!" Durito screamed. "I didn't dictate that part to you—"

"Which?" I asked him, with feigned ingenuousness. "The part about the sublime artist?"

"Very funny," he said, putting all his multiple hands on his hips.

And here I, the Sup, stop writing, because Durito has taken the word by force.

(Durito speaking)

"What's up, bro?

"How's it going?

"Ah, no. Ahem. Ahem.

"Damsels and Knights:

"As Don Diego has decreed the return to feudal times, it is imperative that all of us enlist in order to make the clock of history run once again. And there shall be none of that where the knights prepare for combat while the damsels wait sighing. To the devil with conventions, and let's go make mountains and slam the door on history.

"And so, attention! Lend an attentive ear and an open heart to what Don Durito has come to tell you:

"A cloth is a cloth, and it will not cease being a cloth, unless the wizard lends a hand and turns it into a flag. To do so, one must have colors, which are around us, but which we do not see until we find them inside ourselves.

"The hand thus takes the colors and, with affection, weaves the cloth, and the cloth is no longer cloth, nor is it yet a flag.

"And it is here where glue comes into action. Glue, contrary to what might be thought, *no pega*, it does not hit, does not beat, does not separate, does not distance; but rather, *pega*, it joins, it unites, it brings closer.[1] Glue is a bridge. But glue alone can do nothing if there is not something and somewhere to glue.

"And then the wand makes its appearance. Yes, I know that the big nose who preceded me in speaking said quite clearly, 'Flags, glue, and hands,' and wands were nowhere to be found, but that was his doing, because I quite clearly told him, 'Flags, glue, wands, and hands.'

"Ergo, do not believe him, but me.

"Now, then, to continue:

"Then the wands appear, and the glue can now glue the colored cloth to the wand, and some might say that it is now a flag, and *tan-tan*, the basic unit is finished and on to the next trimester . . . but error! There is still no flag. The hand is missing which, after cutting the cloth, painting it in colors, and gluing it to the wand, holds it up high. Then, and only then, will there be flag.

"But a flag by itself can only be lonely, even if it has many colors, even if it is raised very high, even if the generous wind flutters its form.

"Because the important thing about a flag, as is obvious, is not the cloth, nor the colors that adorn it, nor the wand, nor the glue, but the hand that makes it a flag when it takes it up and raises it.

"And one hand alone is incomplete. It needs another hand and another and another and many, and, when many hands raise many flags, much beauty can be seen, much color, much movement, much joy, much tomorrow.

"But the hands that raise them cannot be seen, even though they are many.

"And in the flags, in the color, in the movement, in the joy, and in the tomorrow, what really matters are the hands, even if they are not seen.

"Thank you very much."

(End of Durito's interruption. The Sup resumes)

Now, then, brothers and sisters of the UAM, what we have come to tell you is that we can be, or not be, flags. But what really matters is you, who are the hands that lift us up and brandish us.

And yes, there will be color and there will be movement and there will be joy and there will be tomorrow, but not because of the flag that we sometimes resemble, but because of the hands that you are.

Thank you, *UAMeros!*[2] Do not let them take away from you what makes you different, because then you will lose dignity, and there will no longer be hands, even if the flags are seen. And that is what the powerful want: to blot out and to silence the hands, because without hands, there are no flags.

Salud, UAM.

From the Xochimilco Unit of the Autonomous Metropolitan University

CLANDESTINE REVOLUTIONARY INDIGENOUS COMMITTEE, GENERAL COMMAND OF THE ZAPATISTA ARMY OF NATIONAL LIBERATION

NOTES

1. *Pegamento* is the Spanish word for "glue." It is based on the verb *pegar,* which has two meanings. *Pegar* can mean to glue together or unite. It can also mean to hit or beat in a violent manner. This sentence plays on the double significance of the word.
2. *UAMeros* is a made-up word, a combination of acronym and suffix, which refers to members of the university community at the Metropolitan Autonomous University (UAM) in Mexico City.

The History of the Search

The afternoon is flickering out in the heat of the night. Shadows come down from the great ceiba, the mother tree and sustenance of the world, and pick a spot to put their mysteries to bed. Along with the afternoon, March is also going out, and not this one which surprises us today . . . I am speaking of another afternoon, in another time and in another land: ours. Old Antonio had returned from hoeing the field, and he sat down in the doorway of his hut. Inside, Doña Juanita was preparing tortillas and words. And as she did so, she was passing them to Old Antonio, putting some in and taking others out, and Old Antonio was muttering while he smoked his hand-rolled cigarette . . .

THE HISTORY OF THE SEARCH

"Our eldest wise men tell that the very first gods, those who birthed the world, had created almost all things, but not everything, because they were aware that a good number of things should be created by men and women. That is why the gods who birthed the world, the very first, went away when the world had been completed. They did not go away leaving things unfinished out of laziness, but because they knew that it was up to a few to begin, but finishing is the work of everyone. The eldest of our elders also tell that the very first gods, those who birthed the world, had a knapsack where they had been keeping all the unfinished things. Not in order to do them later, but in order to remember what must come when men and women have finished the world that had been born incomplete.

"And then the gods went away. They left like the afternoon, as if putting themselves out, as if covering themselves in shadows, as if they were not there even though they were. Then the rabbit, who was angry with the gods because they had not made him big, went and nibbled at the gods' knapsack. But the rabbit was noisy as he nibbled, so the gods noticed, and they pursued him to punish him for the crime he had committed. The rabbit ran quickly. That is why rabbits eat as if they had committed a crime and run away quickly if anyone sees them. The fact is, even though the rabbit was unable to entirely rip open the knapsack of the gods, he had managed to make a hole. When the gods went away, all of their unfinished things fell out of the hole in their knapsack, and they did not even realize it. Then came the one whom they called *wind*, who took to blowing and blowing, and the unfinished things went all over the place, and since it was night, no one knew where to find the unfinished things, which needed more work in order for the world to be complete.

"When the gods became aware of the mess, they made a huge racket and they became very sad, and some of them even wept. That is why they say that, when it is going to rain, first the sky makes a lot of noise, and then the water comes. The men and women of maize, the true ones, heard the bawling, because when the gods cry it can indeed be heard far away. The men and women of maize then went to see why the very first gods were crying, those who birthed the world. Between sobs, the gods recounted to them what had happened. And then the men and women of maize said: 'Do not cry anymore. We are going to look for the unfinished things that were lost, because we already know that there are things undone and that the world will not be complete until everything is made and fixed up.'

"And the men and women of maize went on to say: 'Then let us ask you whether you remember any of the unfinished things that were lost, so that we may be able to tell them apart from things that have already been completely birthed.'

"The gods did not reply then, because their bawling was preventing them from speaking. Later, while they were rubbing their eyes to clean away their tears, they said: 'An unfinished thing is each person finding themself.'

"That is why our most ancient say that when we are born, we are born lost, and then, as we grow up, we go about seeking ourselves, and that living is seeking, looking for ourselves.

"Calmer now, the gods who birthed the world went on to say: 'All those things yet to be born in the world have to do with each person finding himself. That is how you will know if what you find is something yet to be born in the world: if it helps you find yourselves.'

"'That is good," said the true men and women, and they set about everywhere seeking the unfinished things that must be created in the world and that would help them find themselves."

Old Antonio finished the tortillas, the cigarette, and the words. He remained still for a while, looking at a corner of the night. After a few minutes, he said: "Since then, we go about seeking, seeking ourselves. We seek when we are working, when we are resting, when we are eating and when we are sleeping, when we are loving and when we are dreaming. When we live we seek seeking ourselves, and seeking ourselves, we seek when we have already died. In order to find ourselves we seek; in order to find ourselves we live and we die."

"And how does one go about finding oneself?" I asked.

Old Antonio kept looking at me, and he said to me, while rolling another cigarette: "An old, wise Zapotec told me how. I am going to tell you, but in Spanish, because only those who have found themselves can speak the Zapotec tongue well, which is the flower of the word, and my word is barely a seed, and there are others that are a stem and leaves and fruit . . . The Zapotec father said: *'Niru zazalu' guira'xixe neza guidxilayu' ti ganda guidxelu' lii'*—'First you shall walk all the paths of all the peoples of the earth, before finding yourself.'"

I took note of what Old Antonio told me that afternoon when March and the afternoon were putting themselves out. Since then, I have walked many paths, but not all, and I am still seeking the face that will be the seed, stem, leaf, flower and fruit of the word. I seek myself with everything and in everything in order to be complete.

A light was smiling in the night above, as if she would find herself in the shadow below.

March is going. But hope is arriving.

From Juchitán, Oaxaca

SUBCOMANDANTE INSURGENTE MARCOS

To Open the Word

APRIL 2, 2001

17 DE NOVIEMBRE AUTONOMOUS MUNICIPALITY, CHIAPAS

Support Bases of the Zapatista Army of National Liberation:
Local and Regional Committees of the Zot'z Choj region of Chiapas:
Clandestine Revolutionary Indigenous Committee:
Compañero, Compañera:

We have arrived now.

We are here in order to return the *comandantes* and *comandantas* of this region.

We have also come here to honor our dead.

We are here to salute the memory of three compañeros who died in 1994.

- The compañero Sebastián Sántiz López.
- The compañero Severiano Sántiz Gómez.
- The compañero Hermelindo Sántiz Gómez.

We are here to report to these dead compañeros.

And also to inform you, compañero, compañera.

You gave us the task of carrying the example of these fallen compañeros.

The example of not surrendering.

The example of not betraying.

The example of not selling oneself.

Carrying these three examples gave us three missions to complete.

The mission of pushing the three signals.[1]

The mission of engaging in dialogue with civil society.

The mission of engaging in dialogue with the Congress of the Union.

And thus I tell you that we have carried out the three missions.

The three remaining military positions will now soon be free.

There are now just a few zapatista prisoners remaining to be released.

The COCOPA[2] law is now being discussed.

We have now spoken with the Congress of the Union.

We also spoke with hundreds of thousands of Mexican men and women.

In Chiapas. In Oaxaca. In Puebla. In Veracruz. In Tlaxcala. In Hidalgo. In Querétaro. In Guanajuato. In Michoacán. In the state of Mexico. In Morelos. In Guerrero. In the Federal District. In Mexico City.

We spoke with workers, campesinos, teachers, students, neighbors, housewives, drivers, fishermen, taxi drivers, office workers, employees, street vendors, brothers, the disabled, market vendors, unemployed, media workers, professional persons, religious persons, homosexuals and lesbians, artists, intellectuals, men, women, boys and girls, young people, old ones.

And we also spoke with many indigenous.

As you commanded us, we were a mirror for the indigenous of the entire country.

And they were also a mirror for us.

They looked at themselves in our rebel dignity.

We looked at ourselves in their rebel dignity.

So it went with us and with them.

We understood that, in order to be looked upon, we have to look.

And in order to look, one must open one's eyes.

And in order to open one's eyes, the word must be opened.

For us, the zapatistas, it was not easy to open the word.

We had to make a war.

Compañeros like Sebastián, Severiano, and Hermelindo had to die.

With those and other deaths, we opened our word.

And with our word, our eyes were also opened.

And in that way we could look at others.

And in that way we could demand that they look at us, that they listen to us.

It cost us war and blood for them to look at us, for them to listen to us.

With the looking and the word given to us by our dead, we made this trip.

When we looked, our dead looked.

When we spoke, our dead spoke.

Now, looking and speaking, we also listened and were looked at.

In our looking we saw many young people and children, because most of those who accompanied and supported the march were young people and children.

They came from all roads.

They gathered together in all the cities.

They came wanting to listen.

They came seeking.

They looked.

Because the one who listens is seeking.

Because the looking is what he is seeking.

He wants to find something.

He wants to find himself.

We spoke to the children and to the young people with the word of truth.

We told them clearly that we were not what they were seeking.

We were not, because we ourselves are also seeking.

We were seeking them and ourselves.

And seeking the one and the other, we found each other.

They found us.

We found them.

And in finding us, we looked at ourselves.

And in them we saw the word that our dead had been speaking to us.

Because they had told us that the young people and the children were what we were seeking.

Hope.
Rebellion.
Generosity.
Commitment.
The morning.

And you must know, compañero, compañera, the children and young people were generous with us.

They committed themselves to us.

They rebelled with us.

And with us they shared the hope for the morning.

That is why I am telling you, compañero, compañera, that we have much to be grateful to our dead for.

And we have much to be grateful to the young people and to the children for.

Because the ones and the others taught us to seek.

The ones and the others helped us to find and to find ourselves.

And thus we are able to tell our dead here that they were indeed right.

That one day it shall indeed dawn.

That on that day there shall be no concealed faces.

That on that day the smile shall not be lost behind a mask.

And on that day our dead shall live.

And that day is going to dawn thanks to the children and to the young people.

And that is why I am asking you, compañero, compañera, for us to salute the children and young people.

The indigenous children and young people.

The nonindigenous young people and children.

Because in saluting them, we are also saluting our dead.

And we salute them exactly as we salute our dead.

With a flower.

With a flower we tell them that they live.

With a flower we are telling ourselves that we live.

That our dead shall always live.

That death always dies.

Sebastián, Severiano, Hermelindo, children, young people:

Here is our salute.

Democracy!
Liberty!
Justice!

From the mountains of the Mexican Southeast

SUBCOMANDANTE INSURGENTE MARCOS

NOTES

1. Before beginning the March for the Color of the Earth, the zapatistas released three demands, prerequisites that the government must complete before dialogue could be resumed between the EZLN and the Mexican authorities. The first demand was government withdrawal from seven specific military positions it had imposed on zapatista territory. The second demand was the release of all zapatista political prisoners. The third demand was the constitutional recognition of indigenous rights and culture in the form of the Commission for Concord and Pacification (COCOPA) law. The three signals are first alluded to in the *Seventh Anniversary of the Zapatista Uprising*, dated January 1, 2001.

2. The Commission for Concord and Pacification (COCOPA) is a bicameral legislative commission established in 1995 to assist in the process of dialogue between the EZLN and the Mexican government. In 1996 the COCOPA oversaw the multilateral signing of the San Andrés Accords, an agreement between the EZLN and the Mexican government. Following the government's immediate betrayal of the San Andrés Accords, the COCOPA began converting the accords, which dealt with indigenous rights and culture, into official legislation. Since then, the government has refused to comply with the COCOPA's legislative proposal.

Soon With the Wind in Its Favor

JULY 2002

To: Fernando Yanez Muñoz, Architect
From: Subcomandante Insurgente Marcos.

Don Fernando:

Greetings from all the zapatista compañeros and compañeras and from the indigenous communities in resistance. We hope that you, and all of those working alongside you, are in good health and of good cheer.

You, as we know, are working alongside other honest men and women in tending to the memory of our people's struggle. An important part of this memory is being kept in the Museum of Doctor Margil, in the city of Monterrey, Nuevo León, Mexico. There are testaments in this museum to a fundamental part of our history as zapatistas, a history of which we are proud and which we are trying, as much as we are able, to honor.

You, and those with whom you work, are zapatistas. And that museum is zapatista. That is why we have wanted to send you a small gift with zapatista earth. It is a modest homage to all of those men and women who died for liberty after living for the Patria. We hope that there is a place in the museum for this modest homage from the EZLN to the Mexican men and women who gave birth to hope, which will turn 33 years old on August 6, 2002.

It will be a great honor for us to have this zapatista earth shine in the Mexican North on August 6, 2002, and for the lines to be listened to, timidly, of this rudimentary attempt at a poem, titled "Account of the Events"—which I wrote eighteen years ago, at the dawn of the EZLN—and which, as is known, already has a place in the Museum of Doctor Margil.

Hoping to see you soon and to once again have the honor of greeting you personally, I bid farewell in the name of all my compañeros and compañeras.

Vale. Salud, and may hope gain new spirit when the three faces the mirror and gives memory the gift of one of the most honorable moments in the history of Mexico.

From the mountains of the Mexican Southeast

SUBCOMANDANTE INSURGENTE MARCOS

ACCOUNT OF THE EVENTS

Today, the sixth day of the month
of August of the year
nineteen hundred and seventy-nine,
as history forewarned,
the coffee bitter,
the tobacco running out,
the afternoon declining
and everything in place for conspiring
against the shadows and darkness
that obscure the world and its sun,
the below signed appear
in front of me, the Patria, in order to
declare the following.

First. That the below signed
renounce their homes, work,

family and studies and all the
comforts that have been
accumulated in the hands of the few
upon the misery of the many.

Second. That the below signed
renounce a future,
paid on time, of
individual enjoyment.

Third. That the below signed
also renounce the shield
of indifference in the face of the suffering
of others and the vainglory of a
place among the powerful.
Fourth. That the below signed
are prepared for all the sacrifices
necessary in order to fight silently
and without rest in order to make me,
the Patria, free and true.

Fifth. That the below signed
are prepared to suffer persecution,
calumny and torture, and even
to die if it is necessary, in order to achieve
what was noted in the Fourth point.

Sixth. That I, the Patria, will know
to keep your place in history
and to watch over your memory
as they watch over my life.

Seventh. That the below signed
will leave enough space under their
names so that all honest men

and women may sign this
document and, when the moment comes,
the entire people shall sign it.

There being nothing left to be said,
and very much to do, the
below signed leave their
blood as example and
their steps as guide.
Valiantly and respectfully,
LIVE FOR THE PATRIA OR
DIE FOR LIBERTY.

Manuel, Salvador, Alfredo, Manolo, María Luisa,
Soledad, Murcia, Aurora, Gabriel, Ruth, Mario,
Ismael, Héctor, Tomás Alfonso, Ricardo . . .
And the signatures will follow
of those who will have to die and
of those who will have to live
fighting, in this
country of sorrowful history
called *Mexico*, embraced
by the sea and, soon,
with the wind in its favor.

THE CAPTAIN

To Bring the
Rainbow Down

EZLN SENDS GREETINGS TO THE
MADRID AGUASCALIENTES, OCTOBER 12, 2002

To: Angel Luis Lara, "the Russian"
From: Sup Marcos

Well, I told you before that the Aguascalientes should be a fiesta of rebellion, a thing that none of the political parties like—

"They are a fraud!" Durito interrupts me.

"But . . . wait, Durito, I'm not even talking about Mexican political parties."

"I'm not talking about those frauds, but Internet porn pages."

"But Durito, in the jungle we don't have Internet."

"We don't have it? . . . I have it! With a little ingenuity I've converted one of my antennas into a powerful satellite modem."

"And may I know, postmodern gentleman, why the Internet porn pages are frauds?"

"Well, because there's not a single photo with lady scarabs in it, not even nude—damn, not even with any of those knickers of 'dental floss,' as they say."

"Knickers?"

"Sure! Fuck! Aren't you writing to those *Spanishistas*?" Durito says while he jams a beret onto his head.

"Knickers?" I repeat, trying to avoid the inevitable, which is that Durito will get a hand into what I'm writing, because for this purpose he's got too many hands and too much impertinence.

"Let's see, hmm-hmm," murmurs Durito, already leaning over my shoulder. "Russian? Are you writing to Putin? I wouldn't recommend it. Don't let it happen that he sends some of those gases, not even the ones you lay when you eat too many beans."

I protest: "Look, Durito, let's not start revealing intimate things, because right here I have the letter that the Pentagon sent you asking for the formula for the development of ultratoxic gases."

"Ah! But I denied it. Because my gas, like my love, is neither bought nor sold, but I give it as a gift, because I am detached and I give things without looking to see if people deserve them," Durito says with a fucked-up Andalusian accent. After a pause, he adds: "And what is the subject of your writing, lad?"

"And nothing, uncle, of what it's going to be, on rebellion and an Aguascalientes that they're going to open near Madrid," I respond, infected by the flamenco spreading through the country.

"Madrid? Which Madrid? The one of Aznar and the Benemérita? Or irreverent Madrid?"

"Irreverent Madrid, of course. Although it wouldn't be strange if Aznar wanted to get his hooves in on it."

"Magnificent!" applauds and dances Durito in a way that revives Federico García Lorca and is made up of the little-known and unedited *Soleá* of the Epileptic Scarab.

When he finishes his dance, Durito orders: "Write! I will dictate my report to you."

"But Durito, you're not in the program. Not even if they have invited you."

"Sure, of course the Russians don't like me. But it doesn't matter. Go, write. The title is 'Rebellion and Chairs.'"

"Chairs? Durito, don't come out with another of your—"

"Shut up! The idea comes from something Saramago and I wrote at the end of the last century, and it's called 'Chairs.'"

"Saramago? Do you mean José Saramago, the writer?" I ask, perplexed.

"Of course. What, is there another? Well, it so happens that that day we drank to the point of falling out of said chair, and when I was on the ground, with the perspective and lucidity of the underdogs, I said: 'Pepe, this wine hits harder than Aznar's mule.' He didn't say anything, because he was looking for his glasses.

"And then I say to him: 'Something's happening to me. Quickly, José, for ideas are like beans with sausage—if you don't take care, someone else will come by and have them for breakfast.

"Saramago finally found his glasses, and together we gave shape to the story. If I remember correctly, it was in the early 1980s. Of course, only his name appears in the credits, because we scarabs battle a lot over authorship rights."

I want to abbreviate Durito's anecdotes, so I urge: "The title's already there, what more?"

"Well, it's about how the attitude that a human being assumes toward chairs is what defines them politically. The Revolutionary (like that, with a capital R) looks with detachment at common chairs, and he says, he tells himself, *I don't have time to sit down; the weighty mission with which History* (like that, with a capital) *has entrusted me impedes me from distracting myself with silliness.* This is the way he passes his life, until he arrives in front of the seat of power, knocks it down with a shot so that he can sit in it, and then sits with a knitted brow, as if he were constipated, and tells himself: *History* (like that, with a capital) *has completed itself. Everything, absolutely everything, acquires meaning. I am in The Chair* (like that, with capitals), *and I am the culmination of our times.* From there, he continues until another Revolutionary (like that, with a capital) arrives and knocks him off, and history (like that, lowercase) repeats itself.

"On the other hand, when the rebel (like that, lowercase) looks at a chair, common and average, he analyzes it fixedly and then goes to another chair, and another, and another, and, within a short time, it looks like a book club because more rebels (like that, lowercase) have arrived and begun to swarm with coffee, tobacco, and words, and then, precisely when they begin to feel comfortable, they become restless, as if they had worms in the cauliflower, and nobody knows if it was the effects of the coffee or the tobacco or the words, but they all rise up and continue on their way. Until they encounter another common and average chair and history repeats itself.

"There is only one variation. When the rebel comes across the Seat of Power (like that, uppercase), he looks at it fixedly, analyzes it. But, instead of sitting, he goes for a fingernail file and, with heroic patience, he files the legs until, as he understands it, they are left so fragile that they will break when someone sits, which happens almost immediately. *Tan, tan.*"

"'*Tan, tan?*' But Durito—"

"Nothing, nothing. I already know that it is too arid and that theory should be velvety, but mine is a metatheory. It could be that they accuse me of being an anarchist but value my report as a humble homage to the old Spanish anarchists, for there are those who silence their heroism and don't shine less for it."

Durito leaves, although I'm sure that he would prefer to come back.

Well, let's leave joking aside. Where was I before that armor-plated impertinence interrupted me?

Ah! . . . I was saying that the Aguascalientes is a fiesta of rebellion.

And then, my dear Chechen, all that's missing is to define rebellion.

To obtain a definition, it could be enough for you to take a look at all the men and women who took it upon themselves to erect that Aguascalientes, and at all those who will attend its inauguration (not the closing ceremony, because I'm sure the police will do that). But since this is a letter, I should attempt to do it with words that, as eloquent as they may be, will never be as forceful as seeing.

So, searching for a text that would serve me for this purpose, I found a book that Javier Elorriaga lent me.

The little book is called *New Ethiopia*, and it is by a Basque poet named Bernardo Atxaga. There is a poem there called "Reggae of the Butterflies," which speaks of butterflies that fly in the inner sea and that will not have a place to land, because the sea has neither islands nor rocks.

Well, pardon me, Bernardo, if the synthesis is not as fortunate as your reggae, but it helps me with what I want to say.

Rebellion is like that butterfly that guides its flight toward this sea without islands or rocks.

It knows that there won't be a place to rest, and despite this, its flight does not falter.

And no, neither the butterfly nor the rebellion is stupid or suicidal. What happens is that they both know that they will have a place to rest, that there is an island out there that no satellite has been able to detect.

And that island is a sister rebellion that will surely come to float correctly when the butterfly begins to faint.

Then the flying rebellion—which is to say, the marine butterfly—will form part of that emerging island and in that way will become a base of support for other butterflies that now begin their flight toward the ocean.

The chances of this happening are more remote than a curiosity you might find in a biology book. But, as someone who I do not remember once said, the flapping of a butterfly's wings can be the cause of great hurricanes.

With its flight, the flying rebellion—which is to say, the butterfly—is saying: No!

No to logic!
No to prudence!
No to immobility!
No to conformity!

And nothing, absolutely nothing, will be as marvelous as seeing the journey of that flight, to estimate the challenge that it represents, to feel how it begins to stir the wind and see how, with that air, it is not the leaves of the trees that tremble, but the knees of the powerful, who until then naively thought that butterflies died in the sea.

Well, yes, in my Muscovite appraisal, it is known that butterflies, like rebellion, are contagious.

And there are butterflies, like rebels, of all colors.

Those who are blue are painted such so to be confused with the sky and the sea.

Those who are yellow are painted such so to be embraced by the sun.

The red ones are painted with rebellious blood.

The brown carry the color of the land in waves.

The green, like always, are painted with hope.

And all are skin, skin that shines regardless of the color that paints it.

And there are flights of each color.

And there are times when butterflies of all colors from all parts of the world get together and create a rainbow.

And the work of butterflies, it is said in any respectable encyclopedia, is to bring the rainbow down in such a way that all children can learn to fly.

And, speaking of butterflies and rebellions, it occurred to me that when you are all in a circus, or rather in the police court, in front of the clown Garzon, and they ask you what you were doing in the Aguascalientes, you can respond: *Flying.*

Even though they will send you flying, deported to Chechnya, the laughter will be heard all the way to the mountains of the Mexican Southeast.

And a laugh, brother, is appreciated as much as music.

SUBCOMANDANTE INSURGENTE MARCOS

P.S. Eva asks if in the Spanish state (I like the way she said it) they have VCRs, because she wants to take her collection of Pedro Infante movies. I told her that they have another system there. She asked me, "You're kidding—they don't have a neoliberal government there?" I didn't respond, but I say to her now, "Comandanta Eva, what other way could it be made?"

Durito on Trains and Pedestrians

JANUARY 2003

Durito (who once was a railroad worker) says the politics of power under neoliberalism ("Write it completely," he tells and orders me, "because it is not a truth for all times, but something for now") is like a train.

Durito says that, in the train of neoliberal politics, the forward coaches are foolishly fought over by those who think they can conduct better, forgetting the fact that it is the locomotive that drives the coaches, and not the other way around.

Durito says that the politicians also don't realize that the locomotive is being driven by someone else (the one who speaks the language of money) and that, if the derailment is to come, the luxury railcars, the ones in front, will indeed be first, but they will be first when the train runs off the tracks.

Durito says that everyday people travel on foot.

Durito says that walking is free, that it's more fun, and that by walking, one can decide where to go and what will happen.

Durito says that the majority of people on foot look with indifference on the passage of the machine that prides itself on determining its path and doesn't realize that it cannot leave the rails imposed by political rules.

Durito says that not only do everyday people not want to drive the train, but that sometimes they question the destination of the journey (which is, in addition, made in their name, "representing" them).

Durito says that, among the people on foot, there are some who are rebels. These not only criticize the destination of the journey and the ridiculous, arbitrary distribution of the tickets. They even question the train's very existence and they ask themselves if trains really are necessary. Because, yes, certainly they arrive more quickly and more comfortably, but one arrives where one does not wish to arrive.

Durito says we zapatistas are some of those rebel pedestrians ("zapestrians"), and we are the object of mockery by those who criticize the fact that we do not want to buy a ticket and travel at top speed . . . to catastrophe.

Durito says we zapatistas are some very otherly pedestrians. Because instead of watching the train's arrogant passage with indifference, a zapatista just approaches the track, smiling, and puts his foot on it. Certainly, he thinks ingenuously that in this way he will make the powerful train derail and have no choice but to go off the tracks.

Durito says that in those coaches—which were once the place of fierce (and miserable) fights for a power that was never there—they are uniting, peering through the windows, mocking the zapatista who, with his dark-skinned foot, is trying to halt the train.

Durito says that in the dawn of January 1, 1994 (it was rainy and cold, and a dense fog covered the city), a zapatista indigenous put down his foot in order to derail the all-powerful train of the PRI.

Durito says that six years later, the PRI was left lying in the bottom of the gully, and its remains are being fought over by those who yesterday mocked that indigenous who is, right now, carefully bandaging his foot, not because it hurts, but because he sees another train coming there, and another and another . . .

Durito says that if the zapatistas have a lot of anything, it is feet, because their feet grow large from walking the long night of sorrow to hope.

Durito says that the zapatistas will not be done walking the night until all those on foot can decide not just the train's existence and path, but also, and above all, until there are, in the walk of the pedestrians of history, many chairs under an apple tree full of fruit . . . for everyone.

"Because that's what this is all about . . . apples, chairs, and trains," Durito says while he sees, with satisfaction, that the seed he sowed some time ago is already raising up a piece of earth, which, complicit and in solidarity, he saved.

SUBCOMANDANTE INSURGENTE MARCOS

On foot and already into the tenth year of the war against forgetting

Another Calendar:
That of Resistance

Place: Mountains of the Mexican Southeast
Date: January 2003
Hour: Dawn
Climate: Cold, rainy, tense
Altitude: Various meters above sea level
Visibility: Without a flashlight you can't see a damn thing

In a hut, a shadow competes against the fragile light of a candle and, between the smoke from the tobacco and that from the campfire, a hand leafs through a 2003 calendar, which recently arrived at the EZLN headquarters.

"There are calendars," the hand says, "and then there are calendars," and it puts two newspaper photographs on the table: In one appears the fetus that will be Fox's grandchild. In the other, some mothers are weeping for their dead children in Comitán, Chiapas.

The hand says: "Here, the calendar of a birth with the blessing of power. And here, another calendar of many deaths due to the irresponsibility of power."

The hand continues to speak: "Calendars of births and deaths, calendars of payments, calendars of national celebrations, calendars of trips by officials, calendars of government sessions. Now, in 2003, the election calendar. As if there were no other calendars. For example: the calendar of resistance. Or perhaps that one is not spoken of because it demands a great deal and does not look like much."

The hand stops for a bit. The calendar remains closed. It appears as if it has been made by zapatista sympathizers. Each month, in addition to photographs on the subject, there are fragments of the many messages from the EZLN during the March for Indigenous Dignity, in February, March, and April 2001.

"That march," says the hand, which is now leafing through a puff of smoke. "The most important thing was not what we said," and it sets the calendar aside. "The most important thing was what, remaining silent, we saw. If those *señores* and *señoras* who call themselves thinkers had seen with our eyes what we saw, remaining silent, perhaps they might have understood our later silence and our current words. But no. They think they think. And they think that we owe them something. But we owe them nothing. Those whom we do owe, and owe a lot, are the silent ones we silently saw. Our silence was for them. Our word is for them. Our gazes and our hands are with them and for them."

And in this way, the hand points to a map of the Mexican Republic.

The gaze follows the hand's path, and the hand rests above a word:

OAXACA

And, on top of this word, the first stele is lifted . . .

Oaxaca, the First Stele

(DESPITE THE NEW OLD PRI, HISTORY
RESISTS IN THE FACE OF DEATH)
JANUARY 2003

(Stele: engraved stone, created using the techniques of bas-relief, which contain representations of individuals, dates, names, events . . . and prophecies)

It is January, the month that summons up the past, present, and future. It is Oaxaca, land where yesterday and today give rise to the future.

Mexican indigenous survive on this soil: Mixtecos, Popolocas, Chochos, Triquis, Amuzgos, Mazatecos, Cuicatecos, Chinantecos, Zapotecs, Chatinos, Mixes, Chontales, Huaves, Nahuas, Zoques, Ixcatecos, and Tacuates, in addition to an agricultural Mexican population that is ignored. In 1990 the National Institute of Statistics, Geography, and Information (INEGI) declared that there were more than 1.3 million indigenous over the age of 5 in Oaxaca. However, if one utilizes broader criteria than the narrow ones of the INEGI, between 60 and 70 percent of the Oaxacan population is indigenous. Out of a total of 570 municipalities, 418 are called "indigenous municipalities," which are governed by their own rules—what some call "uses and customs"—of government.

It is January, and it is Oaxaca, and the sun advances above a hill that has a truncated summit and is combed with pre-Hispanic buildings.

Different times have given different names to this mountain. And so it was named Hill of the Tiger, and they called it Hill of Precious Stones, and it was spoken of as Hill of the Pure Bird. Those present now call it Monte Albán.

Monte Albán. At its feet glitters the proud disorder of the city of Oaxaca, the capital of this province which, like all of them in Mexico, makes the news only when it experiences a passing hurricane, earthquake, or false governor, or when oppressive poverty follows the path of armed rebellion.

As if history counts only when it narrates the defeats—desperation and misery of those who are below—and forgets the fundamental: resistance.

The sun continues its path.

Also arriving from the east, a macaw flies above the Tlacolula Valley, it circles the Etla Valley, and, in the Zaachila Valley, after covering the four compass points, it heads toward Monte Albán. It glides above the complex of buildings, all of them oriented along a north–south axis.

All but one. Resembling an arrow, one building breaks the supposed harmony, pointing its apex toward the southeast.

Like an out-of-place piece in the complicated jigsaw puzzle of Mesoamerican archeology, this building might have marked an astronomical, visual, or even auditory point. But it also leads one to think of something arrested, and not just in spatial terms, but also, and above all, in temporal terms. It looks like a call to attention, an outburst of the absurd in the midst of apparent order.

How absurd is the image of that macaw and what is seen beneath his vigilant and protective flight. In the southern platform of Monte Albán, in front of the seventh stele, a history is recounted which comes from a cave which is all caves . . .

"Indigenous blood knows that the earth conceals the fertile womb that produced all times, and indigenous Zapotec wise men recount that it was inside a hill where time and life began their laborious path.

"Prior to that, that which cannot be touched with thought, the Coqui Xee, slept in a cave. That was the grotto of time without time, where there was no place for the beginning nor for the end.

"The desire to move the world then entered the heart of the Coqui Xee, and, given that the moon was concealed, he looked inside himself and birthed Cosana and Xonaxi, which is what the ancient Zapotec call *light* and *darkness*.

"With one foot from each of them, the world then took its first steps. He who had no beginning, the one untouchable by reason, Coqui Xee, gave birth to himself as a new moon, and thus began his long passage in the world of the night, while by day he rested in the land of the Mixe, in Cempoaltépetl.

"Cosana, the *señor* of the night and of fire who gave birth to the sun, made himself into a tortoise in order to walk the earth, and that was how he went about creating men, from the hand of Xonaxi, who made himself into a macaw in order to walk the skies, to look after the men and women, and to see that they were created with care.

"Flying the night, Xonaxi painted his path with light so that he would not lose his way, and today his trail of fragmented light is called the Milky Way.

"From the embrace of light and darkness, from sky and earth, came the lightning bolt Cocijo, good father, maker of the good earth and guide of those who work it and make it bear food.

"Giver of health, healer of illness, gentleman of war and death, with the Thirteenth Flower on his flag, Cocijo split into four parts in order to be in the four points that mark the world. In order to name death and pain, he inhabited the north and dressed in black. To give name to happiness, he established himself in the east in orange clothing. In the west, he put on a white cloak in order to mark destiny. And in order to speak war, he dressed in blue and walked in the south.

"The lightning, our father, married the woman of the *huipíl*[1] decorated with flowers and serpents, she who was called Serpent Thirteen, Nohuichana. She, our mother, giver of life in the womb of women, in the beds of rivers and lakes, in the rain, she who goes hand in hand with men and woman from birth to death, was and is a good queen for those who gave and give color to the color of the earth.

"And those who know and are silent tell that every so often, the lightning and the rain return, and with them love and life return, whenever the absurd poses obstacles for any woman and man, perhaps only to heighten the sparkle in their eyes.

"If it is true, as in fact it is, that life first walked as liquid in the caves that abound in indigenous lands, that the caves were and are the womb that the first gods gave to themselves in order to birth themselves and to make themselves, and that grottoes are the hollows left by the flowering of life like scars in the land, then it is within the land where we can read, in addition to the past, the paths that shall take us to tomorrow.

"In this January, the creator couple, Cosana and Xonaxi, embraced the womb of the earth, and they soothed it, in order to turn it into fertile sown fields. Not only so that the rebel struggle, which is collective— because that is the only way it can be rebel—might be renewed, but also so that the dream might be born with the color of those of us who are the color of the earth.

"Silent history now. And what is silent is always greater than that which speaks. Silence . . ."

Above, a storm greets the macaw's determined flight with lightning . . .

Below, Monte Albán remains, with its arrow building breaking the monotony of the entire ceremonial complex, warning that there are pieces missing, preventing us from understanding what we are seeing. As if to remind us that what is missing is greater and more marvelous than what we are seeing.

Because when we see what we are now seeing, vainglorious Monte Albán, we futilely seek continuity. In reality, we are seeing only a photograph, one instant, an image of a clock that stopped running on a particular date.

But it is a discontinuous clock. Only for the powerful is history an upward line, where their today is always the pinnacle. For those below, history is a question that can be answered only by looking both backward and forward, thus creating new questions.

And so we must question what is in front of us. Ask, for example, who is absent yet nonetheless made possible the presence of images of gods, *caciques*, and priests.

Ask who is silent when these ruins speak.

There are not just a few stelae in Monte Albán. They mark calendars that are not yet understood. But let us not forget that they present the calendars of those who held power in those times, and those calendars did not anticipate the date when a rebellion from below would bring their world down. Like an earthquake, the discontent of that time shook the entire social structure, and, while leaving the buildings standing, it did away with a world that was removed from everyone's reality.

Since ancient times, the governing elites have been fashioning calendars according to the political world, which is nothing but the world that excludes the majority. And the disparity between those calendars and those of the lives below is what provokes the earthquakes from which our history abounds.

For every stele that the power sculpts in its palaces, another stele rises from below. And, if those stelae are not visible, it is because they are not made of stone but of flesh, blood, and bone, and, being the color of the earth, they are still part of the cavern in which the future is ripening.

Those buildings that, like plumes, crown the Hill of the Tiger did not belong to those who raised and maintained them with their effort and wisdom:

Monumental architecture, in instances such as Monte Albán and other sites of Mesoamerican cultural interest, was a response to the need for a space dedicated to ceremonies, which corresponded to the organizational demands of a priestly social class with a much higher status than that of the average agricultural population. And so the buildings of Monte Albán, from their first period, were used for reinforcing the political system based in religious worship and for maintaining the ruling class in power. The populace in the villages and towns were charged with supplying all the consumer goods for that class, as well as with providing labor for constructing the buildings and for their continuous maintenance. Another obligation was that of providing all the supplies necessary for carrying out the ceremonies and the indispensable human material for those ceremonies. (Nelly Robles García, *Monte Albán* [CODEX Editores])

It was the powerful who enjoyed the work of those from below, the work that raised these buildings, these buildings that are less surprising than the arrogance that destroyed them. Because Monte Albán, as often happens in those spaces where power resides, collapsed as a result of rebellion from below, which was, in turn, provoked by the indifference of those who governed.

For the Spanish conquistadors, the twofold lesson of Monte Albán (the advanced development of a culture and the neglect caused by government arrogance) passed unnoticed. For the Spanish crown of the sixteenth century—like the neoliberalism of the beginning of the twenty-first century—the only culture is the one they dominate. Indigenous lands were nothing but an abundant source of labor for the Spanish powers, as they are now for savage capitalism. Under Spanish power, condemned to barbaric forced labor in the mines, almost 90 percent of the indigenous population of Oaxaca disappeared. But their suffering continued underground, and rebellion was forged in the grottoes, rebellion that today nourishes the color of the earth.

And what happened to the Indian peoples of Oaxaca also happened to the rest of the indigenous of Mexico: Their cultural wealth was, and is, discounted (sometimes through direct destruction, other times through ignorance, yet other times through racism, and always through condemnation of the different) by those who are power and dominion.

If, upon seeing the remains of the so-called pre-Hispanic cultures, the average spectator marvels and imagines their splendor, he would marvel even more upon seeing the cold cruelty and savage stupidity of those who have destroyed it (and contempt and commercialization are also a form of destruction) and ignored it.

And so it is quite wrong to blame the Spanish race, or any other, for the long pain of the Indian peoples of Mexico. It was, and is, the powerful who, regardless of the race to which they belong, reaffirm their dominion with the destruction of the identity of those under their control.

Following Mexico's liberation from Spanish dominion, the owners of money and their politicians have carried forward the destruction of indigenous culture with a brutality equal to or greater than that of the Spanish conquistadors in the sixteenth century.

Recently, intelligent voices have risen to prevent the Salinas reform of Article 27 of the Constitution (which allows the sale of ejidal land to individuals) from having a serious impact on the archeological monument zones. One of these zones is Monte Albán, where it so happens that part of its original land will now be in the hands of private business. Or at least that is what the neoliberal governments are attempting.

But there are resistances. The residents of the municipalities of San Pedro Ixtlahuaca, Santa Cruz Xoxocotlán, and Santa María Atzompa have organized to prevent that privatization of history. Gathering together ejiditarios, *comuneros*, small business owners, and residents, the Zapatista Front Against Privatization and Neoliberal Seizure includes its mission in its name.

Since mid-2001, these Oaxacans have been denouncing the coming privatization of Monte Albán. Behind these government programs, there was no interest in preserving archeological zones; rather, there was an interest in selling them in order to build hotels, convention centers, and commercial premises.

One year later, in 2002, Governor Murat took a step toward realizing Salinas de Gortari's dream: the Twenty-first Century Monte Albán project—privatizing ejidal lands in the areas surrounding the archeological complex and repressing those who were opposed to this commercialization of history. The resistance, however, was maintained, even though it was banished from the media. "We are the true defenders of the archeological zone of Monte Albán, because it is our home, and also the home of all Mexicans. But, in this continuous struggle to try to care for it and protect it, we are resisting culturally and we are confronting those who are trying to destroy it, restricting the use and enjoyment of our lands for the benefit of large investors," these rebel indigenous said, and committed themselves.

Nonetheless, and in spite of the repression, some of the strongest examples of anti-neoliberal resistance are in Oaxaca, and all of them are being carried out in spite of the political parties, and against them.

Last December, a group of young people, united around culture, was attacked by the Juchitán police, and their members are still being persecuted by the "democratic" municipal government.

In the Northern Mountains of Oaxaca, the Ricardo Flores Magón Popular Indigenous Council has taken heavy hits for refusing to surrender or to join the factions of Murat, Diódoro (the one who, when he was secretary of government in Zedillo's administration, "orchestrated" the PRI defeat in the 2000 lections), or Heladio.

In the Southern Mountains (but not only there), the Zapatista Magonista Alliance, the Coalition of Organizations of the State of Oaxaca, the Defense Committee for the Rights of the People, the Coalition of Independent

Organizations of Cuenca, the Broad Front of Popular Struggle, the Civil Front of Teojomulco, the Sole Front of Indigenous Defense, the Indian Organizations for Human Rights of Oaxaca, the Union of Poor Campesinos, and the Revolutionary Youth of Mexico have all joined together in the Oaxacan Popular Magonista Anti-Neoliberal Coordinating Group. They are building one of the most interesting processes of resistance.

And not only those. The Oaxacan resistance abounds in wisdom, decisiveness, and names: Services of the Mixe People, Union of Organizations of the Sierra Juárez of Oaxaca, Union of Indigenous Communities of the Isthmus Region, the State Coordinating Group of Coffee Producers of Oaxaca, and the Unified Movement of the Trique Struggle are just a few of the many that exist on Oaxacan soil.

And resistance not infrequently takes on the name of the municipalities where it arises. Thus appear Quetzaltepec-Mixe, San Pedro Yosotatu, Union Hidalgo, Yalalag, and others that people the Oaxacan geography with rebellion.

You would find it difficult to see any members of these organizations or municipalities running for office. Their vocation is not power, but service. That was mandated by the ancient ones who raised the grandeur of Monte Albán and whose rebellion toppled those who governed with arrogance.

But if the neoliberals of the PRI or the PAN or the PRD manage to get away with it, we will be facing the possibility that the history of Mexico will be turned into one more business listed on the stock exchange. What other value, besides the staging of tourism, can capital place on pre-Hispanic archeology?

When the front men for big money (Diego Fernández de Cevallos and his *patiños* Manuel Bartlett and Jesús Ortega, of the PAN, PRI, and PRD, respectively) scuppered the constitutional recognition of indigenous rights and culture in the Mexican Congress, they were not only imitating the *encomenderos*[2] of the colonial period, they were also, and above all, stating that the history of Mexico was one more commodity in the international market. If the manner in which they did it resembled a vaudeville act, it is because politicians can never resist the temptation to do the ridiculous.

The powerful purchase history not only to possess it, but also to prevent it from being read as it should be—that is, looking ahead.

The history of above continues saying "were" to those who still are. It does so because up there the only thing that matters is the exchange of those who are in power. And so time ends for the powerful only when another power replaces it.

Below, however, time continues to flow.

By responding to the unknown posited by the historic past, those below decipher crooked lines, ups and downs, valleys, hills, and hollows. That is how they know that history is nothing more than a jigsaw puzzle that excludes them as primary actor, reserving for them only the role of victim.

The missing piece in national history is that which corrects the false image of a single possible world, replacing it with the image of a world that includes everyone in its true size: The constant struggle continues between those who think they are the culmination of the ages and those who know that the last word is built through resistance, sometimes in silence, far from the media and the centers of power.

Only in that way is it possible to understand that the current world is neither the best nor the only one possible, and that other worlds are not merely possible but, above all, those new worlds are better and necessary. As long as that does not happen, history will remain nothing but an anarchic collection of dates, places, and different-colored vanities.

The grandeur of Monte Albán will not be completed with the discovery of more temples, tombs, and treasures, nor even through the exact reconstruction of its undeniable splendor. Monte Albán will be complete—and along with that, it will be part of the real history of our country—when it is understood that the ones who made it possible, who raised and maintained it, and whose rebellion undermined the arrogance that inhabited it, are still living and struggling, not so that Monte Albán and its power will be renewed and history will make an impossible backward turn, but for the recognition of the fact that the world will not be complete unless it includes everyone in the future.

The indigenous movement in which zapatismo is inscribed is not trying to return to the past, nor to maintain the unfair pyramid of society, changing only the skin color of the one who mandates and rules from above. The struggle of the Indian peoples of Mexico is not pointing backward. In a linear world, where above is considered eternal and below inevitable, the Indian peoples of Mexico are breaking with that line and pointing toward something that is yet to be deciphered but that is already new and better.

Whoever comes from below and from so far away in time has, most certainly, burdens and problems imposed by people who made wealth their gods and alibis. Those who come from such a long way can see a great distance, and there is another world in that distant point that their heart divines, a new world, a better one, a necessary one, one where all worlds fit . . .

If, in their long and idiotic march, the neoliberals say, "There is no culture other than ours," then below, with the underground Mexico that resists and struggles, the Indian peoples of Oaxaca are warning: *There are other grottoes like ours.*

From the mountains of the Mexican Southeast

SUBCOMANDANTE INSURGENTE MARCOS

NOTES

1. A *huipíl* is a hand-woven blouse worn by indigenous women throughout southern Mexico and in some parts of Central America.
2. An *encomendero* is the manager of an *encomienda*, a labor system used during the Spanish colonization of the Americas. *Conquistadores* were granted trusteeship over the indigenous people they conquered, an expansion of feudal institutions. The official *encomienda* system was established in 1493 and abolished in 1791.

Puebla, the Second Stele

February: Candle and shadow continue to tremble. Brushing aside the smoke and the "January" page in the calendar, the hand reveals, contradictory and luminous, February, and with it another gaze, another hand, and another word: *Puebla.*

It is February, a month that summons up history, with all its lights and contradictions. It is Puebla, land where contradictions presage hope.

Puebla. According to the INEGI, it had more than five million inhabitants in the year 2000, among whom more than half a million over the age of 5 were indigenous-language speakers. Indigenous Nahuas, Totonacos, Mixtecos, Otomís, and Popolocas are living and resisting in what today are their lands.

It is February and it is Puebla. Above Tehuacán, a little blue cloud, delicate like a princess, frames, not conceals, the sun.

As if it were her vassal, the little cloud forces the sun not to follow its stubborn westward route but instead to fly toward the north. There, in the midst of the Mixtec Sierra, looms a hill surrounded by ravines. Above it, ramparts can be discerned, as if this were a place prepared to protect resistance. It seems to be Tepexi El Viejo. The Nahuas called it Cleft Rock, and the Popolocas named it Small Mountain. Here they rest and frolic while the sun recounts to the cloud a history that causes her to blush, and teaches her:

"The ancient Mixtecos tell that the world was created from the union of two great trees, in the solitary Apoala, at the foot of a grotto, in the Achiutl River. Joined at their roots, these two first trees created the first Mixtec couple, and from the children of their children was born Yacoñooy, the archer of the sun.

"These ancient ones recount that Yacoñooy was a small *guerrero*, courageous and bold, who feared nothing, no matter how large and powerful it might appear.

"Because, these indigenous wise men say, stature is carried in the heart, and it often happens that those who seem small on the outside are great in the greatness of their hearts. And those whose appearance seems strong and powerful are, in fact, small and weak in heart.

"And they also say that the world is large and full of immense marvels because people small in stature know how to find the strength inside themselves to make the earth become large.

"They then told that time was walking the first months of the calendar of humanity and that Yacoñooy left to look for new lands in order to make them grow through work and the word. He found them, and he saw that the sun appeared to be the sole and powerful owner of everything illuminated by its light. At that time, the sun was killing the life of the different, and it accepted things only that mirrored it and bore tribute to his grand greatness.

"And they recount that, upon seeing this, Yacoñooy challenged the sun, saying: 'You, who with your force dominate these lands, I challenge you in order to see who is the greatest and who can therefore bring greatness to these lands.'

"The sun laughed, confident in his power and strength, and he ignored the small being who, from the ground, was challenging him. Yacoñooy challenged him anew and said: 'The strength of your light does not frighten me. I have time as a weapon, which is growing in my heart.'

And he drew his bow taut, pointing the arrow at the very center of the arrogant sun.

"The sun again laughed, and then he tightened his heat's dazzling belt of fire about the rebel, to make the small one even smaller.

"But Yacoñooy protected himself with his shield, and thus resisted while noon gave way to afternoon. He saw the sun becoming impotent, its strength diminishing with the passage of time, and the small rebel continued there, protected and resisting behind his shield, waiting for the hour of the bow and the arrow.

"Seeing that the sun was weakening with the passage of time turned dusk, Yacoñooy left his place of refuge and, taking up the bow, pierced the great sun seven times. As twilight fell, the entire sky was stained red, and the sun finally fell, mortally wounded, to the ground of the night.

"Yacoñooy waited for a time and, seeing that the night prevented the sun from continuing the combat, said: 'I have won. I resisted your attack with my shield. I made time and your arrogance my allies. I conserved my strength for the necessary moment. I have won. Now the earth shall have the greatness that our heart sowed in its bosom.'

"And they recount that on the next day the sun returned, recuperated, to try and reconquer the land. But it was already too late. The people of Yacoñooy had already harvested what had been sown in the night.

"That was how, by being victors in the sky, the Yacoñooy is called 'The Archer of the Sun' and the Mixtecos were named inhabitants of the clouds.

"Ever since then, the Mixtecos have painted Yacoñooy's victory on gourds, not to boast of the victory, but in order to remember that greatness is carried in the heart and that resistance is also a form of combat."

From the mountains of the Mexican Southeast

SUBCOMANDANTE INSURGENTE MARCOS

The Federal District,
the Twelfth Stele

(FIRST IMAGE: THE CITY BETWEEN ILLUSION
AND REALITY), JANUARY 2003

It is once again dawn when the hand and eyes touch the calendar. On top it says "December," and below, "Mexico Federal District."

Cloud and stone rise up in order to draw near other parts of Mexico City.

This city presents an illusion. It appears to be inhabited by broken-down automobiles, by sterile shopping centers, by news programs that are torn between lies and facile scandal (although sometimes they are combined), by television programs that reward the ridiculous on primetime, by swift convoys replete with bodyguards transporting officials or tycoons who are not going anywhere, but who are moving because they believe it is necessary to remind the city that they exist.

Mexico City. A multitude of cities in transit to other cities (at their own, and always external, rate). A city that has lost its capacity for being astonished in the face of cynicism and corruption. A city that the dawn continues to catch naked and surprised. A city that everyone has wanted to tame, to domesticate, to kill, and that nonetheless continues to rebel—indomitable, unpredictable. Because this city has the virtue of being a light sleeper. And it wakes up quickly if a misfortune—its own or foreign—clouds the days and nights that illusions conceal.

But now, at this hour of the dawn, it appears empty . . .

Where are those who make it run? Where are those who nurture it, give it light, color, rhythm, life?

Where are the brothers and sisters who, generously and uncondition-ally, turn their hearts and eyes to those who, like them, are the color of the earth? Where are those who, in March of 2001, heard in the Zócalo: *Do not allow another dawn to break without that flag having a place for those of us who are the color of the earth.*

Where is the rebel city in solidarity?

Where are the social movements that incorporate and shelter the resist-ances and rebellions that emerge all over from the Mexico of below?

Where are the humble people who, having little, give everything to the one who needs it?

The cloud looks and the stone looks. They look and, looking, they find. Scattered and fragmented, not because that is their fate, but because that is how they are born. Rebellion and resistance are sheltered in those who, being below, do not matter to those who are above.

They find it difficult to get their bearings, but, looking above and look-ing below, stone and cloud are learning to distinguish between the lights and the mere reflections provided by a puddle of dirty water.

That still-pale light, for example, is going to great efforts to build an alternative culture that is, by definition, critical, and that is construct-ing its questions with ingenuity and imagination. Their colors are many. From the rainbow that, sometimes in clerical garb, is demand-ing not only free sexual preference, but also the right to be without masks or closets. To those who join machete and art in order to give voice and ear to the marginalized. To those cultural groups and spaces that, outside official circuits, are exercising the old and forgotten right to learn and to teach, enjoying and coexisting, like in that auditorium where Alicia contemplates us through the mirror.

Now it is night in the city.

On a corner, an anonymous voice is proclaiming: "In the beginning there was the word, and the word was made Word, and, in order to make the world run better, the Word was made . . . rock and roll," and then, for lack of a guitar, the orator frets his gum with his teeth, and now one can distinctly make out that tune that goes, "*Papa* was a rolling stone." And, swinging their hips with a rhythm that would be loved at any table dance, cloud and stone continue, "like a rolling stone," to seek and find more lights.

There, constantly escaping from schemes and budgets, the young are making their dress, their dance, and their speech a continuous "performance" that repeats rebellion. And there are the goths, the street, the punks, the skins, the metalheads, the skaters, the ravers, the rockers, the many names with which the young clothe themselves. And in that way they are defending an identity that is stolen from them by a society that criminalizes, even more than their clothing or the cut or color of their hair, their age.

And speaking of youth and rebellion . . .

During every election, young people are treated like recyclable garbage for the system. Young people, who carry their distrust as IDs. Young people, who refuse to buy a life with the false coin of cynicism. Young people, who are fodder for jail, for raids, for beatings, for rapes, for contempt, for humiliation, for lies, for death. Irreverent young people, uncompromising . . . invincible as long as they do not forget that a young person without rebellion is . . . well, what can I say, *bro*?

The early morning advances, and the unclad city begins enrobing itself in the modest apparel of street vendors.

Determined to build an honest way of life, small-shop-keepers in the streets and the markets have more to put up with than the police and inspectors. They must also contend with the large shopping centers that, knowing that the vendors' merchandise is better in quality and price, are employing all their resources to eliminate them and drive them into indigence or crime.

There one can see Viana, which, of course, is not the least expensive. Further along is Wal-Mart, Señora Sahagún's accomplice in deceiving consumers. In addition to robbing them through the prices and the quality of their products, Wal-Mart is snatching pennies from those who fall into their nets. The propaganda says that those pennies (which turn into millions as the days and clients accumulate) are for education, but they are, in fact, for the Let's Go Mexico Foundation, that Super-Department of State led by Marta Sahagún de Fox.

Between the big shopping centers and the little corner stores, it is the little corner shops and bodegas that are better and cheaper (and much more honest).

If cloud and stone have any memory of what solidarity is with the unknown in misfortune, it is memory of the poorest and most persecuted people in this city. Stall holders; taxi drivers; truckers; prostitutes; waitresses; *luchadores* (of *lucha libre* and of life);[1] criers and boxers; fire swallowers/clowns/corner windshield cleaners; homosexuals; transvestites; transsexuals; sellers of ice cream, *tortas*, hot dogs, *licuados* – *uno* – *de* – *nuez* – *por* – *favor* – *hoy* – *no* – *se* – *fía* – *mañana* – *quién* – *sabe* – *dama* – *caballero* – *por* – *esta* – *única* – *ocasión* – *le* – *vengo* – *a* – *ofrecer* – *esta* – *oportunidad* – *llévese* – *10* – *plumas* – *10* – *calidad* – *de* – *importación* – *a* – *solo* – *10* – *pesitos* – *próxima* – *parada* – *estación* – *indios* – *verdes* – tiruri . . .[2]

Why is it that, at the hour of need, the ones who have the least give the most? When hurricanes, droughts, and earthquakes paint the land of the humble with misery, it is the poorest people who stand in line at the collection places in order to donate the rice, beans, oil, and salt that they are undoubtedly lacking at their own tables. While in the charity telethons, the powerful are handing out checks with many zeros and no dignity.

The humble give what they have, stone and cloud reflect, and the powerful give what is left over, what is in their way, what is already used, the expired, the unusable.

The stone walks. The cloud flies. How many cities concealed by this city! How many of them have the dignity that the powerful lack!

From the mountains of the Mexican Southeast

SUBCOMANDANTE INSURGENTE MARCOS

NOTES

1. *Luchadores* are professional wrestlers. *Lucha libre* is a term commonly used to refer to professional wrestling throughout Latin America.
2. This passage may prove confusing to readers who are unfamiliar with Mexico City slang. We have temporarily left the English-speaking world to enter *Chilangolandia*, the capital city of Mexico. The last word, "tituri," is onomatopoetic of the sound of a subway door opening.

Durito and One about False Options

Durito says that all the multiple options being offered by power conceal a trap.

"Where there are many paths, and we're presented with the chance to choose, something fundamental is forgotten: all those paths lead to the same place. And so, liberty consists not in choosing the destination, the pace, the speed, and the company, but in merely choosing the path. The liberty that the powerful is offering is, in fact, merely the liberty to choose who will walk representing us," Durito says.

And Durito says that, in reality, power offers no liberty other than that of choosing from multiple options of death. You can choose the nostalgic option, that of forgetting. That is the one being offered to the Mexican indigenous as the most suitable for their idiosyncrasies.

Or you can also choose the modernizing option, that of frenetic exploitation. This is the one being offered, for example, to the Latin American middle classes as most suitable for their patterns of consumption.

Or, if not, you can choose the futuristic option, that of twenty-first-century weapons. This is the one being offered by the guided missiles in Iraq and which, so that there may be no doubt as to their democratic spirit, kill Iraqis as well as North Americans, Saudi Arabians, Iranians, Kurds, Brits, and Kuwaitis.

There are many other options, one for almost every taste and preference. Because if there is anything neoliberalism is able to pride itself on, it is on offering an almost infinite variety of deaths, and no other political system in the history of humanity can say that.

Then Durito puts a vase with water on the little table, which is made of sticks, tied together with *bejuco*,[1] and he says: "The powers tell us, for example, that we have to choose between being optimists or pessimists. The pessimist sees the glass as being half empty. The optimist sees the glass as half full. But the rebel realizes that neither the vase nor the water it contains belongs to him. It is someone else, the Powerful, who fills it and empties it at his whim. The rebel, on the other hand, sees the trap. But he also sees the spring from which the water issues forth.

"And so, when the rebel faces the option of choosing between various paths, he looks farther ahead and he looks twice: He sees that those routes lead to the same place, and he sees that there is no path to the place where he wishes to go. Then the rebel, instead of agonizing over polls that say that one path is better than the other because such and such a percent cannot be wrong, begins building a new path," says Durito, while handing out many "No"s on little pieces of paper of all colors in front of North American embassies throughout the world, which, as everyone knows, look suspiciously like plastic burger shops.

From the mountains of the Mexican Southeast

SUBCOMANDANTE INSURGENTE MARCOS

NOTE

1. *Bejoco* refers to climbing vines, commonly found in tropical areas of Central and South America, and the West Indies.

Chiapas, the Thirteenth Stele

PART ONE: A CARACOL

July 2003, Mexico
Dawn in the mountains of the Mexican Southeast

Slowly, with an unhurried but continuous movement, the moon allows the dark sheet of night to slip off her body and to finally reveal the erotic nudity of her light. She then reclines across the length of the sky, desirous of looking and being looked at, that is, of touching and being touched. If light does anything, it delineates its opposite, and so, down below, a shadow offers the cloud its hand while murmuring:

"Come with me, look with your heart at what my eyes show you, walk in my steps, and dream in my arms. Up above, the stars are making a *caracol*, with the moon as origin and destiny. Look and listen. This is a dignified and rebel land. The men and women who live in it are like many men and women in the world. Let us walk, then, in order to look at and listen to them now, while time hovers between night and day, when dawn is a queen and a lady in these lands.

"Take care with the puddle and the mud. Better to follow the tracks that, like in so many other things, are the most knowing. Do you hear that laughter? It is from a couple who are repeating the ancient rite of love. He murmurs something, and she laughs, she laughs as if she were singing. Then silence, then sighs and muted moans. Or perhaps the other way around, first sighs and moans, afterward murmurs and laughter. But let's continue on ahead, because love needs no witnesses other than glances turned flesh, and, since it is sunlight regardless of the hour, that undresses shadows.

"Come. Let us sit for a bit and let me tell you things. We are in rebel lands. Here live and fight those who are called 'zapatistas.' And these zapatistas are very otherly . . . and they frustrate more than one. Instead of weaving their history with executions, death, and destruction, they insist on living. And the vanguards of the world tear at their hair, because, as for 'victory or death,' these zapatistas neither vanquish nor die, but neither do they surrender, and they despise martyrdom as much as capitulation. Very otherly, it's true. And then there is the one who is said to be their leader, one Sup Marcos, whose public image is closer to that of Cantinflas and Pedro Infante than to Emiliano Zapata and Che Guevara. And it's a waste of time to say that no one will take them seriously that way, because they themselves are the first to joke about their being so otherly.

"They are rebel indigenous. Breaking, thus, the traditional preconception, first from Europe and afterward from all those who are clothed in the color of money, that was imposed on them for looking and being looked at.

"And so they do not adapt to the 'diabolical' image of those who sacrifice humans to appease the gods, nor to that of the needy indigenous, with his hand extended, expecting crumbs or charity from he who has everything. Nor that of the good savage who is perverted by modernity, nor that of the infant who entertains his elders with gibberish. Nor that of the submissive peon from all those haciendas that lacerated the history of Mexico. Nor that of the skillful craftsperson whose products will adorn the walls of he who despises him. Nor that of the ignorant fool who should not have an opinion about what is further than the limited horizon of his geography. Nor that of someone who is fearful of heavenly or earthly gods.

"Because you must know, blue repose, that these indigenous become angry even at those who sympathize with their cause. And the fact is that they do not obey. When they are expected to speak, they are silent. When silence is expected, they speak. When they are expected to lead, they step to the back. When they are expected to keep going back, they're off on another side. When it's expected that they alone speak, they break out talking of other things. When they're expected to be satisfied with their geography, they walk the world and its struggles.

"It's as if they please no one. And it doesn't seem to matter much to them. What does matter to them is for their heart to be content, and so they follow the paths shown by their heart. That's what they seem to be doing now. Everywhere there are people on paths. They are coming and going, barely exchanging the usual greetings. They are spending long hours in meetings or assemblies or whatever. They go in with frowning faces, and they leave, smiling in complicity.

"Mmh . . .

"Whatever it is, I am sure that many people will not like what they are going to do or say. In addition, as the Sup says, the zapatistas' specialty is in creating problems and then seeing later who is going to solve them. And so one shouldn't expect much from those meetings other than problems . . .

"Perhaps we can guess what it is about if we look carefully. The zapatistas are very otherly—I don't know if I already told you that—and so they imagine things before they exist, and they think that, by naming them, those things will begin to have life, to walk . . . and, yes, to create problems. And so I am sure they have already imagined something, and they are going to begin to act as if that something already exists, and no one is going to understand anything for some time, because, in effect, once named, things begin to take on body, life, and a tomorrow.

"Then we could look for some clue . . . No, I don't know where to look . . . I believe their way is looking with their ears and listening with their eyes. Yes, I know it sounds complicated, but nothing else occurs to me. Come, let's keep on walking.

"Look, the stream is turning into a whirlpool there, and in its center the moon is shimmering its sinuous dance. A whirlpool . . . or a *caracol*.

"They say that the most ancient say that the even more ancient said that the first people of these lands valued the *caracol*'s shape. They say that they say that they said that the *caracol* represents entering the heart, which is what the most ancient called understanding. And they say that they say that they said that the *caracol* also represents leaving the heart to walk the world, which is what the most ancient called life. The *caracol* was used to summon the collective so that the word could travel between one and the other—so that agreement could be born. They also say that the *caracol* helped to hear even the most distant word. That is what they say they say they said. I'm not sure. I am merely walking with you—hand in hand—showing you what my ears see and what my gaze hears. I see and I hear a *caracol*, the *pu'y*, as they say in their language here.

"*Sshhhhh.* Silence. The dawn has already yielded to the day. Yes, I know it's still dark, but look how the huts are filling, little by little, with light from fire in the stoves. Since now we are shadows in the shadow, no one sees us, but if they did see us, I am sure they would offer us a cup of coffee, which, with this cold, would be appreciated. As I appreciate the pressure of your hand in my hand.

"Look, the moon is already slipping away to the west, concealing its pregnant light behind the mountain. It is time to leave, to cover the step in the shadow of a cave, there, where desire and weariness are soothed with another, more pleasant weariness. Come, here, I will murmur to you with flesh and words:

> *And, ay, how I would wish to be*
> *a joy among all joys,*
> *one alone, the joy you would take joy in!*
> *A love, one single love:*
> *the love you would fall in love with.*
> *But*
> *I am nothing more than what I am*

—PEDRO SALINAS, "LA VOZ A TI DEBIDA"

"We will no longer be looking at each other there, but in the half-sleep of desire, moored in a safe harbor, we will be able to listen to what is stirring these zapatistas now, those who insist on subverting even time and who are once again raising, as if it were a flag, another calendar . . . that of resistance.

"Shadow and light go. They have not noticed that in a hut a faint light has been kept up all through the night. Now, inside, a group of men and women are sharing coffee and silence, as they shared the word previously.

"For several hours, these humans with their dusk-colored hearts have traced a great *caracol* with their ideas. Starting from the international, their eyes and their thoughts have turned within, passing successively through the national, the regional, and the local, until they reached what they call "El Votán"—the guardian and heart of the people, the zapatista people. In this way, from the *caracol*'s most external curve, words like the following are contemplated: "globalization," "war of domination," "resistance," "economy," "city," "countryside," "political situation," and others that the eraser eliminates after the rigorous question is asked: "Is it clear or are there questions?" At the end of the path from outside in, at the center of the *caracol*, only some initials remain: "EZLN." Afterward, there are proposals, and they paint, in thought and in heart, windows and doors that only they see (among other reasons, because they still don't exist). The disparate and scattered word begins to make common a collective path.

"Someone asks: 'Is there agreement?'

"'There is,' the now-collective voice responds affirmatively.

"The *caracol* is traced again, but now in the opposite path, from the inside out. The eraser also continues the reverse path until only one sentence remains, filling the old chalkboard, a sentence that is madness to many, but that is, to these men and women, a reason for struggle: 'A world where many worlds fit.' A little bit later, a decision is made.

"Now is silence and waiting. A shadow goes out into the night rain. A spark of light barely illuminates the eye. Once again, smoke rises from his lips in the darkness. With his hands behind his back, he begins a coming and going without destination. A few minutes ago, there, inside, a death has been decided.

(To be continued)

From the mountains of the Mexican Southeast

SUBCOMANDANTE INSURGENTE MARCOS

PART TWO: A DEATH

Mexico, July of 2003

A few days ago, the Zapatista Army of National Liberation decided on the death of the so-called Aguascalientes of La Realidad, Oventik, La Garrucha, Morelia, and Roberto Barrios. All of them located in rebel territory. The decision to disappear the Aguascalientes was made after a long process of reflection.

On August 8, 1994, during the Democratic National Convention held in Guadalupe Tepeyac, Comandante Tacho, in the name of the Clandestine Revolutionary Indigenous Committee, General Command of the Zapatista Army of National Liberation, inaugurated, before some 6,000 persons from various parts of Mexico and the world, the so-called Aguascalientes, and he handed it over to national and international civil society.

Many people did not know that first Aguascalientes, whether because they couldn't go, or because they were very young in that year (if you are 24 now, or turning 25, you would have been 14 then, or turning 15), but it was a formidable ship. Run around on the side of a hill, its huge white sails hoped to travel the seven seas. The flag, with its ferocious skull and crossbones, waved fiercely and defiantly above the bridge. Two huge national flags were unfurled at the sides, like wings. It had its library, infirmary, lavatories, showers, background music (which alternated obsessively between "Red Bow" and "Marked Cards"), and, it is said, even a place for attacks. The layout of the buildings looked, as I have related once, like a huge *caracol*, thanks to what we called the "crooked house." The "crooked house" wasn't crooked; it had a crack that appeared at first glance to be an architectural error but that, from above, allowed one to observe the spiral formed by the buildings. The crew of the first Aguascalientes was made up of individuals without face, clear transgressors of maritime and terrestrial laws. And their captain was the handsomest pirate who has ever sailed the oceans: a patch over his missing right eye, a black beard glistening with strands of platinum, a pronounced nose, hook in one hand, saber in the other, a leg of flesh and one of wood, pistol in his belt, and pipe in his mouth.

The process that led to the building of that first Aguascalientes was fortuitous . . . and painful. And I am not referring to the physical construction (which was carried out in record time and without television "spots") but to the conceptual construction. Let me explain:

We had prepared ourselves for ten years for killing and dying, for handling and firing weapons of all kinds, for making explosives, for executing strategic and tactical military maneuvers—in sum, for making war. After the first days of combat, we found ourselves invaded by a genuine army. First an army of journalists, but later one of men and women from the most diverse social, cultural, and national backgrounds. It was after those "Cathedral Dialogues," in February–March of 1994. The journalists continued to appear intermittently, but what we call "civil society"—in order to differentiate it from the political class, and so as not to categorize it in social classes—was always constant.

We were learning, and I imagine civil society was, as well. We learned to listen and to speak, the same, I imagine, as civil society. I also imagine that the learning was less arduous for us.

After all, that had been the EZLN's fundamental origin: a group of "illuminati" who came from the city to "liberate" the exploited and who looked, when confronted with the reality of the indigenous communities, more like burned-out lightbulbs than illuminati. How long did it take us to realize that we had to learn to listen, and, afterward, to speak? I'm not sure, but I calculate two years at least. Meaning that what had been a classic revolutionary guerrilla force in 1984 (armed uprising of the masses, the taking of power, the establishment of socialism from above, many statues and names of heroes and martyrs everywhere, purges, et cetera—in sum, a perfect world), by 1986 was already an armed group, overwhelmingly indigenous, listening attentively, and barely babbling its first words with a new teacher: the Indian peoples.

What I mean by this is that the main founding act of the EZLN was learning to listen and to speak. I believe, at that time, we learned well and we were successful. With the new tool we built with the learned word, the EZLN quickly turned into an organization not just of thousands of fighters, but one which was clearly "merged" with the indigenous communities.

To put it another way, we ceased to be "foreigners," and we turned into part of that corner forgotten by the country and by the world: *the mountains of the Mexican Southeast.*

A moment arrived, I can't say precisely just when, in which it was no longer the EZLN on one side and the communities on the other, but when we were all simply zapatistas. I'm simplifying, necessarily, when remembering this period. There will be another occasion, I hope, and another means, for going into details about that process, which, in broad terms, was not without contradictions, setbacks, and backsliding.

The fact is, that's how we were, still learning (because, I believe, learning never ends), when the now "newly appeared" Carlos Salinas de Gortari (then president of Mexico, thanks to a colossal election fraud) had the "brilliant" idea of making reforms that did away with the campesinos' right to the land.

The impact in the communities that were already zapatista was, to say the least, brutal. For us (note that I no longer distinguish between the communities and the EZLN), the land is not merchandise. It has cultural, religious, and historic connotations that don't need to be explained here. And so, our regular ranks grew, quickly and exponentially.

And there was more. Poverty also grew, and along with it death, especially of children under the age of 5. As part of my responsibilities, it was up to me at that time to check in with the now hundreds of villages by radio, and there wasn't a day when someone didn't report the death of a little boy, of a little girl, of a mother. As if it were a war. Afterward, we understood that it was, in fact, a war. The neoliberal model that Carlos Salinas de Gortari commanded in such a cynical and carefree fashion was, for us, an authentic war of extermination, an ethnicide, given that it was entire Indian peoples who were being destroyed. That is why we know what we are talking about when we speak of the "neoliberal bomb."

I imagine (there are serious studies here that will recount with precise figures and analysis) that this took place in all the indigenous communities in Mexico. But the difference was that we were armed and trained for a war. Mario Benedetti says, in a poem, that one doesn't always do what one wants, that one can't always, but he has the right to not do what he doesn't want. And in our case, we did not want to die . . . or, more accurately, we didn't want to die like that.

I have previously, on some occasion, spoken of the importance memory has for us. And therefore, death by forgetting was (and is) the worst of deaths for us. I know it will sound apocalyptic, and that more than one person will search for some touch of martyrdom in what I am saying, but, in order to put it in simple terms, we found ourselves facing a choice, but not between life or death, but between two kinds of death. The decision, collective and in consultation with each one of the then tens of thousands of zapatistas, is already history, and it was the spark for that dawn of the First of January of 1994.

Mmm. It seems to me as if I'm wandering, because what this is supposed to be about is our decision to get rid of the zapatista Aguascalientes. Ah, well, be generous and keep reading.

Cornered, we left on that dawn in 1994 with only two certainties: One was that they were going to tear us to shreds. The other was that the act would attract the attention of good persons toward a crime that was no less bloody because it was silent and removed from the media: the genocide of thousands of indigenous Mexican families. And, as I've said, it could sound as if we were inclined to being martyrs who sacrificed themselves for others.

I would lie if I said yes. Because even though, looking at it coldly, we had no chance militarily, our hearts weren't thinking of death, but of life. Given that we were (and are) zapatistas and, ergo, our doubts include ourselves, we thought we could be wrong about being torn to shreds and that perhaps the entire people of Mexico would rise up. But our doubts, I should be sincere, didn't extend so far as imagining that what actually happened could have happened.

And what happened was precisely what gave rise to the first Aguascalientes, and then to the ones that followed. I don't believe it's necessary to repeat what happened. I'm almost sure (and I'm not usually sure about anything) that anyone reading these lines had something, or much, to do with what happened.

And so make an effort and put yourself in our place: Entire years preparing for firing weapons, and it so happens that it's words that have to be fired. When it's said like that, and now that I read what I just wrote, it seems as if it were almost natural, like one of those syllogisms they teach in high school. But believe me, at that time nothing was easy. We struggled a lot . . . and we continue to do so. But it so happens that a *guerrero* doesn't forget what he learns, and, as I explained earlier, we learned to listen and to speak. So then, history—as someone, I don't recall who, once said—grew tired of moving and repeated itself, and we were once again like we were in the beginning. Learning.

And we learned, for example, that we were different, and that there were many who were different from us, but who were also different among themselves. Almost immediately after the bombs ("they weren't bombs, but rockets," those connected intellectuals—the ones who criticize the press when it talks of "bombing indigenous communities"—will then hasten to clarify), a multiplicity fell on top of us that made us think, not a few times, that it would have been better, effectively, if they had torn us to shreds.

A fighter defined it, in very zapatista terms, in April of 1994. He came to report to me about the arrival of a caravan from civil society. I asked him how many there were (they had to be put up somewhere) and who they were (I didn't ask each one of their names, but what organization or group they belonged to). The rebel considered the question first, and then the answer he would give. That generally took a while, so I lit my pipe. After considering, the compañero said: "They're *un chingo*,¹ and they're absolute chaos." I believe it is useless to expound on the quantitative universe embraced by the scientific concept of "*un chingo*," but the rebel wasn't using "absolute chaos" disapprovingly, or as a means of characterizing the state of mind of those who were arriving, but rather of defining the composition of the group. "What do you mean, absolute chaos?" I asked him. "Yes," he answered. "There's everything . . . t's absolute chaos," he ended up saying, insisting that there was no scientific concept whatsoever that could better describe the multiplicity that had taken rebel territory by storm. The storm was repeated again and again. Sometimes they were, in effect, a *chingo*. Other times they were two or three *chingos*. But it was always, to use the neologism utilized by the rebel, "absolute chaos."

We intuited then that, oh, well, we had to learn, and this learning must be for the most possible. And so we thought about a kind of school, where we would be the students and the "absolute chaos" would be the teacher. This was already June of 1994 (we weren't very quick at realizing we had to learn), and we were about to make public the Second Declaration of the Lacandon Jungle, which called for the creation of the National Democratic Convention (CND).

The history of the CND is another story, and I'm mentioning it now only to orient you in time and space. Space. Yes, that was part of the problem with our learning. That is, we needed a space in order to learn and to listen and to speak with that plurality that we call "civil society." We agreed then to build the space and to name it "Aguascalientes," given that it would be the seat of the National Democratic Convention (recalling the Convention of the Mexican revolutionary forces in the second decade of the twentieth century). But the idea for the Aguascalientes went further. We wanted a space for dialogue with civil society. And "dialogue" also means learning to listen to the other and learning to speak with him.

However, the Aguascalientes space had been born linked to a current political initiative, and many people assumed that once that initiative had run its course, the Aguascalientes would lose meaning. Very few returned to the Aguascalientes of Guadalupe Tepeyac. Later came Zedillo's betrayal on February 9, 1995, and the Aguascalientes were almost totally destroyed by the federal army. They even built a military barracks there.

But if anything characterizes zapatistas, it's tenacity ("stupidity," more than one person might say). And so, not even a year had passed before new Aguascalientes arose in various parts of rebel territory: Oventik, La Realidad, La Garrucha, Roberto Barrios, Morelia. Then, yes, the Aguascalientes were what they should be: spaces for *encuentro*[2] and dialogue with national and international civil society. In addition to being the headquarters for great initiatives and *encuentros* on memorable dates, they were the place where civil society and zapatistas met every day.

I told you that we tried to learn from our *encuentros* with national and international civil society. But we also expected them to learn. The zapatista movement arose, among other things, to demand respect. And it so happened that we didn't always receive respect. And it's not that they insulted us, or at least not intentionally. But for us, pity is an affront and charity is a slap in the face. Because, parallel with the emergence and operation of those spaces of *encuentro* that were the Aguascalientes, some sectors of civil society have maintained what we call "the Cinderella syndrome."

Right now I'm taking out of the chest of memories some excerpts from a letter I wrote more than nine years ago:

We are not reproaching you for anything (to those from civil society who came to the communities), we know that you are risking much to come and see us and to bring aid to the civilians on this side. It is not our needs that bring us pain, it's seeing in others what others don't see, the same abandonment of liberty and democracy, the same lack of justice. . . . I saved an example of "humanitarian aid" for the Chiapaneco indigenous, which arrived a few weeks ago as a benefit in this war: a pink stiletto heel, imported, size six and a half . . . without its mate. I always carry it in my backpack in order to remind myself, in the midst of interviews, photo reports, and attractive sexual propositions, that since the First of January what we are to the country is a Cinderella. . . . These good people who, sincerely, send us a pink stiletto heel, size six and a half, imported, without its mate . . . thinking that, poor as we are, we'll accept anything, charity and alms. How can we tell all those good people that no, we no longer want to continue living Mexico's shame? In that part that has to be prettied up so it doesn't make the rest look ugly. No, we don't want to go on living like that.

That was April 1994. Then we thought it was a matter of time that the people were going to understand that the zapatista indigenous were dignified and they weren't looking for alms, but for respect. The other pink heel never arrived, and the pair remained incomplete, and piling up in the Aguascalientes were useless computers, expired medicines, extravagant (for us) clothes, which couldn't even be used for plays (*señas*, as they call them here), and, yes, shoes without their mate. And things like that continue to arrive, as if those people were saying, "Poor little things, they're very needy. I'm sure anything would do for them, and this is in my way."

And that's not all. There is a more sophisticated charity. It's the one that a few NGOs and international agencies practice. It consists, broadly speaking, in their deciding what the communities need and, without even consulting them, imposing not just specific projects, but also the times and means of their implementation. Imagine the desperation of a community that needs drinkable water and they're saddled with a library. The one that requires a school for the children, and they give them a course on herbs.

A few months ago, an intellectual of the left wrote that civil society should mobilize to achieve the fulfillment of the San Andrés Accords[3] because the zapatista indigenous communities were suffering greatly (not because it would be just for the Indian peoples of Mexico, but so that the zapatistas wouldn't suffer any more deprivation).

Just a moment. If the zapatista communities wanted, they could have the best standard of living in Latin America. Imagine how much the government would be willing to invest in order to secure our surrender and to take lots of pictures and make a lot of "spots" where Fox or Martita could promote themselves, while the country fell apart in their hands. How much would the now "newly appeared" Carlos Salinas de Gortari have given in order to end his term, not with the burden of the assassinations of Colosio and Ruíz Massieu, but with a picture of the rebel zapatistas signing the peace and the Sup handing over his weapon (the one God gave him?) to the one who plunged millions of Mexicans into ruin? How much would Zedillo have offered in order to cover up the economic crisis in which he buried the country, with the image of his triumphal entrance into La Realidad? . . .

No. The zapatistas have received many offers to buy their consciences, and they keep up their resistance nonetheless, making their poverty (for he who learns to see) a lesson in dignity and generosity. Because we zapatistas say "Everything for everyone, nothing for ourselves," and if we say it, it is what we live. The constitutional recognition of indigenous rights and culture, and the improvement of living conditions, is for all the Indian peoples of Mexico, not just for the zapatista indigenous. The democracy, liberty, and justice to which we aspire are for all Mexicans, not just for us.

We have emphasized to not just a few people that the resistance of the zapatista communities is not meant to engender pity, but respect. Here, now, poverty is a weapon that has been chosen by our peoples for two reasons: in order to bear witness that it is not welfare that we are seeking, and in order to demonstrate, with our own example, that it is possible to govern and to govern ourselves without the parasite that calls itself government. But fine, the issue of resistance as a form of struggle isn't the purpose of this text, either.

The support we are demanding is for the building of a small part of that world where all worlds fit. It is then political support, not charity.

Part of indigenous autonomy (to which the "COCOPA Law" certainly speaks) is the capacity for self-governance, that is, for conducting the harmonious development of a social group. The zapatista communities are committed to this effort, and they have demonstrated, not a few times, that they can do it better than those who call themselves the government. Support for the indigenous communities should not be seen as help for mental incompetents who don't even know what they need, or for children who have to be told what they should eat, at what time and how, what they should learn, what they should say, and what they should think (although I doubt that there are children who would still accept this). And this is the reasoning of some NGOs and a good part of the financing bodies of community projects.

The zapatista communities are in charge of the projects (not a few NGOs can testify to that), they get them up and running, they make them produce and thus improve the collectives, not the individuals. Whoever helps one or several zapatista communities is helping not just to improve a collective's material situation, it is helping a much simpler but more demanding project: the building of a new world, one where many worlds fit, one where charity and pity for another are the stuff of science fiction novels . . . or of a forgettable and expendable past.

With the death of the Aguascalientes, the "Cinderella syndrome" of some civil societies and the paternalism of some national and international NGOs will also die. At least they will die for the zapatista communities, who, from now on, will no longer be receiving leftovers, nor allowing the imposition of projects.

For all these reasons, and for other things that will be seen later, on August 8, 2003, the anniversary of the first Aguascalientes, the death of the Aguascalientes will be decreed. The fiesta (because there are deaths that must be celebrated) will be in Oventik, and all of you are invited who, over these ten years, have supported the rebel communities, whether with projects or with peace camps, or with caravans, or with an attentive ear, or with the compañera word, whatever it may be, as long as it not be with pity and charity.

On August 9, 2003, something new will be born. But I will tell you of that tomorrow. Or, more accurately, in a bit, because it is dawn here now, in the mountains of the Mexican Southeast—a dignified corner of the Patria, rebel land, lair of the transgressors of the law (including the one of seriousness), and a small piece of the great world jigsaw puzzle of rebellion for humanity and against neoliberalism.

(To be continued)

From the mountains of the Mexican Southeast

SUBCOMANDANTE INSURGENTE MARCOS

PART THREE: A NAME

Mexico, July 2003

It's raining, as it does here in July, the seventh month of the year. I'm shivering next to the stove, turning around and around, as if I were a chicken on a rotisserie, to see if I can dry off a bit. It so happened that the meeting with the committees ended quite late, at dawn, and we were camped a good distance from where the meeting took place. It wasn't raining when we left, but, as if it were waiting for us, an almighty downpour was unleashed right when we were halfway there, when it would have been the same distance to go back or to keep on going. The rebels went to their respective huts to change out of their wet uniforms. I didn't, not out of bravery but out of idiocy, because it so happens that, seeking to lighten the weight of my backpack, I wasn't carrying a change of clothes. And so, here I am, making like a "Sinaloa-style chicken." Uselessly, to boot, because for some reason I'm not able to fathom, my cap acts like a sponge, absorbing the water when it rains and exuding it only when it's inside. The fact is, inside the hut where the stove is, I have my own personal rain. These absurdities don't astonish me. After all, we're in zapatista lands, and here the absurd is as frequent as the rain, especially in the seventh month of the year. Now I've really thrown too much wood on the fire, not figuratively, and the flames are threatening to burn the roof. "There's no bad that can't get worse," I say to myself, remembering one of Durito's refrains, and it's best that I leave.

Outside there isn't any rain above, but there's a deluge under my cap. I'm trying to light a pipe with the bowl turned down when Major Rolando arrives. He just watches me. He looks at the sky (which, at this altitude, is already completely clear and with a moon that looks, believe me, like a noonday sun). He looks at me again. I understand his confusion and say: "It's the cap." Rolando says "Mmh," which has come to mean something like "Ah." More rebels come over and, of course, a guitar (and yes, that's dry), and they start singing. Rolando and yours truly burst into a duet, "La Chancla," in front of a confused public, because the hit parade here leans toward *cumbias, corridos,* and *norteñas.*[4]

Having seen a repeat of my failed launch as a singer, I withdrew to a corner and followed the wise counsel of Monarca, who, just like Rolando, kept looking at me, looked at the sky, looked at me again, and just said: "Take off your cap, Sup." I took it off and, of course, my private rain stopped. Monarca went over to where the others were. I told Captain José Luis (who acts as my bodyguard) to go rest, that I wasn't going to be doing anything now. The captain went, though not to rest, but rather to join in with the singing.

And so I was left alone, still shivering but now without rain above me. I went back to trying to light my pipe, now with the bowl turned up, but then I discovered that my lighter had gotten wet, and it wouldn't even flicker. I murmured: "Son of a bitch, now I can't even light my pipe," certain that my "sex appeal" would be going to hell. I was searching in my pants pockets (and there are quite a few), not for a paperback edition of the *Kama Sutra*, but for a dry lighter, when a flame was lit quite close to me.

I recognized the face of Old Antonio behind the light, I moved the bowl of my pipe to the lit match and, still puffing, I said to Old Antonio: "It's cold."

"It is," he responded, and he lit his hand-rolled cigarette with another match. By the light of the cigarette, Old Antonio kept looking at me, then he looked at the sky, then he looked at me again, but he didn't say anything. I didn't, either, certain that Old Antonio was already accustomed, as I was, to the absurdities that inhabit the mountains of the Mexican Southeast. A sudden wind put out the flame, and we were left with just the light of a moon that was like an ax, jagged from use, and smoke scratching at the darkness. We sat down on the trunk of a fallen tree. I believe we were silent for a time, I don't remember very well, but the fact is that, almost without my noticing, Old Antonio was already telling me . . .

The History of the Upholder of the Sky

"According to our earliest ones, the sky must be held up so that it does not fall. The sky is not firm; every once in a while it becomes weak and faints, and it just lets itself fall like the leaves fall from the trees, and then absolute disasters happen, because evil comes to the milpa, the rain breaks everything, the sun punishes the land, war rules, the lie conquers, and death walks and sorrow thinks.

"Our earliest ones said that it happens like this because the gods who made the world, the very first, put so much effort into making the world that, after they finished it, they did not have much strength left for making the sky, the roof of our home, and they just put whatever they had there, so the sky is placed above the earth just like one of those plastic roofs. Thus the sky is not firm; at times it comes loose. And you must know that when this happens, the winds and waters are disrupted, fire grows restless, and the land gets up and walks, unable to find peace.

"That is why those who came before we did said that four gods, painted in different colors, returned to the world. They placed themselves at the four corners of the world in order to grab hold of the sky so that it would not fall and it would stay still and good and even, so sun and moon and stars and dreams could walk without difficulty.

"However, those who first stepped on these lands also recount that sometimes one or more of the *bacabes*,[5] the upholders of the sky, would start to dream or would be distracted by a cloud, and then he would not hold up his side of the earth's roof tightly, and then the sky would come loose and would want to fall over the earth, and the sun and the moon would not have an even path and neither would the stars.

"That is how it happened from the beginning; that is why the first gods, those who birthed the world, left one of the upholders of the sky in charge, and he had to stay alert, in order to read the sky and to see when it began coming loose, and then this upholder had to speak to the other upholders to awaken them, so they would tighten up their side and put things straight again.

"And this upholder never sleeps—he must always be alert and watchful, in order to awaken the others when evil falls to the earth. And the most ancient of the walk and the word say that this upholder of the sky carries a *caracol* hanging from his chest, and he listens to the sounds and silences of the world with it, and he calls the other upholders with it, so that they do not sleep or in order to awaken them.

"And the very first ones say that this upholder of the sky, so that he would not sleep, came and went inside his own heart, by way of the paths he carried in his chest, and those ancient teachers say that this upholder taught men and women the word and its writing, because they say that while the word walks the world, it is possible for evil to be quieted and for the world to be just right.

"That is why the word of the one who does not sleep, the one who is alert to evil and its wicked deeds, does not travel directly from one side to the other but instead walks toward herself, following the lines of reason. The knowledgeable ones from before say that the hearts of men and women have the shape of a *caracol*, and those of good heart and thoughts walk from one side to the other, awakening the gods and men so that they will be alert to whether the world is just right. That is why the one who stays awake when the others are sleeping uses his *caracol*, and uses it for many things, but especially in order to not forget."

With his last words, Old Antonio had taken a wand and sketched something in the dirt. Old Antonio goes, and I go, as well. The sun was just barely peeking through the horizon in the east, as if it were just looking, as if checking to see if the one who is staying awake has not gone to sleep and if there is someone staying alert for the world to become fine again.

I returned there at the hour of *pozol*,[6] when the sun had already dried the earth and my cap. At one side of the fallen trunk, I saw the sketch Old Antonio had made on the ground. It was a firmly traced spiral—a *caracol*.

The sun was halfway through its journey when I returned to the meeting with the committees. The death of the Aguascalientes having been decided the previous dawn, now being decided was the birth of the "*Caracoles*," with other functions in addition to the ones the now-dying Aguascalientes had.

And so the Caracoles will be like doors for going into the communities and for the communities to leave. Like windows for seeing us and for us to look out. Like speakers for taking our word far and for listening to what is far away. But, most especially, for reminding us that we should stay awake and be alert to the rightness of the worlds that people the world.

The committees of each region have met together in order to name their respective Caracoles. There will be hours of proposals, discussions on translations, laughter, anger, and voting. I know that takes a long time, so I withdraw and tell them to let me know when an agreement has been reached.

In the barracks now, we are eating, and then, sitting around the table, Monarca says that he has found a really "fantastic" pool for bathing . . . The fact is that Rolando, who doesn't bathe even in his own self-defense, gets enthusiastic and says, "Let's go."

I've been listening with some skepticism (it wouldn't be the first time that Monarca has been up to tricks), but, since we have to wait anyway for the committees to reach agreement, I say "Let's go" as well. José Luis stays and will catch up with us later, because he hasn't eaten, and so the three of us—Rolando, Monarca, and me—leave first. We cross a pasture, and nothing. We cross a milpa, and nothing. I tell Rolando: "I think we're going to arrive when the war is already over." Monarca replies that "we're just about there."

We finally arrive. The pool is in a shallow part of the river where cattle cross and is therefore muddy and surrounded with cow and horse dung. Rolando and I protest in unison. Monarca defends himself: "It wasn't like this yesterday." I say: "Besides, it's cold now—I don't think I'm going to bathe." Rolando, who lost his enthusiasm during the walk, remembers that dirt, like Piporro[7] put it so well, also protects against bullets, and he joins in with a "I don't think I will, either." Monarca lets out with a speech about duty and I don't know what else and says that "privations and sacrifices don't matter." I ask him what duty has to do with his bloody pool. And then he delivers a low blow and says: "Ah, then you're backing out."

He shouldn't have said it. Rolando was grinding his teeth like an angry boar while he was taking his clothes off, and I was chewing my pipe as I undressed completely, down to completely revealing my "other" average personal details. We dove into the water, more out of pride than desire. We bathed somehow, but the mud left our hair in such a state that we would have been the envy of the most radical punk. José Luis arrived and said, "The water's a mess." Roland and I said to him, in stereo, "Ah, then you're backing out." And so José Luis also got into the muddy pool. When we got out, we realized that no one had brought anything to dry ourselves off with. Rolando said, "Then we'll dry off in the wind." And so we put on only our boots and our pistols, and we started back, absolutely stark naked, with our minutiae exposed, drying ourselves in the sun.

Suddenly José Luis, who was marching in the vanguard, alerted us, saying, "People are coming." We put on our ski masks and continued on ahead. It was a group of compañeras who were going to wash clothes in the river. Of course they laughed, and someone said something in their language. I asked Monarca if he'd heard what they said, and he told me, "There goes the Sup." Hmm . . . I say they recognized me by the pipe, because, believe me, I haven't given them any reason to have recognized me from the "other" average personal details.

Even though we were still wet, before we got to the barracks we got dressed, because we didn't want to disturb the rebels. They then advised us that the committees had already finished. Each Caracol now had a name assigned:

The Caracol of La Realidad, of Tojolabal, Tzeltal, and Mame zapatistas, will be called *Madre de los Caracoles del Mar de Nuestros Sueños* or *S-NAN XOCH BAJ PAMAN JA TEZ WAYCHIMEL KU'UNTIC*—"Mother of Caracoles of the Sea of Our Dreams."

The Caracol of Morelia, of Tzeltal, Tzotzil, and Tojolabal zapatistas, will be called *Torbellino de Nuestras Palabras*, or *MUC'UL PUY ZUTU'IK JU'UN JC'OPTIC*—"Whirlwind of Our Words."

The Caracol of La Garrucha, of Tzeltal zapatistas, will be called *Resistencia Hacia un Nuevo Amanecer*, or *TE PUY TAS MALIYEL YAS PAS YACH'IL SACAL QUINAL*—"Resistance for a New Dawn."

The Caracol of Roberto Barrios, of Chol, Zoque, and Tzeltal zapatistas, will be called *El Caracol Que Habla Para Todos*, or *TE PUY YAX SCO'PJ YU'UN PISILTIC* (in Tzeltal), and *PUY MUITIT'AN CHA 'AN TI LAK PEJTEL* (in Chol)—"The Caracol that Speaks for All."

The Caracol of Oventik, of Tzotziles and Tzeltales, will be called *Resistencia y Rebeldía por la Humanidad*, or *TA TZIKEL VOCOLIL XCHIUC JTOYBAILTIC SVENTA SLEKILAL SJUNUL BALUMIL*—"Resistance and Rebellion for Humanity."

That afternoon it didn't rain, and the sun was able to come out without any problems, traveling through a level sky, toward the house it has behind the mountain.

The moon came out then, and even though it seems incredible, the dawn warmed the mountains of the Mexican Southeast.

(To be continued)

From the Mountains of the Mexican Southeast

SUBCOMANDANTE INSURGENTE MARCOS

PART FOUR: A PLAN

July 2003

The zapatista indigenous communities have been committed for several years now to a process of building autonomy. For us, autonomy is not fragmentation of the country or separatism, but the exercise of the right to govern and govern ourselves, as established in Article 39 of the Constitution of the United Mexican States.

From the beginning of our uprising, and even long before, we zapatista indigenous have insisted that we are Mexicans . . . and that we are indigenous. This means that we demand a place in the Mexican nation, but without ceasing to be what we are.

The purported zapatista project for a "Mayan Nation" exists solely in the papers of some of the stupidest military persons in the Mexican Federal Army, who, knowing that the war they are waging against us is illegitimate, are using this poor argument to convince their troops that by attacking us, they are defending Mexico. The high military command and their intelligence services know, however, that the aim of the EZLN is not to separate itself from Mexico but is, as its initials say, for "national liberation."

The separatist project for the Mexican Southeast does indeed exist, on the other hand, in the implementation of the neoliberal doctrine in our lands, and it is being directed by the federal government. The now-ill-fated "Plan Puebla-Panama" was nothing more than a plan for fragmenting the country, assigning the Mexican Southeast the function of "reserve" for world capital.

In the fragmentation project that is being implemented by the government (this, and not the one that appears in the press, is the real agenda of the political parties and the three branches of the government), Mexico will be divided into three parts: The North, with its states incorporated into the economic and commercial framework of the American Union; the Center, as provider of consumers with middle- and high-level purchasing power; and the South/Southeast, as a territory to be conquered for the appropriation of natural resources that, in the globalized destruction, are increasingly important: water, air, and land (wood, oil, uranium . . . and people).

Being simple and laconic, we would hold that the plan is to make the North into a great *maquila*,[8] the Center into a gigantic mall, and the South/Southeast into a large finca.

Plans on paper are one thing, and reality is another. Capital's voracity, the corruption of the political class, the inefficiency of public administration, and the increasing resistance of groups, collectives, and communities have all prevented the plan from being fully implemented. And where it is able to be established, it demonstrates the solidity of a shaky cardboard stage set.

Since "suicides" seem to be fashionable for power of late, we might say that there is no better concept for defining the plan that politicians and businesspersons have for our country: It's a suicide.

The globalization of capital needs the destruction of the nation-state. For some time the nation-state has been (among other things) the trench where local capital has taken refuge in order to survive and grow. But there is only a bit of rubble left of the trench.

In the countryside, small and mid-size producers have been succumbing in the face of large agro-industry. They will soon be followed by the large national producers. In the cities, the "malls," the commercial centers are not only destroying small and midsize businesses, they are also "swallowing up" the large national companies. Not even to mention national industry, which is already in its last death throes.

In response to this, the strategy of national capital has been naive, if not stupid. It has been distributing coins on one side and the other of the spectrum of the political parties, thus ensuring (or at least believing) that it does not matter what color is governing, because it will always be at the service of the color of money. And so, big Mexican businessmen finance the PRI, the PAN, and the PRD equally, as well as any political party that might have a chance in the governmental and parliamentary rackets.

During their meetings (like in the times of the mafia in North America, weddings are generally a pretext for the great gentlemen to sign agreements and settle conflicts), the Mexican *señores* of money congratulate one another. They have the entire national political class on the payroll.

But I regret to give them some bad news: As the now-silenced "Friends of Fox" scandal demonstrated, the heavy-duty money comes from the other side. If the one who pays governs, the one who pays more governs more. And so those politicians will promote laws commensurate with the checks they receive. Sooner or later, big foreign capital will be appropriating everything, starting by bankrupting and absorbing those who have the most, and all of this with the protection of "ad hoc" laws.

Politicians are now, and have been for some time, docile employees . . . of whoever pays more. National businessmen are quite wrong if they think that foreign capital will be satisfied with the electricity industry and oil. The new power in the world wants everything. And so there will be nothing left of national capital but nostalgia and, if they're lucky, some minor positions on the boards of directors.

Dying national capital, in its historical blindness, looks at any form of social organization with terror. The houses of rich Mexicans are protected with complicated security systems. They fear that the hand that is going to snatch what they have away from them is going to come from below. By exercising their right to schizophrenia, rich Mexicans are revealing not only the real source of their prosperity, but also their shortsightedness. They will be dispossessed, yes, not by improbable popular rage, but rather by an avarice that is even larger than theirs, that of the rich who are even wealthier than they. Misfortune will not enter by assaulting the great mansions at dawn, but through the front door and during office hours. The thief will not have the physique of the destitute, but of the prosperous banker.

The one who will be stripping everything from Slim, the Zambranos, Los Romo, the Salinas Pliegos, the Azcárragas, the Salinas de Gortaris, and the other surnames from the limited universe of wealthy Mexicans, do not speak Tzeltal, Tzotzil, Chol, or Tojolabal, nor do they have dark skin. They speak English, their skin is the color of money, they studied in foreign universities, and they are thieves with cultivated manners.

That is why armies and police forces will be of no use to them. They are preparing and entrenching themselves in order to fight against rebel forces, but their greatest enemy, the one that will annihilate them completely, practices the same ideology: savage capitalism.

The traditional political class, for its part, has already begun to be displaced. If the state is viewed as a business, it is better if managers, not politicians, run it. And in the "nation-state.com" neobusiness, the art of politics is of no use.

The politicians of yesteryear have now realized that fact, and they are positioning themselves for ambush in their respective regional or local trenches. But the neoliberal hurricane will also go there to seek them out.

Meanwhile, national capital will continue with their sumptuous feasts. And they might never realize that one of their guests will be their gravedigger.

That is why those who are longing for the defense of the nation-state to come from national businessmen, from politicians, or from "the institutions of the Republic" are waiting in vain. The one, the other, and the other have all been intoxicated by the hologram of national power, and they do not realize that they will soon be thrown out of the mansion they now have.

We, the zapatistas, have referred on some occasions to the so-called Plan Puebla–Panama as something already extinct. This has been for various reasons:

One is that the plan has already been undermined, and even the attempt at its implementation will do nothing but worsen social uprisings.

Another is that the plan expects us to accept that things have already been decided in the north and center of the country and that no one is opposed. This is false. The routes of resistance and rebellion cross the entire national territory, and they are also surfacing there, where modernity seems to have completely triumphed.

Another reason is that, at least in the mountains of the Mexican Southeast, its implementation will not, for any reason, be permitted.

· · ·

Those who govern governing have forgotten that the virtue of a good plan is that it should be simple.

And so, in response to the "Plan Puebla–Panama" in particular, and against all global plans for the fragmentation of the Mexican nation in general, the Zapatista Army of National Liberation is now launching the . . . "Plan La Realidad–Tijuana" (or "RealiTi").

The plan involves linking all the resistances in our country and, along with them, rebuilding the Mexican nation from below. There are men, women, children, and old ones in all the states of the federation who do not surrender and who, even though they go unnamed, are fighting for democracy, liberty, and justice. Our plan involves speaking with them and listening to them.

The "La Realidad–Tijuana" plan has no budget whatsoever, nor officials, nor offices. It has only those people who, in their place, in their time, and in their way, are resisting dispossession and who remember that the Patria is not a business with branch offices, but a common history. And history is not something that is just the past. It is also, and above all, the future.

Like the Corrido of the White Horse, but in Shadow-Light and departing one Sunday from La Realidad (and not from Guadalajara), the zapatista word and ear will cross the entire national territory, from Cancún and Tapachula, to Matamoros and La Paz, it will arrive in Tijuana at the light of day, it will pass through Rosarito, and it will not back off until it sees Ensenada.

And not just that. Given that our modest aim is to contribute in some way to the building of a world where many worlds fit, we also have a plan for the five continents.

For the north of the American continent, we have the "Morelia–North Pole Plan," which includes the American union and Canada.

For Central America, the Caribbean, and South America, we have the "La Garrucha–Tierra del Fuego Plan."

For Europe and Africa, we have the "Oventik–Moscow Plan" (traveling to the east and passing through Cancún this September).

For Asia and Oceania, we have the "Roberto Barrios–New Delhi Plan" (traveling to the west).

The plan is the same for the five continents: fighting against neoliberalism and for humanity.

And we also have a plan for the galaxies, but we still don't know what name to give it (the "Earth–Alpha Centauri Plan"?). Our intergalactic plan is as simple as the previous ones, and it involves, in broad strokes, it not being shameful to call oneself a "human being."

It is obvious that our plans have several advantages: They are not onerous, they have no directors, and they can be carried out without ribbon cuttings, without boring ceremonies, without statues, and without the music group having to repress its desire to play—now to the rhythm of the *cumbia* and while the respectable kick up their heels—the one that goes, "*Ya se mira el horizonte . . .*"9

From the mountains of the Mexican Southeast

SUBCOMANDANTE INSURGENTE MARCOS

Chiapas, Mexico, American Continent, Planet Earth, Solar System, Galaxy . . .

P.S. Speaking of evil plans, this July 25, it will be nine years since the attack on the procession of the then candidate for governor of Chiapas, Amado Avendaño Figueroa, in which social activists Agustín Rubio, Ernesto Fonseca, and Rigoberto Mauricio lost their lives. Justice is still pending. I don't know about you, but we have not forgotten.

PART FIVE: A HISTORY

July 2003

The history of the Rebel Zapatista Autonomous Municipalities (the MAREZ) is relatively young—seven years old, going on eight. Although the municipalities were declared at the time the December 1994 siege was broken, the MAREZ still took a while to become reality.

Today, the exercise of indigenous autonomy is a reality in zapatista lands, and we are proud to say that the change has been led by the communities themselves. The EZLN has been engaged in this process only in order to accompany and intervene when there have been conflicts or deviations. That is why the EZLN's spokesperson has not been the same as that of the autonomous municipalities. The autonomous municipalities have directly communicated their *denuncias*,[10] requests, agreements, "twinnings" (not a few rebel Zapatista Autonomous Municipalities maintain relationships with municipalities in other countries, primarily in Italy). If the autonomous have now asked the EZLN to fulfill the duties of spokesperson, it is because they have entered a higher stage of development and, having broadened, announcements are not the purview of one municipality, or several. That is the reason for the agreement that the EZLN would announce these current changes.

The problems of the autonomous authorities, in the period that is now over, can be divided into two types: those having to do with their relationship with national and international civil society, and those having to do with self-governance, that is, with relations between zapatista and nonzapatista communities.

In their relationship with national and international civil society, the primary problem has been an unbalanced development of the autonomous municipalities, of the communities located within them, and even of the zapatista families who live there. The most well-known autonomous municipalities (like those that were the seats of the now-defunct Aguascalientes) or those closer at hand (closer to urban centers or with highway access) have received more projects and more support. The same thing has taken place with the communities. The most well known and those along the highway receive more attention from "civil societies."

In the case of zapatista families, what happens is that when civil society visits the communities or works on projects or sets up a peace camp, they usually build special relationships with one or more families in the community. Those families will obviously have more advantages—assignments, gifts, or special attention—than the rest, even though they are all zapatistas. Nor is it unusual for those who interact with civil society because of the position they occupy in the community, in the autonomous municipality, in the region, or in the area, to receive special attention and gifts, which often gives rise to talk in the rest of the community and does not follow the zapatista criterion of "each according to his needs."

I should clarify that it is not a bad relationship, nor what someone proudly called "well-intentioned counterinsurgency," but rather something natural in human relations. It can, however, produce imbalances in community life if there are no counterbalances to that privileged attention.

Regarding the relationship with zapatista communities, the "govern obeying" principle has been administered without distinction. The authorities must see that community agreements are carried out. Their decisions must be regularly informed, and the collective "weight," along with the "word of mouth" that functions in all the communities, becomes a kind of monitoring that is difficult to avoid. Even so, instances take place of persons managing to get around this and to become corrupt, but it does not get very far. It is impossible to conceal illicit enrichment in the communities. The guilty party is punished by being compelled to do collective work and to repay to the community whatever he wrongfully took.

When an authority goes amiss, becomes corrupt, or, to use a local expression, *"está de haragán,"*[II] they are removed from their position, and a new authority replaces them. In the zapatista communities, the position of authority is not remunerated at all (during the time that the person is in authority, the community helps to support him). It is conceived as work in the collective interest, and it is rotated. The assignment to a position of authority is not infrequently enforced by the collective in order to punish laxness or indifference of some of its members—for example, when someone misses a lot of the community assemblies, they might be punished by being given a position such as municipal agent or ejidal commissioner.

This "form" of self-governance (of which I am giving just the sketchiest summary) is not an invention or contribution of the EZLN. It comes from further back in time. When the EZLN was born, it had already been operating for a good while, although only at the level of each community.

It was because of the enormous growth of the EZLN (as I have already explained, this was at the end of the 1980s) that this practice moved from the local to the regional. Functioning with local *responsables*[12] (those in charge of the organization in each community), regional ones (a group of communities), and area ones (a group of regions), the EZLN saw that those who did not discharge their duties were, in a natural fashion, replaced by others. Although here, the political-military command makes the final decision.

What I mean by this is that the EZLN's military structure in some way "contaminated" a tradition of democracy and self-governance. The EZLN was, in a manner of speaking, one of the "undemocratic" elements in a relationship of direct community democracy (another antidemocratic element is the Church, but that's a matter for another paper).

When the Autonomous Municipalities began operating, self-governance did not move just from the local to the regional. It also emerged from the "shadow" of the military structure. The EZLN does not intervene at all in the designation or removal of autonomous authorities. And it has limited itself by pointing out that—given that the EZLN, by principle, is not fighting for the taking of power—none of the military command or members of the Clandestine Revolutionary Indigenous Committee can occupy a position of authority in the community or in the autonomous municipalities. Those who decide to participate in the autonomous governments must definitively resign from their organizational position within the EZLN.

I am not going to expand much on the operations of the Autonomous Councils. They have their own methods of acting ("their way," as we say) as guarantor, and there are not a few witnesses (national and international "civil societies" who have seen them functioning and who work with them directly).

I do not, however, want to leave the impression that it is something perfect or that it should be idealized. The "govern obeying" principle in
zapatista territories is a tendency, and it is not exempt from ups and
downs, contradictions and errors. But it is a dominant tendency. Its having managed to survive in conditions of persecution, harassment, and
poverty that have rarely existed in the history of the world speaks to the
fact that it has benefited the communities. In addition, the autonomous
councils have managed to carry forward, with the fundamental support
of "civil societies," a colossal labor: the building of the material conditions for resistance.

Charged with governing a territory in rebellion, that is, without any
institutional support and under persecution and harassment, the
autonomous councils have focused their efforts on two fundamental
aspects: health and education.

In health, they have not limited themselves to building clinics and phar-
macies (always helped by "civil societies," it must not be forgotten); they
also train health workers and maintain constant campaigns for community health and disease prevention.

One of those campaigns came very close, once, to costing me being criticized in assembly (I don't know if you know what it's like being criticized in an assembly, but if not, it's enough to tell you that hell must be
something like that) and being "looked at" by the community (the people "look" at you, but with one of those looks that make you tremble—
in sum, a kind of purgatory). It so happened that—I think I was in La
Realidad—I was passing through and I spent the night in one of the
huts the compas have for these cases. The community's "health committee" was going around checking out the latrines in each house (there
was an agreement that the latrines had to be regularly blocked with lime
or ash to prevent the spread of disease). Our latrine, of course, had neither lime nor ash. The health committee told me, kindly, "Compañero
Subcomandante Insurgente Marcos, we're checking out the latrines by
agreement of the community, and your latrine doesn't have lime or ash,
so you have to put it in, and we're going to come tomorrow to see if it

has it then." I began babbling something about the trip, the lame horse, the communiqués, military movements, the paramilitaries, and I don't remember what all else. The health committee listened patiently until I stopped talking and said only, "That's all, Compañero Subcomandante Insurgente Marcos." When the health committee came by the next day, the latrine, of course, had ash, lime, sand, but not cement, only because I couldn't find any and seal up the latrine forever . . .

Regarding education—in lands where there had been no schools, let alone teachers—the Autonomous Councils (with the help of "civil societies," I will not tire of repeating) built schools, trained education promoters, and in some cases even created their own curricula. Literacy manuals and textbooks are created by "education committees" and promoters, accompanied by "civil societies" who know about those subjects. In some areas (not in all, it's true), they have managed to see to it that girls—who have been traditionally deprived of access to learning—go to school. Although they have also seen to it that women are no longer sold and may freely choose their mates, what feminists call "gender discrimination" still exists in zapatista lands. The "Women's Revolutionary Law"[13] still has a long way to go in being fulfilled.

Continuing with education, in some places the zapatista bases have made agreements with teachers from the democratic section of the teachers' union (those who aren't with Gordillo) that they will not do counterinsurgency work and will respect the curricula recommended by the Autonomous Councils. Zapatistas, in fact, these democratic teachers accepted the agreement and have fully complied with it.

Neither the health nor the educational services take in all the zapatista communities, it's true. But a large number of them, the majority, now have a means of obtaining medicine and of being treated for illness and have a vehicle to take them to the city in case of serious illness or accident. Literacy and primary education are hardly widespread. But one region already has an autonomous secondary school that, incidentally, recently "graduated" a new generation made up of men and *indigenous women*.

A few days ago, they showed me the diplomas and school-leaving certificates from the Rebel Autonomous Zapatista Secondary School (ESRAZ). My humble opinion is that they should have made them out of chewing gum, because at the top they have "EZLN. Zapatista Army of National Liberation," and then they read (in "Castillo" and in Tzotzil), "The Rebel Autonomous Zapatista Educational System of National Liberation [referring to how it operates in Los Altos, because there are other educational systems in other areas] certifies that student so-and-so has satisfactorily completed the three grades of the Autonomous Secondary School, in accordance with the Zapatista Plans and Programs in ESRAZ, Rebel Autonomous Zapatista Secondary School, 'January 1, 1994,' obtaining a general average of _____. Therefore our Educational System recognizes your efforts, your contributions to the resistance struggle, and invites you to share with our peoples what the people have given you." And it then says, "For a liberating education! For a scientific and popular education! I put myself at the service of my people." And so, in the event of persecution, the student will not only be unable to show it, she will also have to eat it—that's why it would be better if it were chewing gum. There is also the report card (which appears as "Recognition"), and there you can read the subjects (in reality, they aren't subjects, but "areas") that were completed: Humanism, Sports, Arts, Reflection on Reality, Social Sciences, Natural Sciences, Reflections on the Mother Language, Communication, Mathematics, and Productions and Services to the Community. There are only two assessments: "A" ("area approved") and "ANA" ("area not approved"). I know that the Anas of the world are going to be offended, but there's nothing I can do, because, like I say, autonomies are autonomies . . .

Education is free, and the "education committees" go to great efforts (I repeat: with the support of "civil societies") to see that each student has his own notebook and her own pencil, without having to pay for it.

In health, efforts are being made to see that it is free, as well. Some zapatista clinics no longer charge compañeros—not for the consultation, not for the medicine, not for the operation (if it's necessary and can be performed in our circumstances)—and others charge only the cost of the medicine, not for the consultation nor the medical care. Our clinics have the help and direct participation of specialists, surgeons, doctors, and nurses from national and international civil society, as well as from students and assistants in medicine from UNAM, from UAM, and from other institutions of higher education. They do not charge one single peso, and not infrequently, they pay out of their own pockets.

I know that some of you will be thinking that this is starting to look like a government report, and the only thing missing is my saying, "The number of poor has been reduced" or some other "Fox-ism," but no, the number of poor has increased here, because the number of zapatistas has increased, and one thing goes with the other.

That is why I want to emphasize that all of this is taking place under conditions of extreme poverty, shortages, and technical and informational limitations, in addition to the fact that the government does everything possible to block those projects that come from other countries.

A short time ago, I was talking with some "civil societies" about the suffering they had to go through in order to bring a freezer that worked off solar energy. The project involved vaccinating children, but the majority of the communities do not have electricity or, if they do have it, they don't have a refrigerator. And so the freezer would allow the vaccine to be maintained until it was administered to those who needed it. Fine, it so happened that, in order to bring the freezer they had to go through an infinity of bureaucratic procedures and, according to their investigation, there was only one organization that could bring what they wanted in from the outside expeditiously: Martha Sahagún de Fox's "Let's Go Mexico Foundation." They did not, of course, resort to that publicity agency. They carried out all the procedures, and the freezer will be installed, although late, and there will be vaccinations.

In addition to education and health, the Autonomous Councils look at problems with land, work, and trade, where they are making a little progress. They also look at the issues of housing and food, where we are in our infancy. Where things are doing a bit well is in culture and information. In culture, the defense of language and cultural traditions is being promoted above all. In information, news in local languages is being transmitted through the various zapatista radio stations. Also being regularly transmitted, alternating with music of all kinds, are messages recommending that men respect the women, and calling for women to organize themselves and to demand respect for their rights. And it may not be much, but our coverage on the war in Iraq was very superior to CNN's (which, strictly speaking, isn't saying much).

The Autonomous Councils also administer justice. The results are erratic. In some places (in San Andrés Sacamchén de los Pobres, for example) even the *Priístas*[14] go to the autonomous authorities because, as they say, "they do take care of it and resolve the problem." In other places, as I will explain now, there are problems.

If the relationship between the Autonomous Councils and the communities is full of contradictions, the relationship with nonzapatista communities has been one of constant friction and confrontation.

In the offices of nongovernmental human-rights defenders (and in the Comandancia General of the EZLN), there are a fair few *denuncias* against zapatistas for alleged human-rights violations, injustices, and arbitrary acts. In the case of the *denuncias* that the Comandancia receives, they are turned over to the committees in the region to investigate their veracity and, when the results are positive, to resolve the problem, bringing the parties together in order to come to agreement.

But in the case of human-rights defense organizations, there is doubt and confusion, because there has been no definition as to whom they should be directed. To the EZLN or to the Autonomous Councils?

And they are right (the human-rights defenders), because there is no clarity on this matter. There is also the problem of differences between statute law and "uses and customs" (as the jurists say) or "path of good thinking" (as we say). The resolution of the latter belongs to those who have made the defense of human rights their lives. Or, as in the case of Digna Ochoa (whom the special prosecutor regarded as nothing more than an office worker—as if being an office worker was somehow less— but who was, and is, a defender for the politically persecuted), their deaths. Regarding a clear definition of whom one should direct oneself to in order to process those *denuncias*, the answer is to the zapatistas. It will be made known soon how they will try to resolve them.

In sum, there are more than a few problems confronting indigenous autonomy in zapatista lands. To try to resolve some of them, important changes have been made in its structure and operation. But I will tell you about these later; now I just want to give a brief sketch of where we're at.

This long explication is given because the process of indigenous auton- omy has not been the work of just the zapatistas. If the process has been carried out exclusively by the communities, its realization has had the support of many, many more.

If the uprising of January 1, 1994 was possible because of the conspira- torial complicity of tens of thousands of indigenous, the building of autonomy in rebel lands is possible because of the complicity of hun- dreds of thousands of persons of different colors, different nationalities, different cultures, different languages—in short, of different worlds.

They, with their help, have made possible (for the good, because the bad is our responsibility alone) not the resolution of the demands of the rebel zapatista indigenous, but their ability to improve their living conditions a bit and, above all, to survive and make grow one more, perhaps the small- est, of the alternatives in the face of a world that excludes all the "others," that is, indigenous, young people, women, children, migrants, workers, teachers, campesinos, taxi drivers, shopkeepers, unemployed, homosex- uals, lesbians, transsexuals, committed and honest religious persons, artists, progressive intellectuals, and _____ (add whoever is missing).

There should also be a diploma for all of them (and those who are not them), which says, "The Zapatista Army of National Liberation and the

Rebel Zapatista Indigenous Communities certify that _____ (name of the accomplice in question) is our brother/sister and has, in these lands and with us, a dusk-colored heart as home, dignity as food, rebellion as flag, and, for tomorrow, a world where many worlds fit. Given in zapatista lands and skies at such and such a day of such and such a month of the year, et cetera." And it would be signed by those zapatistas who know how to do so, and those who can't would leave their mark. I, in a corner, would put:

From the mountains of the Mexican Southeast

SUBCOMANDANTE INSURGENTE MARCOS

SEVENTH AND LAST PART: A POSTSCRIPT

Here it is again! It's back! After a tragic period when it didn't delight us with its incomparable style! The much longed for! The . . . recurring . . . postscript! Yes! Yippee! Hurray! Bravo! Cheers! (It may be assumed that at this point the audience is erupting in joyful applause.)

P.S. Which Extends the Hand and the Word

It's official: You are formally invited to the celebration of the death of the Aguascalientes and to the fiesta for naming the "Caracoles" and the beginning of the "Good Government Juntas." It will be in the Autonomous Municipality of Oventik, San Andrés Sacamchén de Los Pobres, Zapatista and Rebel Chiapas, on August 8, 9, and 10 of 2003. Or, as we say here, arrival is on the 8th, the fiesta on the 9th, and departure on the 10th. There is a sign at the entrance to the Caracol of Oventik that reads: "You are in Rebel Zapatista Territory: here the people govern, and the government obeys" (I want to put up a similar one in our camps, but it would say: "Here the Sup governs, and everyone can do whatever they like." Sigh.).

• • •

P.S. Which Tunes In

If you have one, bring your shortwave radio (or "borrow" one, but don't buy it unless it's from a stall seller or a small shop—they work better than those from the big malls), because on August 9, at a time we still haven't decided, the first intergalactic broadcast of "Radio Insurgente" will be heard. Even if you decide to punish us with the whip of your disdain, wherever you are, you will be able to tune us in. The exact shortwave band and frequency are: 5.8 megahertz on a band of 49 meters. Since it is to be expected that the supreme power of Mexico will interfere with the transmission, move the dial with the same swinging of hips as in a *cumbia* and search until you find us.

Vale. Salud, and if you can't come, don't worry, you'll still be with us.

(No longer to be continued)

From the mountains of the Mexican Southeast

SUBCOMANDANTE INSURGENTE MARCOS

NOTES
1. *Un chingo* is Spanish slang. It is an exclamation denoting a large quantity, comparable to the phrase "a shitload."
2. An *encuentro* is a gathering. The zapatistas have hosted local, national, international, and intergalactic *encuentros* in what were formerly the Aguascalientes and what are now the *caracoles*.
3. The San Andrés Accords were an agreement signed by the EZLN and the Mexican government on February 16, 1996. The accords dealt primarily with the protection of indigenous rights and culture, and represented an important first step toward peace negotiations. However, then-president Ernesto Zedillo ignored the agreement and instead escalated federal military presence in Chiapas, with political support from Mexico's three primary political parties: PRI, PAN, and PRD. The accords were later drafted as official legislative proposals, which the government continues to ignore.
4. *Cumbias, corridos*, and *norteñas* are all genres of music. *Cumbias* originated in modern-day Colombia, through the mixture of indigenous and African slave cultures. *Cumbias* eventually mixed with European musical influences and today are a popular form of dance music throughout Latin America. *Corridos* are a form of Mexican folk music that combine elements of storytelling, poetry, and ballad. *Norteñas* are a genre originating from northern Mexico. Traditionally, *norteño* bands played *corridos*, polkas, and rancheras.
5. The *bacabes* are a group of four gods venerated by the Yucatec Maya. The ancient Yucatec Maya recitations, known as the "Rituals of the Bacabs," combine eroticism, magic, and tra-

ditional medicine. At times sung or chanted, this oral tradition was captured in the Roman alphabet at the end of the eighteenth century. The incantations describe various illnesses and invoke the medicinal help of the four cosmic quadrants, their deities, sacred trees, flowers, and animals.

6. *Pozol* is a corn drink of Mesoamerican origin that continues to be prepared throughout Mexico and Central America, particularly in indigenous communities. It is made with fermented corn and water. Often salty in taste, it may be mixed with cocoa. The pozol is a very nutritional and filling meal and keeps for long periods of time without refrigeration.

7. Eulalio González Ramirez was an actor in Mexican radio soap operas in the 1950s. He gained fame through his role as the character "el Piporro" in Pedro Infante's radio series, "Ahí Viene Martín Corona." Eulalio "el Piporro" continued his career starring as his own protagonist in many popular Mexican films. Eulalio Ramirez died in Monterrey City on September 1, 2003.

8. *Maquila*—or *maquiladora*—is defined by *Merriam-Webster's 11th Collegiate Dictionary* as "a foreign-owned factory in Mexico at which imported parts are assembled by lower-paid workers into products for export." The term is increasingly used to describe similar factories throughout Latin America.

9. *"Ya se mira el horizonte."* are the first words of the "Himno Zapatista." The verse translates as "The horizon can now be seen."

10. A *denuncia* is a denouncement, often responding to political corruption, human-rights abuses, or other forms of social injustice.

11. In Spanish, a person who is *haragán* is lazy, inactive, or careless.

12. *Responsables* refers to individuals charged with authority within autonomous zapatista communities.

13. EZLN: Women's Revolutionary Law. In their just fight for the liberation of our people, the EZLN incorporates women in the revolutionary struggle regardless of their race, creed, color, or political affiliation, requiring only that they meet the demands of the exploited people and that they commit to the laws and regulations of the revolution. As well as taking account of the situation of the woman worker in Mexico, the revolution incorporates their just demands of equality and justice in the following Women's Revolutionary Law.

    First: Women, regardless of their race, creed, color, or political affiliation, have the right to participate in the revolutionary struggle in any way that their desire and capacity determine.

    Second: Women have the right to work and receive a just salary.

    Third: Women have the right to decide the number of children they have and care for.

    Fourth: Women have the right to participate in the matters of the community and take charge if they are free and democratically elected.

    Fifth: Women and their children have the right to Primary Attention in their health and nutrition.

    Sixth: Women have the right to education.

    Seventh: Women have the right to choose their partner and are not obliged to enter into marriage.

    Eighth: Women have the right to be free of violence from both relatives and strangers. Rape and attempted rape will be severely punished.

    Ninth: Women will be able to occupy positions of leadership in the organization and hold military ranks in the revolutionary armed forces.

    Tenth: Women will have all the rights and obligations which the revolutionary laws and regulations give.

14. A *Priísta* is a member of the Institutional Revolutionary Party (PRI).

Three Shoulders

(EXCERPT FROM AN EIGHT-PART SERIES OF COMMUNIQUÉS
TITLED "READING A VIDEO"), MEXICO, AUGUST 2004

The moon appeared on the shoulder of the night, but for barely a moment. The clouds separated, like curtains being drawn apart, and then the nocturnal body flaunted its edge of light. Yes, like the mark a tooth leaves on the shoulder when, in the flight of desire, you don't know whether you're falling or rising.

Twenty years ago, after struggling up the first hill to go into the mountains of the Mexican Southeast, I sat down at a bend in the road. The hour? I don't remember exactly, but it was when the night says it was already-full-of-crickets-I'd-better-get-to-sleep, and the sun won't get anyone up. It was the dawn.

While I tried to calm down my racing heart and breathing, I thought about the advisability of choosing a more serene profession. After all, these mountains had done quite well without me before I'd arrived, and they wouldn't miss me.

I should say that I did not light my pipe. In fact, I didn't even move. And not out of military discipline, but because my entire, at that time splendid, body was hurting. Beginning a custom that I have maintained (with rigid self-discipline) up to the present time, I began cursing my flair for getting myself into problems.

That's what I was doing—the sport of gripe-gripe-gripe—when I saw a gentleman with a sack of maize on his back going up the hill. They had taken the load away from me halfway up the hill so the march wouldn't be held up. But it was life that was weighing me down, not the pack. Anyway, I don't know how long I was sitting there, but after a while the gentleman passed by again, going downhill now, and now without his burden. But the gentleman was still walking hunched over. *"Chin!"* I thought (which was the only thing I could do without hurting all over), "that's how I'm going to end up. My manly demeanor is going to be destroyed, and my future as a sex symbol will be like the elections, a fraud."

And sure enough, in a few months I was already walking like a question mark, not because of the weight of the pack, but so I wouldn't catch my nose in the branches and the vines.

About a year later I met Old Antonio. I went to his hut one dawn to pick up tostadas and *pinole.*[1] At that time we weren't showing ourselves to the people, and only a few indigenous knew about us. Old Antonio offered to accompany us to the camp, and so he divided up the load into two sacks and attached the *mecapal*[2] to his. I put the bag in my pack, because I won't have anything to do with the *mecapal*. We made the trek with the flashlight until we reached the edge of the dirt path, where the trees began. We stopped in front of a stream, waiting for dawn to break.

I don't quite remember how it came up in our talk, but Old Antonio explained to me that the indigenous always walk as if they were hunched over, even if they aren't carrying anything, because they carry the good of the other on their shoulders.

I asked how that was, and Old Antonio told me that the first gods, the ones who gave birth to the world, made the men and women of maize in such a way that they always walked collectively. And he told me that walking collectively also meant thinking about the other, about the compañero. "That is why the indigenous walk bent over," Old Antonio said, "because they are carrying on their shoulders their hearts and the hearts of everyone."

I then thought that two shoulders wouldn't be enough for that weight.

Time passed, and with it passed what passed. We did not prepare for battle, and our first defeat was in the face of these indigenous. They—and we—walked bent over, but we did so because of the weight of pride, and they because they were also carrying us (although we didn't realize it). Then we became them, and they became us. We began to walk together, bent over, but all of us knowing that two shoulders were not enough for that weight. And so we rose up in arms one first day of January in the year of 1994 in order to seek another shoulder that would help us walk, that is, to exist.

Vale. Salud, and, if the *piñata* has Bush's face, I'll ask for a go at it.

From the mountains of the Mexican Southeast

SUBCOMANDANTE INSURGENTE MARCOS

P.S. My birthday will be light to moderate. There will be bitter *pozol*, and not because I like it, but because then the compañeros get to act dumb.

NOTES

1. *Pinole* is a Mexican candy of pre-Hispanic origin. The candy is made from toasted and sweetened corn flour. The Spanish word originates from the Náhuatl word *pinolli*, which means corn flour.
2. A *mecapal* is a kind of head band attached to a sack, bag or bundle. It is a means for transporting objects that has been used by indigenous people for centuries.

The Speed of Dreams

MEXICO, SEPTEMBER 2004

PART ONE: BOOTS

Dawn does not make haste in the mountains of the Mexican Southeast. As if it were in no hurry, it takes delight in each and every corner, like a patient and dedicated lover. The fog knows no bounds, with its long dress of cloud, and it manages to smother the most determined light. It lays siege to it and surrounds it with its snow-white wall, encircles it in a diffuse loop. From the middle of the sky, the moon is making its retreat. A column of smoke mingles with the mist, slowly, with the same languor with which the cloud wraps the scattered huts under the wide skirts of her petticoat. Everyone is sleeping. Everyone except the shadow. Everyone is dreaming. Especially the shadow. As soon as it extends its hand, it catches a question.

What is the speed of dreams?

I don't know. Perhaps it's . . . But no, I don't know . . .

The truth is that what is known here is known collectively.

We know, for example, that we are at war. And I'm not referring just to the real zapatista war, the one that has not totally satisfied the blood-thirstiness of some of the media and some intellectuals "on the left." The former are focused on the numbers of those killed, injured, and disappeared, and the latter on translating deaths into errors "for not having done what I told them."

It is not just that. I'm also speaking about what we call the "Fourth World War," which is being waged by neoliberalism against humanity. The one that is taking place on all fronts everywhere, including in the mountains of the Mexican Southeast. As well as in Palestine and in Iraq, in Chechnya and in the Balkans, in Sudan and in Afghanistan, with more or less regular armies. The one that fundamentalism of both camps is carrying to all corners of the planet. The one that, taking on nonmilitary forms, is claiming victims in Latin America, in Social Europe, in Asia, in Africa, in Oceania, in the Near East, with financial bombs that are causing entire nation-states and international bodies to disappear into little pieces.

This war which, according to us, is attempting to destroy/depopulate lands; to rebuild/reorder local, regional, and national maps; and to create, by blood and fire, a new world cartography. This one which is leaving its signature in its path: death.

Perhaps the question "What is the speed of dreams?" should be accompanied by the question "What is the speed of nightmares?"

Just a few weeks prior to the terrorist attacks of March 11, 2004, in Spain, a Mexican political journalist-analyst (one of those to whom they give a piece of candy and then they break into ridiculous praise) was lauding José Maria Aznar's "vision of the state."

The analyst said that Aznar, by accompanying the United States and Great Britain in the war against Iraq, had gained promising ground for the expansion of the Spanish economy, and the only cost he had to pay was repudiation by a "small" part of the Spanish population, "the radicals who are never lacking, even in a society as buoyant as the Spanish one," said the "analyst." He went on to note that the only thing the Spanish had to do was to wait for a while until the reconstruction business of Iraq got underway, and then yes, they would be getting boatloads of money. In short, a dream.

It didn't take long until reality demanded the real price for Aznar's "vision of the state." That morning of March 11, the fact that Iraq is not in Iraq came true. I mean Iraq is not only in Iraq, but in the entire world. In short, the Atocha Station is a synonym for nightmare.

But before that, the nightmare was the dream, the neoliberal dream. The war against Iraq had been set in motion a good deal prior to the terrorist attacks of September 11, 2001, in U.S. lands.

In order to go back to that beginning, there is nothing like a photograph . . .

Flat, reddish ground. It looks hard. Perhaps clay or something similar. A boot. Alone, without its mate. Abandoned. Without a foot to wear it. Some scattered pieces of rubble. The boot, in fact, looks like one more piece of rubble. It's all that there is in the image, and so it's the bottom of the picture that clarifies what Iraq is about. The date? September 2004.

One can't discern whether the boot is from someone who died, if it was abandoned in flight, or if it is just a discarded boot. Nor is it known if the boot belongs to a U.S. or British soldier, or to a resistance fighter, to an Iraqi civilian, or to a civilian from another country.

Nonetheless, despite the lack of information, the image presents an idea of what Bush's "postwar" Iraq is: violence, death, destruction, desolation, confusion, chaos.

All of it a neoliberal program.

If the false arguments that the war against Iraq was a war "against terrorism" have collapsed, the real reasons are now emerging, more than a year after Hussein's statue was pulled down—aided by the tanks of the U.S. war—and a euphoric Bush erected another one to himself, declaring an end to the war. (Apparently, the Iraqi resistance didn't listen to Bush's message: The number of U.S. and British soldiers killed and injured has only increased since "the war ended," and now added to that are the losses of civilians from various nations.)

Neoconservative ideology in the United States has a dream: building a neoliberal "Disneyland." In place of a "village model," a reflection of the counterinsurgency manuals of the 1960s, it has to do with building a "nation model." The land of ancient Babylon was then chosen.

The dream of building an "example" of what the world should be (always according to the neoliberals) was fueled by the most prized belief of the ideological architects of the war (against Iraq): that greed is good. Not just good for them and their friends, but good for humanity and certainly good for the Iraqis. Greed creates profits, which create growth, which creates jobs, products, and services and anything else anyone could possibly need or want:

> The role of good government, then, is to create the optimal conditions for corporations to pursue their bottomless greed, so that they in turn can meet the needs of the society. The problem is that governments, even neoconservative governments, rarely get the chance to prove their sacred theory right: despite their enormous ideological advances, even George Bush's Republicans are, in their own minds, perennially sabotaged by meddling Democrats, intractable unions, and alarmist environmentalists.
>
> Iraq was going to change all that. In one place on Earth, the theory would finally be put into practice in its most perfect and uncompromised form. A country of 25 million would not be rebuilt as it was before the war; it would be erased, disappeared. In its place would spring forth a gleaming showroom for laissez-faire economics, a utopia such as the world had never seen. (Naomi Klein, "Baghdad Year Zero: The Pillage of Iraq After a Neo-conservative Utopia," *Harper's*, September 2004)

Instead of that, Iraq is indeed an example, but an example of what is waiting for the entire world if the neoliberals win the great war, the Fourth World War: unemployment of almost 70 percent, industry and commerce paralyzed, an exorbitant increase in foreign debt, anti-car-bomb walls everywhere, the exponential growth of fundamentalism, civil war . . . and the exporting of terrorism to the entire planet.

I'm not going to inundate you with something that appears in the news every day: military offensives by the coalition (in a war that has "already ended"), mobilization of the Iraqi resistance, attacks, attacks on military and civilian objectives, kidnappings, executions, new offenses by the coalition, new mobilization of the Iraqi resistance, et cetera. I'm sure you can find plenty of information in the press of the entire world. The best source in Spanish, beyond a shadow of a doubt, is the Mexican newspaper *La Jornada*, which has among its analysts some of the most serious and best informed on the issue of Iraq.

The truth is we have already seen this video in other places . . . and we are continuing to see it: Chechnya, the Balkans, Palestine, and Sudan are only examples of this war that destroys nations in order to try and "restructure" them into paradises . . . and they end up being turned into hells.

An abandoned boot on the ground in "liberated" Iraq sums up the New World Order: the destruction of nations, the obliteration of any trace of humanity, reconstruction as the chaotic reordering of the ruins of a civilization.

There are, however, other boots, even if they are just a few . . .

Broken boots. Worn-out boots. Yes, Insurgenta Erika's boots are worn-out. The sole is detached from the right toe, making the boot look like an unsatisfied mouth. The toes aren't visible yet, so Erika doesn't seem to have realized that her boots, especially the right one, are worn-out.

From my first days on the mountain, I made it my custom to look down. Footwear is often one of the *guerrillero*'s dreams/nightmares (others include sugar and keeping your feet dry and other rather damp obsessions, since he devotes a good deal of his attention to it. Perhaps that's why one acquires that obsession of always looking at other people's feet.

Insurgenta Erika has come to advise me that they've now finished edit-

ing the story of "The Magical Orange" (Radio Insurgente's latest production, which is about . . . well, better if you listen to it).[1] I respond to
her that her boot is worn-out. She lowers her gaze and tells me, "You,
too." She salutes me and leaves.

Erika is going to change clothes, because two teams of *insurgentas* are
soon going to be playing football. One is called "8 de Marzo" and the
other "The Princesses of the Jungle." I don't know much about football,
but my understanding is that the "Princesses" play in a style rather far
removed from the good manners of the *corte real* and the "8 de Marzo"
play as if it were the First of January uprising. In other words, a good
number of them end up in the insurgent medical station. In fact, every
time they're going to play, the medical people have the stretcher on one
side of the field. "So we don't have to turn around," they say.

They tied—the *insurgentas* tied in football. They went to penalties without breaking the tie. Insurgenta Erika came and told me this. Erika is
the romance counselor to the *insurgentas*, but this time she didn't come
to tell me that a compañera's "heart was hurting" from lovesickness,
but that the match was over now and she was going to give a talk to the
villages, more specifically, to the women of the villages. She was going
as a civilian, or in civilian clothing. Well, that's what she said. Because
I saw that she was wearing boots made in zapatista workshops, and they
had "EZLN" embossed on one side.

"Hmm, if you're going to wear those boots, it would be better if you wore
the complete uniform," I told her, trying to be sarcastic. Erika left. She
returned shortly with her uniform on. "Where are you going?" I asked
her. "To the village," she responded. "But whatever made you change
into uniform?" I asked/scolded her. "Because that's what you told me,"
she said. Understanding that it's useless to try and explain the qualities
of subtle irony, I just ordered: "No, put civilian clothes on, and take off
those boots." She left. She returned shortly in civilian clothing . . . and
barefoot. I sighed; what else could I do?

Don't believe Erika. My boot isn't worn-out. The stitching is coming apart, which isn't the same. Besides, it's an eye that's split, and so the way the laces are intertwined looks like the political system under neoliberalism: It's a mess, and you don't know where the right is going or where the left is going. I was explaining this to Rolando, when who should arrive but . . .

First-Generation Toñita, or Toñita I (she of the kiss denied because "it was too scratchy," she of the little broken cup, she of the stalk of maize fashioned into a doll) is 15 years old now. "Or she finished 14, but she turned 15 and now she's going on 16," her papa, who is one of the oldest zapatista *responsables* among us, tells me.

I concur, not confessing that I have never understood the higher mathematics that rule the calendars in the rebel zapatista communities (after trying to explain it to me, to no avail, Monarca resigned herself and just added: "I think it's because that's our way, which is just quite otherly").

The papa of Toñita I (or First-Generation Toñita) had come so I could see her, because it's been more than ten years since I'd last met her. Ten years had not passed in vain, since Toñita I not only didn't deny me a kiss, but, without my saying anything, she gave me a hug and planted a kiss on the padded cheek of my ski mask and turned all colors (Toñita I, not the ski mask). I didn't say anything, but I thought, "Hmm, I'm not doing well this year . . . and I haven't taken off my ski mask even to bathe myself."

Then Toñita I took some boots out of her backpack and put them on. I was going to ask her why she was putting on her boots after walking barefoot for six hours from her village, but Toñita spoke first, asking me if she could go "there"—and she pointed to where there was a group of *insurgentas*. Toñita I knows what a kiss, even if it's on a ski mask, can achieve, so she didn't wait for an answer and left.

While Toñita I was running over to see if they would let her play in the football match, her papa told me about their village (which I have always called, taking care that no one would hear me, "Stormy Peaks"). I had seen the scar that's on Toñita I's left arm, and I asked him about it.

Toñita I's papa told me that a young man from the village had wanted to take her to the latrine. (Note: Let me explain to the unlikely reader of these lines that in some villages, the latrine fulfills not only its smelly hygienic functions, but it's often also the place for couples to meet. There are not a few marriages in the communities that have originated in the not-at-all romantic location of the latrine. End of note.) What happened was that Toñita I did not want to go to the latrine. "It wasn't her pleasure," her papa informed me. And then the boy tried to force her, and then, "since it wasn't her pleasure"—her papa repeated—they struggled. Toñita I managed to escape, but, as they then said, the matter was made public and the matter reached the village assembly. Toñita I's papa told me that they had wanted to put her in jail. I interrupted: "But why, if he attacked her, and she even had a scratch on her arm?"

"Ah, Sup, you should see how the young man ended up," the papa told me. "He was left flat-out unconscious. Toñita is, as they say, quite fierce."

Toñita I has, in addition to an attractive face, a sturdy figure, or—how can I explain it to you? Well, for you to understand me, I'll just tell you that Rolando wanted her to play defense center on the zapatista football team.

"But the *insurgentas*' team is already complete," I said to Rolando. He just added: "Maybe so, but I wanted her for the men's team." Just then the people from the medical unit were going by with two quite battered *insurgentas*. Toñita I was crying, because it was her fault that her team had been given two penalties. I understood Rolando and turned around to her papa and asked him: "Has Toñita I said whether she wanted to be an *insurgenta*?"

Toñita I took off her boots and put them in her backpack. She left with her papa, walking barefoot.

It wasn't long before, accompanied by her mother . . . Second-Generation Toñita, or Toñita II, showed up.

Elena is the name of Toñita II's mama. She is an insurgent medical lieutenant, and she has to her credit the fact that in January of 1994 she saved the lives of various insurgents and militants who were left wounded in the fighting in Ocosingo. In a more than modest field hospital, Elena operated on bullet wounds and extracted pieces of shrapnel from the bodies of zapatistas. "A compa[2] died," she said when she made her report. She didn't mention the more than thirty combatants, who are now living and struggling in these lands, whom she saved.

Toñita II is 3 years old. "Or she's finished 2 and she's going on 4?" I asked, anticipating Elena's explanation. She laughed. I mean Elena laughed. Because Toñita II was shrieking at a level worthy of a more serious cause. And it so happened that, putting on my most flirtatious face (number seven from my exclusive "catalog of seductive gazes"), I had asked her for a kiss. Toñita II didn't even say "too scratchy" (not even an improved version); she just started crying with such vehemence that she had a group of *insurgentas* at her side offering her caramels and a little purse with a rabbit face (although it looked to me as if it were a possum face—the purse, you understand)—they were even singing to her the one about the baby goat, a song that is an uncommon success among zapatista boys and girls.

"They don't love you," Major Irma told me, making matters worse. I answered: "Bah, she's crazy for me," and I acted as if my heart were not broken.

Leaving the shop, Rolando handed me one of those needles called *capoteras* and a roll of nylon thread.

In the hut of the EZLN Comandancia General now, I wonder . . .

I don't know what the speed of dreams is, nor do I know whether to mend my boots or my heart.

(To be continued)

From the mountains of the Mexican Southeast

SUBCOMANDANTE INSURGENTE MARCOS

PART TWO: SHOES, SNEAKERS, FLIP-FLOPS, SANDALS, AND HEELS

September is the ninth month of the year, and above it's as if the moon has a tummy. She even blushes a bit when she lets herself fall over the west. The rain and the clouds almost make an appearance, but they grow lazy and remain behind the mountain, the one that rises to the east. Below, on the tape player, Tania Libertad is singing that song that goes, "They're not going to stand in our way . . . we shall grow despite the autumn." Mixed up in the shadows, the shadow is writing a letter. After "Zapatista Army, et cetera," and the date, September of 2004, can be read . . .

To: Pierluigi Sullo
Editorial Office of the Carta Weekly
Italy, European Continent, Planet Earth
Pedro Luis, brother:
Greetings from the mountains of the Mexican Southeast. I suppose you might think the "Pedro Luis" strange, but I have been influenced by the compas' "way" of "zapatizing" names, and so I'm using "Pedro Luis" for "Pierluigi."

Well, then, I received the letter you wrote and that you didn't send. I received the letter in *Carta* (August 26–September 1, 2004, year VI, number 31). Since my Italian doesn't extend even to the point of looking like the "Itañol" of the "*turbineros* and *turbineras*"[3] (who have been working hard for years to bring light to La Realidad), I had to ask for someone to do me the favor of translating it. And they did it, but in a neolanguage that we call "Itazapañol" here and that, if my memory doesn't fail me, Vanessa inaugurated when, always disobedient, she remained for years, living in the zapatista reality. Things being as they were, I had to resort to some dictionaries they had sent us some time ago (I don't quite remember who—I believe it was Mantovant or Alfio). In order to do that, first I had to look for the dictionaries and find them. They were, as was to be expected, leveling one of the legs of one of the tables of one of the *comandancia generales* of the one and only EZLN. It took me longer to intuit than to know what the letter in *Carta* said.

Perhaps I am wrong, but I managed to understand that the objective of your letter was to greet us . . . and to posit problems.

The epistolary genre is, in my humble opinion, one of the best means of debating (another, better yet, is political practice).

You didn't say so openly, but anyone could notice that your letter basically poses, now from rebel Italy, the same problem of the speed of dreams. And even though you don't say so explicitly, either, from the Italy which struggles, or dreams, you also answer, "I don't know."

Well, I can answer the problems you're raising with the axiom of the ineffable and great (of ego) Don Durito of the Lacandon: "There's no problem so great it can't be mulled over."

That appears to me to be an excellent recipe (it has given me good results on more than one occasion). I sincerely believe that you are not searching for a solution, but rather for a discussion.

The question, *What to do in Italy?* is, in effect, a problem. And to my way of thinking, it is part of the problem of what to do in the world?

Now our response, from us, the zapatistas, is . . . "We don't know."

I know that you don't expect anything else of us, knowing us as well as you know us. However, from our land and our struggle, we can say the following:

First. In the Mexico of today, all politicians—even those who are leading in the opinion polls, in the front pages of the news stories, or in the number of demonstrators, regardless of the color of the rhetoric they brandish or the sign of their party organization—can count on the sullen mistrust of us, the zapatistas, with our skepticism and incredulity. Based solely on their words, promises, intentions, figures, opinion studies, they will absolutely not receive anything good from us. Nothing, not even the benefit of the doubt. Like the chief of the Liberation Army of the South, General Emiliano Zapata in front of Francisco I. Madero, our hostility toward the politicians of the center will be an invariable rule and, like Emiliano Zapata in front of the presidential chair, we shall continue turning our backs on the National Palace and on those who aspire to take that seat. And the same thing goes for the self-styled "Congress of the Union" and the circus Judicial Branch of the Federation.

Second. In the specific case of the official self-proclaimed leftist political parties in Mexico (and which, it should not be forgotten, are not the only political organizations of the left that exist in our country), we cannot stop laughing bitterly when their party officials, leaders, deputies, senators, and little-paid canaries throw Vicente Fox's failure to fulfill his campaign promise of resolving the Chiapas "problem" in fifteen minutes in his face. We do not forget that those who are criticizing are the same ones who voted for a law that, in addition to failing to act on a breach of elemental justice, was in fundamental contravention of the cries of the Indian peoples of Mexico and of millions of persons in our country and in other parts of the planet.

They are the same ones who are encouraging paramilitary groups to harass and attack the zapatista communities. They are the same ones who are striving to appear pleasant to a right (whether it's called the ecclesiastical or the business high hierarchy) that, it must be said, feels no attraction for them. They are the same ones who are carrying under their arms the economic and police plans that have been drawn up in the boardrooms of international greed.

Even with all of this, we cannot endorse, with our silence, the legal dirty business with which they are trying to prevent the person who heads the Mexico City government from running in 2006 for the presidency of the country. It seems to us to be an illegitimate act, poorly wrapped up in legal fallacies, an attack against the right of Mexicans to decide if one or the other or no one shall govern them. The commission of a felony of that nature would mean neither more nor less than the invalidation of Article 39 of the Mexican Constitution, which establishes the right of Mexicans to decide their form of government. It would be, to put it in simple terms, a "soft" coup d'état.

By pointing this out, we are not putting ourselves on the side of a person or a government program. Even less does it translate into support for a party that is not only not of the left and is not progressive, but is not even republican. Quite simply, we are putting ourselves on the side of the history of the struggle of our peoples.

Third. Elections pass, governments pass. The resistance remains as it is, one more alternative for humanity and against neoliberalism. Nothing more, but nothing less.

However, consistent with the aversion we profess for dogmas, we will always admit that we could be wrong, and it could be, in effect, as the fashionable hacks are now predicting, necessary, urgent, essential, to deliver ourselves up unconditionally into the arms of those who, from above, are promoting changes that can be achieved only from below.

We could be wrong. When we realize it, because stupid reality gets in the way of our path, we will be the first to recognize that mistake in front of everyone, those who are with us and those who are opposed to us. It will be that way because we believe, among other things, that honesty in front of the mirror is necessary for all of those who, in word or in fact, are committed to the building of a new world.

In any event, we give life to our wise moves and to our mistakes. I sincerely believe that, ever since the dawn of the First of January of 1994, we have won the right to decide for ourselves our path, its rhythm, its speed, its accompaniment, continuous or sporadic.

We shall not cede that right. We are willing to die to defend it.

Fourth. We shall continue doing what we believe is our duty. And without regard to the "ratings" our actions receive, the space we occupy in the news, or the threats and prophecies that they are good enough—

from both sides of the political spectrum—to prescribe for us every time we don't do what they want us to do or we don't say what they want us to say (something that happens all the time).

We will not join in the hysterical clamor of the political class and of their fans in the "political analysis" columns. Those people who try to impose, always from above, an agenda that has nothing to do with what is happening below in our country, the implacable dismantling of the foundations of national sovereignty.

Nor will we flail about concerning the calendar, hastening 2006 and its uncertainty, its festival of vanities, its cynical squandering of resources, and its stupidity. Even less will our actions be guided by those who are demanding that we contribute the names of prisoners, disappeared, and dead, while they contribute names to the nominating lists.

Fifth. This does not mean that we do not listen. We do, and we shall continue to do so. From all over the world we receive words of encouragement and criticism, advice and warnings, support and condemnation. We listen to everything, and we keep it in the collective heart which we are. Anyone, anyplace in the world, can be certain that the zapatistas will listen to them.

But it is one thing to listen and another thing to obey.

We don't give a damn about the "polemics" as to whether the zapatistas are revolutionaries or reformers, "lights" or "heavies," naive or malicious, good or bad. They are like the mosquitoes in the long nights of the Mexican Southeast, they are not what keeps us awake.

The transnationals do not govern in zapatista lands, nor does the IMF,[4] nor the World Bank,[5] nor imperialism, nor the empire, nor governments of any sign. Here the communities make the fundamental decisions. I don't know what that is called. We call it "zapatismo."

But ours is not a liberated territory, nor a utopian commune. Nor an experimental laboratory for nonsense, nor the paradise of an orphaned left.

This is a rebel territory, in resistance, invaded by tens of thousands of federal soldiers, police, intelligence services, spies from the various "developed" nations, counterintelligence officials, and opportunists of all types. A territory composed of tens of thousands of Mexican indigenous, harassed; persecuted; attacked for refusing to stop being indigenous, Mexican, and human beings—that is, citizens of the world.

Sixth. As far as the rest of the planet goes, our ignorance is encyclopedic (it would, in fact, take up more volumes than the complete works of the external and internal words of the neozapatistas, which, incidentally, abound), and there is little or nothing we can say about political organizations of the left that are struggling, or say they are struggling, under other skies.

There, as everywhere, we prefer to look downward, to movements and trends of resistance and the building of alternatives. We turn our gaze upward only if a hand from below points us there.

Seventh. We are trying, with our clumsiness and our wise actions, definitions, or vagueness, just trying, but putting life into it, to build an alternative, full of imperfections and always incomplete, but our alternative.

If we have arrived where we have arrived, it has not, however, been just because of our abilities and decisions. It has been because of the support of men and women from throughout the world who have understood that in these lands there are not a bunch of needy people, eager for handouts and pity, but human beings, just like them, who are yearning and working for a better world, one where all worlds fit.

I believe that such an effort deserves the sympathy and support of every honest and noble person in the world.

And I believe that, more often than not, this sympathy and support find their most fortunate version in the struggle people are undertaking or maintaining in their respective realities, whatever their culture, their language, their flag, or their kind of footwear—shoes, sneakers, trainers, flip-flops, sandals, or heels.

In this sense, you are closer, in our geography, to the real zapatista communities than the distances noted on maps.

The Europe of below is thus closer: disobedient and self-managing Italy; the Greece which communicates with smoke signals; the France of the flip-flops and of those without papers and without homes, but with dignity; rebel and solidarity Spain; Euskal Herria, which resists and does not surrender; rebel Germany; committed Switzerland; compañera Denmark; persistent Sweden; conscientious Norway; the Patria denied to the Kurds; the marginal Europe which the immigrants suffer; the entire Europe of the young people who refuse to buy shares in the markets of cynicism . . . and the Mazahua Mexican indigenous women.

Rebellions and resistances that we feel are closer than the endless distances that separate us from the arrogant city of San Cristóbal de Las Casas and from the political parties who talk with the left and act with the right.

Well, that's all for now, compa Pedro Luis. Believe me, I have no regrets about running a risk of "being judged as someone who's crazy, who doesn't see reality" through what I'm writing you. However it may be, the fundamental problem remains, to wit, that of determining the speed of dreams.

While it's being resolved, best wishes, and the next time you write, send, in addition to the letter in *Carta*, a translation, even if it's in "Itañol."

Vale, salud, and may the clamor from above not prevent the murmur from below from being heard.

(To be continued)

From the mountains of the Mexican Southeast

SUBCOMANDANTE INSURGENTE MARCOS

NOTES

1. Audio files of Marcos reading "The Magical Orange" are posted on Radio Insurgente's Web site at http://www.radioinsurgente.org/index.php?name=archivo_2004

2. Compa is an abbreviated form of compañera or compañero. See editors' note for an explanation about why we chose not to italicize this word.

3. *Turbineros* and *turbineras* refer to the Italians who helped install a generator in the zapatista jungle community La Realidad.

4. The International Monetary Fund (IMF) is an organization of 185 countries that promotes global neoliberalism. The IMF provides or imposes loans and economic management for indebted countries. Loans are distributed under strict conditions, known as Structural Adjustment Programs. These conditions include emphasizing the economy on direct export and resource extraction; trade deregulation; privitization of national resources and enterprises; and enhancing rights for foreign investors.

5. The World Bank consists of five international organizations that provide economic advice, grants, and loans to "developing countires." The World Bank claims to promote education, health, agricultural development, environmental protection, urban development, and good governance. However, the World Bank's emphasis on western neoliberal models of development tend to perpetuate many of the problems it claims to address.

Sixth Declaration of the Lacandon Jungle

This is our simple word that seeks to touch the hearts of humble and simple people like ourselves, but people who, like ourselves, are also dignified and rebel. This is our simple word for recounting what our path has been and where we are now, in order to explain how we see the world and our country, in order to say what we are thinking of doing and how we are thinking of doing it, and in order to invite other people to walk with us in something very great, which is called Mexico, and something greater, which is called the world. This is our simple word to inform all honest and noble hearts what it is we want in Mexico and the world. This is our simple word, because it is our idea to call on those who are like us and to join together with them, everywhere they are living and struggling.

WHAT WE ARE

We are the zapatistas of the EZLN, although we are also called "neozapatistas." Now, we, the zapatistas, rose up in arms in January of 1994 because we saw how widespread had become the evil wrought by the powerful who only humiliated us, stole from us, imprisoned us, and killed us, and no one was saying anything or doing anything. That is why we said, *"¡Ya Basta!"*—that we were no longer going to allow them to make us inferior or to treat us worse than animals. We also said that we wanted democracy, liberty, and justice for all Mexicans, although we were concentrating on the Indian peoples, because it so happened that we, the EZLN, were almost entirely indigenous people from Chiapas. But we did not want to struggle just for our own good, or just for the good of the indigenous of Chiapas, or just for the good of the Indian peoples of Mexico. We wanted to fight along with everyone who was humble and simple like ourselves, who was in great need, and who suffered from exploitation and thievery by the rich and their bad governments, here in our Mexico and in other countries around the world.

Our small history is that we grew tired of exploitation by the powerful, and we organized in order to defend ourselves and to fight for justice. In the beginning there were not many of us, just a few, going this way and that, talking with and listening to other people like ourselves. We did that for many years, and we did it in secret, without making a stir. In other words, we joined forces in silence. We remained like that for about ten years, and when we had grown, we were many thousands. We trained ourselves quite well in politics and weapons, and, suddenly, when the rich were throwing their New Year's Eve parties, we fell upon their cities and just took them over. And we left a message for everyone that we are here, that they had to notice us. Then the rich sent their great armies to do away with us, just like they always do when the exploited rebel. But we were not done away with at all, because we had prepared ourselves quite well prior to the war, and we made ourselves strong in our mountains. And there were the armies—looking for us and launching their bombs and bullets at us—and then they were making plans to kill off all the indigenous at one time, because they did not know who was a zapatista and who was not. We were running and fighting, fighting and running, just like our ancestors had done. Without giving up, without surrendering, without being defeated.

Then the people from the cities went out into the streets and began shouting for an end to the war. And then we stopped our war, and we listened to those brothers and sisters from the city who were telling us to try to reach an arrangement or an accord with the bad governments, so that the problem could be resolved without a massacre. We paid attention to them, because they were what we call "the people," or the Mexican people. So we set aside the fire and took up the word.

And it so happened that the governments said that they would indeed be well behaved, that they would engage in dialogue, that they would make accords and would fulfill them. We said that it was good, but we also thought it was good that we knew those people who went out into the streets in order to stop the war. Then, while we were engaging in dialogue with the bad governments, we were also talking with those people, and we saw that most of them were humble and simple like us, and both—they and we—understood quite well why we were fighting. And we called those people "civil society" because most of them did not belong to political parties; rather, they were common, everyday people, like us—simple and humble people.

But it so happened that the bad governments did not want a good agreement; rather, it was just their underhanded way, to say they were going to talk and to reach accords while they were actually preparing their attacks in order to eliminate us once and for all. And they attacked us several times, but they did not defeat us, because we resisted quite well, and many people throughout the world mobilized. And then the bad governments thought that the problem was that many people saw what was happening with us, and they began acting as if nothing were going on. Meanwhile, they were quick to surround us, and they laid siege to us in hopes that, since our mountains are indeed remote, people would then forget, since zapatista lands are so far away. And every so often the bad governments tested us and tried to deceive us or to attack us, like in February 1995, when they launched a huge number of troops at us. But they did not defeat us, because we were not alone; many people helped us, and we resisted well.

Then the bad governments had to make accords with the EZLN, and those accords were called the "San Andrés Accords," because the municipality where those accords were signed was called San Andrés. During the dialogues, we were not all alone in speaking with people from the bad governments. We invited many people and organizations who were, or are, engaged in the struggle for the Indian peoples of Mexico, and everyone spoke their word and reached agreement as to how we were going to speak with the bad governments. And that is how that dialogue was, not just the zapatistas on one side and the governments on the other. Instead, the Indian peoples of Mexico and those who supported them were with the zapatistas. Then the bad governments said in those accords that they were indeed going to recognize and respect the rights and culture of the Indian peoples of Mexico, and to make everything law in the Constitution. But then, once they had signed, the bad governments acted as if they had forgotten what they had agreed to, and many years passed, and the accords were not fulfilled at all. Quite the opposite: the government attacked the indigenous in order to make them back out of the struggle, as it did on December 22, 1997, the date on which Zedillo ordered the killing of forty-five men, women, old ones, and children in the Chiapas town called Acteal. This immense crime was not so easily forgotten, and it was a demonstration of how the bad governments color their hearts in order to attack and assassinate those who rebel against injustices. And while all of that was going on, we zapatistas were putting our all into fulfilling of the accords and resisting in the mountains of the Mexican Southeast.

We also spoke with other Indian peoples of Mexico and their organizations, and we made agreements with them that we were going to struggle together for the same thing, for the recognition of indigenous rights and culture. We are also being helped by many people from all over the world, including people whose word is great because they are well-respected intellectuals, artists, and scientists from Mexico. We also held international *encuentros*. In other words, we are joining together to talk with people from America and Asia, from Europe, Africa, and Oceania, and we are learning about their struggles and their ways. We say they are "intergalactic" *encuentros*, just to be silly and because we also invite those from other planets, but it appears they have not come. Or perhaps they have come, but they haven't made it clear.

But the bad governments do not keep their word anyway, and so we made a plan to talk with many Mexicans so they would help us. And then, in 1997, we held our "March of the 1,111" to Mexico City (which was called that because a compañero or compañera was sent from each zapatista town), but the bad government paid no attention. Then, in 1999, we held a *consulta*[1] throughout the country that showed the majority of people were indeed in agreement with the demands of the Indian peoples, but again the bad governments paid no attention. And then, lastly, in 2001, we held what was called the "March for Indigenous Dignity," which had support from millions of Mexicans and people from other countries and which went to where the deputies and senators were—the Congress of the Union—to demand recognition of the Mexican indigenous.

But it happened that the politicians from the PRI, the PAN, and the PRD reached an agreement among themselves, and they simply did not recognize indigenous rights and culture. That was in April 2001, and the politicians demonstrated quite clearly that they had no decency whatsoever, that they were swine who thought only about making their good money like the bad politicians they were. This must be remembered, because you will now see them say they will indeed recognize indigenous rights, but it is a lie they tell so we will vote for them. They had their chance, and they did not keep their word.

We saw quite clearly that there was no point in dialogue and negotiation with the bad governments of Mexico. It was a waste of time for us to be talking with the politicians, because neither their hearts nor their words were honest. They were crooked, and they said that they would keep their word, but they did not. In other words, on that day when the politicians from the PRI, PAN, and PRD approved a law that was no good, they killed dialogue once and for all; they clearly stated it did not matter what they had agreed to and signed, because they did not keep their word. And then we had no further contact with the federal government, because we understood that dialogue and negotiation had failed as a result of those political parties. We saw that blood did not matter to them, nor did death, suffering, mobilizations, consultas, efforts, national and international statements, *encuentros*, accords, signatures, commitments. And so the political class not only closed the door—one more time—on the Indian peoples, they also delivered a mortal blow to a peaceful resolution, through dialogue and negotiation, to the war. We can no longer believe that agreements will be respected. Take that into account so you can learn from what has happened to us.

When we saw that the government was not going to keep its word, we wondered in our hearts what we were going to do.

The first thing we saw was that our heart was not the same as before, when we began our struggle. It was larger, because now we had touched the hearts of many good people. And we also saw that our heart was more hurt; it was more wounded. It was not wounded by the deceits of the bad governments, but because, when we touched the hearts of others, we also touched their sorrows. It was as if we were seeing ourselves in a mirror.

WHERE WE ARE NOW

Then, like the zapatistas we are, we thought it was not enough to stop engaging in dialogue with the government, but that it was necessary to continue in the struggle, in spite of those lazy parasites, the politicians. The EZLN then decided to unilaterally carry out the San Andrés Accords regarding indigenous rights and culture. For four years—from the middle of 2001 until the middle of 2005—we have devoted ourselves to this and to other things we are going to tell you about.

We began to encourage the autonomous rebel zapatista municipalities— which is how the people are organized in order to govern and to govern themselves—to make themselves stronger. This method of autonomous government was not simply invented by the EZLN; it comes from several centuries of indigenous resistance and from the zapatistas' own experience. It is the self-governance of the communities. In other words, no one from outside comes to govern, but the people decide, among themselves, who governs and how, and if those who govern do not obey the people, they are removed from authority and others come in.

But then we saw that the autonomous municipalities were not equal. Some were more advanced and had more support from civil society, whereas others were more neglected. Some action had to be taken to balance the situation. And we also saw that the EZLN, with its political-military component, was involving itself in decisions that belonged to the democratic authorities, "civilians," as they say. The problem here is that the political-military component of the EZLN is not democratic, because it is an army. And we saw that the military being above, and the democratic authority below, was not good, because democratic authority should not be decided militarily. It should be the reverse: the democratic–political authority governing above, and the military obey-

ing below. Or perhaps it would be better with nothing below, just completely level, without any military, and that is why the zapatistas are soldiers, so that one day there will be no soldiers.

What we then did about this problem was to begin separating the
political-military from the autonomous and democratic aspects of organization in the zapatista communities. Actions and decisions that had previously been made by the EZLN were being passed, little by little, to the
democratically elected authorities in the villages. It is easy to say, of
course, but it was very difficult in practice, because many years had
passed—first in the preparation for the war and then the war itself—and
the political-military aspects have become customary. But regardless, we
did so because it is our way to do what we say, because, if not, why should
we go around saying things if we do not then do them?

That was how the "Good Government Juntas" were born, in August
2003. Through them, we continued the self-education and exercise of
"governing by obeying."

From that time, the EZLN leadership has no longer involved itself in
giving orders in the villages' civil matters, but it has accompanied and
helped the authorities democratically elected by the people. It has also
kept watch that the people, and national and international civil society,
are kept well informed concerning the aid that is received and how it is
used. Now we are passing the work of safeguarding good government to
the zapatista support bases, with temporary rotating positions, so everyone learns and carries out this work. We believe a people that doesn't
watch over its leaders is condemned to be enslaved; and we fight to be
free, not to change masters every six years.

The EZLN, during the last four years, also handed over to the Good
Government Juntas and the autonomous municipalities the aid and
contacts we had attained throughout Mexico and the world during these
years of war and resistance. At the same time, the EZLN was also building economic and political support to allow the zapatista communities
to make progress toward autonomy and improved living conditions. It's
not much, but it's far better than what they had prior to the January
1994 uprising. If you look at one of the government-sponsored studies,
you will see that the only indigenous communities that have improved

their living conditions—whether in health, education, food, or hous-ing—were those in zapatista territory, which is what we call the area where our villages are. All of this has been possible because of the progress made by the zapatista villages and because of the very large support that has been received from good and noble people, whom we call "civil societies," and from their organizations throughout the world. It is as if all of these people have made "another world is possible" a reality—but not just with empty words, but through real action.

The villages have made good progress. Now there are more com-pañeros and compañeras who are learning to govern. And little by little, more women are going into this work, although there is still a lack of respect for the compañeras and a need for them to participate more in the work of the struggle. Also, through the Good Government Juntas, coordination has improved between the autonomous municipalities and in the resolution of problems with other organizations and official authorities. There has also been much improvement in the projects in the communities, and the distribution of projects and aid donated by civil society from all over the world has become more equal. Health and education have improved, although there is still a good deal lacking in order for them to be what they should. The same is true for housing and food, and in some areas there has been much improvement with the problem of land, because the lands recovered from the *finqueros*[2] are being distributed. But there are areas that continue to suffer from a lack of land to cultivate. There has been great improvement in the support from national and international civil society, because previously every-one went wherever they wanted, but now the Good Government Juntas direct them to where the greatest need exists. Similarly, everywhere there are more compañeros and compañeras who are learning to relate to peo-ple from other parts of Mexico and the world. They are learning to respect and to demand respect. They are learning that there are many worlds, that everyone has their place, their time, and their way, and that therefore there must be mutual respect between everyone.

We, the zapatistas of the EZLN, have devoted this time to our pri-mary force, to the people who support us. The situation has indeed improved. No one can say that the zapatista organization and struggle has been pointless. Rather, even if the government were to do away with us completely, our struggle will indeed have been of some use.

But it is not just the zapatista villages that have grown; the EZLN has also grown. What has happened during this time is that new generations have renewed our entire organization. They have added new strength. The *comandantes* and *comandantas* who were in their maturity at the beginning of the uprising in 1994 now have the wisdom they gained in the war and in the twelve years of dialogue with thousands of men and women from throughout the world. The members of the Comité Clandestino Revolucionario Indígena (CCRI)—the zapatista political-organizational leadership—are now counseling and directing the new ones entering our struggle, as well as those who are holding leadership positions. For some time now, the "committees" have been preparing an entirely new generation of *comandantes* and *comandantas* who, following a period of instruction and testing, are beginning to learn the work of organizational leadership and how to discharge their duties. Our insurgents, *insurgentas*, militants, local and regional *responsables*, as well as support bases, who were youngsters at the beginning of the uprising, are now mature men and women, combat veterans, and natural leaders in their units and communities. Those who were children in January 1994 are now young people who have grown up in the resistance. They have been trained in rebel dignity, lifted up by their elders throughout these twelve years of war. These young people have a political, technical, and cultural training that we who began the zapatista movement did not have. These youth are now sustaining our troops more and more, as well as assuming leadership positions in the organization. All of us have seen the deceits of the Mexican political class and the destruction its actions have caused in our country. And we have seen the great injustices and massacres that neoliberal globalization causes throughout the world. But we will speak to you of that later.

The EZLN has resisted through twelve years of war—of military, political, ideological, and economic attacks, of siege, of harassment, of persecution—and we have not been vanquished. We have not sold out or surrendered, and we have made progress. More compañeros from many places have entered into the struggle so that instead of being weaker after so many years, we have become stronger. Of course there are problems that can be resolved by more separation of the political-military from the civil-democratic authority. But there are still things—the most important ones, the demands for which we struggle—that have not been fully achieved.

By our way of thinking, and what we see in our hearts, we have reached a point where we cannot go any further, and we could possibly lose everything we have if we do nothing more to move forward. The hour to take a risk has come once again, to take a step that is dangerous but worthwhile. United with other social sectors who suffer from the same wants as ours, it will perhaps be possible to achieve what we need and what we deserve. A new step forward in the indigenous struggle is possible only if the indigenous join together with workers, campesinos, students, teachers, employees: the workers of the city and the countryside.

HOW WE SEE THE WORLD

This is how we, the zapatistas, see what is going on in the world. We see that capitalism is dominant right now. Capitalism is a social system, a way in which a society goes about organizing things and people: who has and who has not, who gives orders and who obeys. In capitalism, some people have money, or capital, and factories, stores, fields, and many other things, and there are others who have nothing to work with but their strength and knowledge. In capitalism, those who have money and things give the orders, and those who have only the ability to work obey.

Capitalism means only a few have great wealth, but they did not win a prize, find a treasure, or inherit from a parent. They obtained that wealth, rather, by exploiting the work of the many. So capitalism is based on the exploitation of the workers, which means the few exploit the workers and take out all the profits they can. This is done unjustly, because they do not pay the workers what their work is worth. Instead, the workers receive a wage that barely allows them to eat a little and rest for a bit; the next day they go back to work in exploitation, whether in the countryside or in the city.

Capitalism also makes its wealth from plunder, or theft, because the wealthy take what they want from others—land, for example, and natural resources. Capitalism is a system where the robbers go free and are actually admired and held up as examples.

In addition to exploiting and plundering, capitalism represses because it imprisons and kills those who rebel against injustice.

Capitalism is most interested in commodities, because when goods are bought or sold, profits are made. And so capitalism turns everything into merchandise; it makes merchandise of people, of nature, of culture, of history, of conscience. According to capitalism, everything must be able to be bought and sold. It hides behind the merchandise, so we don't see the exploitation that exists. The merchandise is bought and sold in a market, and the market, in addition to being used for buying and selling, is also used to hide the exploitation of the workers. In the market, for example, we see coffee in its little package or its pretty little jar, but we do not see the campesino who suffered in order to harvest the coffee, and we do not see the *coyote*³ who paid him so cheaply for his work, nor do we see the workers in the large company working their hearts out to package the coffee. Or we see a device for listening to music like *cumbias*, *rancheras*, or *corridos*, or whatever, and that is very good because it has good sound, but we do not see the worker in the maquiladora who struggled for many hours, putting the the device together, while she is barely paid a pittance, lives far away from work, and spends a lot on the commute. In addition, she often runs the risk of being kidnapped, raped, and killed, as is happening to the women in Ciudad Juárez in Mexico.⁴

We see merchandise in the market, but we do not see the exploitation with which it was made. And capitalism needs many markets, or a very large market: a world market.

Capitalism today is not the same as before, when the rich were content to exploit the workers in their own countries. Now it is on a path called *neoliberal globalization*. This globalization means that capitalists no longer control the workers in one or several countries; now they are trying to dominate everything all over the world.

Neoliberalism is the idea that capitalism is free to dominate the entire world, and so, tough, you have to resign yourself, conform, and not make a fuss—in other words, not rebel. So neoliberalism is like the theory, the plan, of capitalist globalization. Neoliberalism has its economic, political, military, and cultural plans. All of those plans have to do with dominating everyone, and they repress or isolate anyone who doesn't obey so that his rebellious ideas aren't passed on to others.

In neoliberal globalization, the great capitalists who live in powerful countries like the United States want the entire world to be made into a big business—a global market—for buying and selling the entire world while hiding the exploitation from the world. The global capitalists insert themselves everywhere, in all countries, in order to pursue their big business, their great exploitation. They respect nothing, and they meddle wherever they wish, as if they were conquering other countries. That is why we zapatistas say that neoliberal globalization is a war of conquest of the entire world, a world war, a war being waged by capitalism for global domination. Sometimes that conquest is by armies who invade a country and conquer it by force. But sometimes it is by way of the economy—in other words, the big capitalists put their money into another country or they lend it money, but on the condition that the country does what they tell it to. They also spread their ideas and their capitalist culture, which is the culture of merchandise, of profits, of the market.

Capitalism does as it wants; it destroys and changes what it does not like and eliminates whatever gets in its way. For example, those who do not produce, buy, or sell modern merchandise get in their way, and so do those who rebel against their order. Capitalists despise those who are of no use to them. That is why the indigenous get in the way of neoliberal capitalism, why capitalists despise them and want to eliminate them. Neoliberal capitalists also get rid of the laws that do not allow them to exploit and make a huge profit. They demand that everything can be bought and sold, and, since capitalism has all the money, it buys everything. Capitalism destroys the countries it conquers with neoliberal globalization, but it also wants to adapt everything, to make it over again, but in its own way, a way that benefits capitalism and doesn't allow anything to get in its way. Neoliberal globalization destroys what exists in these countries, their culture, their language, their economic system, and their political system. It also destroys the ways in which the people who live in those countries relate to one another. Everything that makes a country a country is left destroyed.

Neoliberal globalization wants to destroy the nations of the world so that only one country remains: the country of money, of capital. Capitalism wants everything its own way; it doesn't like things that are different, so it persecutes and attacks them, or puts them off in a corner and acts like they don't exist.

In short, the capitalism of global neoliberalism is based on exploitation, plunder, contempt, and repression of those who refuse. The same system as before, but now globalized, worldwide.

But it is not so easy for neoliberal globalization, because the exploited of each country become discontent. They do not say, "Oh, well, too bad"; instead, they rebel. Those who remain and are in the way resist, and they don't allow themselves to be eliminated. That is why we see, all over the world, those who are being screwed over not putting up with it; in other words, they rebel, and not just in one country but wherever they abound. As there is a neoliberal globalization, so there is a globalization of rebellion.

Not just the workers of the countryside and of the city appear in this globalization of rebellion. Others also appear, who are much persecuted and despised for the same reason, for not letting themselves be dominated, like women, young people, the indigenous, homosexuals, lesbians, transsexual persons, migrants, and many other groups who exist all over the world but who remain unseen until they shout, *¡Ya basta!*, enough of being despised. Then they rise up, and we see them, we hear them, and we learn from them.

Then we see that all those groups of people who are fighting against neoliberalism, against the capitalist globalization plan, are struggling for humanity.

We are astonished when we see the stupidity of neoliberals who want to destroy all humanity with wars and exploitation, but it also makes us happy to see resistance and rebellions such as ours appearing everywhere. We see this all over the world, and now our hearts learn that we are not alone.

HOW WE SEE OUR COUNTRY, MEXICO

What we see going on in our Mexico is our country being governed by neoliberals. As we already explained, our leaders are destroying our nation, our Mexican Patria. These bad leaders don't look after the well-being of the people; instead, they are concerned only with the well-being of the capitalists. For example, they make laws like the North American Free Trade Agreement, which end up leaving many Mexicans—such as campesinos and small producers—destitute because they are "gobbled up" by the big agro-industrial companies. Workers and small business-people cannot compete with the large transnationals who come in without anybody saying anything to them, some even thanking them, and set their salaries low and their prices high. So much of the economic foundation of our Mexico, which includes the countryside, industry, national commerce, is being destroyed, and only a bit of rubble—which will certainly be sold off, too—remains.

These are great disgraces for our Patria. Food is no longer being produced in our countryside—just what the big capitalists sell—and the good land is being stolen through trickery and with the help of the politicians. What is happening in the countryside is the same as *Porfirismo*,[5] but instead of *hacendados*,[6] now there are a few foreign businesses that have truly screwed the campesino. Where before there were credits and price protections, now there is just charity—and sometimes not even that.

As for the workers in the city, the factories close, and they are left without work, or capitalists open what are called maquiladoras, which are foreign and which pay a pittance for many hours of work. Then the price of the goods people need, whether they are expensive or cheap, doesn't matter, since there is no money. If someone was working in a small or mid-size business, now they are not, because it was closed, or it was bought by a big transnational. If someone had a small business, it disappeared as well, or the owners went to work clandestinely for big businesses that exploit workers terribly and even put boys and girls to work. If the workers belonged to a union in order to demand their legal rights, now the same union tells them they will have to put up with their wages being lowered or their hours or benefits being taken away, because, if not, the business will close and move to another country. Then there is the *microchangarro*,[7] which is the government's economic program for putting all the city's workers on street corners selling gum or telephone cards. In other words, absolute economic destruction in the cities as well.

With the people's economy being totally screwed in the countryside as well as in the city, many Mexican men and women have to leave their Patria, Mexican lands, and seek work in another country, the United States. And they are not treated well there. Instead they are exploited, persecuted, treated with contempt, and even murdered. Under neoliberalism, the economy has not improved. Quite the opposite: The countryside is in dire need, and there is no work in the cities. Mexico is being turned into a place where people are working for the wealth of foreigners, mostly rich gringos, a place you are just born into for a little while, and where in another little while you die. That is why we say that Mexico is dominated by the United States.

Neoliberalism has also changed the Mexican political class, the politicians, because it made them into something like employees in a store, who have to do everything possible to sell everything and to sell it very cheaply. You have already seen that they changed the laws in order to remove Article 27 from the Constitution, so that ejidal and communal lands could be sold.[8] Salinas de Gortari and his gangs said it was for the good of the countryside and the campesinos, that they would prosper and live better. Has it been like that? The Mexican countryside is worse than ever, and the campesinos are more screwed than under Porfirio Díaz.[9] They also say they are going to privatize—sell to foreigners—the companies held by the state to help the well-being of the people, because the companies don't work well and need to be modernized. But instead of being improved, the state of the rights that were won for the people in the revolution of 1910 now makes one sad—and angry. They also said the borders must be opened so foreign capital can enter to fix all the Mexican businesses. But now we see that there aren't any national businesses; foreigners gobbled them all up, and the things that are sold are inferior to those that were made in Mexico.

Mexican politicians now also want to sell PEMEX, the oil that belongs to all Mexicans, and the only disagreement is that some say everything should be sold and others that only a part of it should be sold. They also want to privatize social security, and electricity and water and the forests and everything, until nothing of Mexico is left, and our country will be a wasteland or a place of entertainment for rich people from all over the world, and we Mexican men and women as their servants, dependent on what they offer: bad housing, without roots, without culture, without even a Patria.

The neoliberals want to kill Mexico, our Mexican Patria. And the political parties—all the political parties, not just some of them—not only do not defend it but are the first to put themselves at the service of foreigners, especially those from the United States. They are the ones who are in charge of deceiving us, making us look the other way while everything is sold, and they are left with the money. Think about whether anything has been done well, and you will see that the answer is no, nothing but theft and scams. Look how all the politicians always have nice houses and nice cars and luxuries. Yet they still want us to thank them and to vote for them again. It's obvious that they are without shame. They do not, in fact, have a Patria; they have only bank accounts.

We also see that drug trafficking and crime have been increasing a lot. Sometimes we think that criminals are like the ones in movies or songs, and maybe some are, but not the real *capos*.[10] The real *capos* go around very well dressed. They study outside the country. They look elegant. They are not in hiding. They eat in good restaurants and they appear in the papers, very attractive and well dressed at their parties. They are, as they say, "good people," and some are even officials, deputies, senators, secretaries of state, prosperous businessmen, police chiefs, generals.

Are we saying that politics serves no purpose? No, what we mean is that *that* politics serves no purpose. It is useless because it does not take the people into account. It does not listen or pay any attention to them; it approaches them only when there are elections. They don't even want votes anymore; the polls are enough to say who wins. There are promises about what this one is going to do and what the other one is going to do, and then it's "Bye, see you later," but you don't see them again, except when they appear in the news when they've just stolen a lot of money and nothing is going to be done to them because the law—which those same politicians made—protects them.

That's another problem: the Mexican Constitution is now completely warped and changed. It's no longer the one that guarded the rights and liberties of working people. Now it protects the rights and liberties of the neoliberals so they can have their huge profits. The judges exist to serve the neoliberals, always ruling in favor of them, and those who are not rich get injustice, jails, and cemeteries.

Well, even with all this mess the neoliberals are making, there are Mexican men and women who are organizing and making a resistance struggle.

We found out that there are other indigenous people—their lands far away from us here in Chiapas—who are establishing their autonomy, defending their culture, and caring for their land, forests, and water.

There are workers in the countryside, campesinos, who are organizing and holding marches and mobilizations to demand credits and aid for the countryside.

There are workers in the city who won't let their rights be taken away or their jobs privatized. They protest and demonstrate so that the little they have isn't taken away and so they don't lose what, in fact, belongs to the country, like electricity, oil, social security, education.

There are students who won't let education be privatized, who are fighting for it to be free, popular, and scientific, so everyone can learn and so they won't learn stupid things in schools.

There are women who won't let themselves be treated as ornaments or be humiliated and despised just for being women, who are organizing and fighting for the respect they deserve.

There are young people who won't accept being stultified by drugs or being persecuted for their way of being; instead, they make themselves aware through their music, their culture, their rebellion.

There are homosexuals, lesbians, transsexuals who won't put up with being ridiculed, despised, mistreated, and even killed for having another way that is different, who do not accept being treated like they are abnormal or criminals, but who make their own organizations in order to defend their right to be different.

There are priests, nuns, and laypeople who are not with the rich and who are not resigned, but who are organizing to accompany the struggles of the people.

There are social activists, men and women who have been fighting all their lives for exploited people, and they are the same ones who participated in the great strikes and workers' actions, in the great citizens' mobilizations, in the great campesino movements, and who suffer great repression. Even though some are old now, they continue without surrendering and go everywhere, looking for the struggle, seeking justice, and making leftist organizations, nongovernmental organizations, human-rights organizations, organizations in defense of political prisoners and for the disappeared, leftist publications, organizations of teachers or students, social struggle, and even political-military organizations. They are not quiet, and they know a lot because they have seen a lot and lived and struggled.

And so we see in general that in our country, which is called Mexico, there are many people who do not put up with things, who do not surrender, who do not sell out: people who are dignified. And that makes us very pleased and happy, because with all those people it's not going to be so easy for the neoliberals to win, and perhaps it will be possible to save our Patria from their great theft and destruction. We think that perhaps our "we" will include all those rebellions . . .

WHAT WE WANT TO DO

We are now going to tell you what we want to do in the world and in Mexico, because we cannot watch everything that is happening on our planet and just remain quiet, as if only we are where we are.

What we want to tell all you who are resisting and fighting in your own ways and in your own countries is that you are not alone—that we, the zapatistas, even though we are very small, are supporting you, and we are going to look at how to help you in your struggles and to speak to you in order to learn—because what we have learned, in fact, is to learn. And we want to tell the Latin American peoples that we are proud to be a part of you, even if it is a small part. We remember quite well how the continent was illuminated some years ago by a light called Che Guevara, a light that had previously been called Bolivar, because sometimes the people take up a name in order to say they are taking up a flag.

We want to tell the people of Cuba, who have now been on the path of resistance for many years, that you are not alone. We do not agree with the embargo the United States is imposing, and we are going to figure out how to send you something, even if it is *maiz*, for your resistance. We want to tell the North American people that we know that the bad governments you have and that spread harm throughout the world are one thing—and those North Americans who struggle in their country, and who are in solidarity with the struggles of other countries, are a very different thing. We want to tell the Mapuche brothers and sisters in Chile that we are watching and learning from your struggles. And to the Venezuelans, we see how well you are defending your sovereignty, your nation's right to decide where it is going. To the indigenous brothers and sisters of Ecuador and Bolivia, we say you are giving a good lesson in history to all of Latin America, because now you are indeed putting a halt to neoliberal globalization. To the *piqueteros*[11] and to the young people of Argentina, we want to tell you that we love you. To those in Uruguay who want a better country, we admire you. And to those who are without land in Brazil, we respect you. And to all the young people of Latin America, what you are doing is good, and you give us great hope.

And we want to tell the brothers and sisters of Social Europe, those who are dignified and rebel, that you are not alone. Your great movements against the neoliberal wars bring us joy. We are watching your forms of organization and your methods of struggle attentively so that we can perhaps learn something. We are considering how we can help you in your struggles, and we are not going to send euros, because they will be devalued as a result of the European Union mess. Perhaps we will send you crafts and coffee so you can market them, to help you a little in the tasks of your struggle. Perhaps we might also send you some *pozol*, which gives much strength in the resistance, but who knows if we will send it to you, because *pozol* is more our way, and what if it were to hurt your bellies and weaken your struggles and then the neoliberals defeated you?

We want to tell the brothers and sisters of Africa, Asia, and Oceania that we know you are fighting also, and we want to learn more of your ideas and practices.

We want to tell the world that we want to make it large, so large that all those worlds will fit, those worlds that are resisting because they want to destroy the neoliberals and because they simply cannot stop fighting for humanity.

What we want to do in Mexico is to make an agreement with people and organizations from the left, because the idea of resisting neoliberal globalization, and of making a country with justice, democracy, and liberty for all, comes from the left. Right now there is justice only for the rich, liberty only for big business, and democracy only for painting walls with election propaganda. We believe that it is only from the left that a plan of struggle can emerge, so that our Patria, which is Mexico, does not die.

What we think is that, with these people and organizations of the left, we can make a plan for going to all those parts of Mexico where there are humble and simple people like ourselves.

And we are not going to tell them what they should do or give them orders.

Nor are we going to ask them to vote for a candidate, since we already know that the ones who exist are neoliberals.

Nor are we going to tell them to be like us, nor to rise up in arms.

What we are going to do is to ask them what their lives and struggles are like, their struggle, what their thoughts about our country are, and what we should do so captialism does not defeat us.

What we are going to do is to take heed of the thoughts of the simple and humble people, and perhaps we will find there the same love that we feel for our Patria.

Perhaps we will find agreement among those of us who are simple and humble and, together, we will organize all over the country and reach agreement in our struggles, which are alone right now, separated from one another. We will find something like a program that has what we all want, and a plan for how we are going to achieve the realization of that program, which is called the "national program of struggle."

With the agreement of the majority of those people to whom we are going to listen, we will then engage in a struggle with everyone, with indigenous, workers, campesinos, students, teachers, employees, women, children, old ones, men, with all of those of good heart who want to struggle so that our Patria called Mexico does not end up being destroyed and sold, and which still exists between the Rio Grande and the Rio Suchiate, and which has the Pacific Ocean on one side and the Atlantic on the other.

HOW WE ARE GOING TO DO IT

This is our simple word that goes out to the humble and simple people of Mexico and of the world, and we are calling our word of today:

The Sixth Declaration of the Lacandon Jungle.

We are here to say, with our simple word, that . . .

The EZLN maintains its commitment to an offensive cease-fire, and it will not make any attack against government forces or any offensive military movements.

The EZLN still maintains its commitment to the path of political struggle through this peaceful initiative we are now undertaking. The EZLN continues, therefore, in its resolve to not establish any kind of secret relations with either national political-military organizations or those from other countries.

The EZLN reaffirms its commitment to defend, support, and obey the zapatista indigenous communities of which it is composed and which are its supreme command. Without interfering in their internal democratic processes, the EZLN will, to the best of its abilities, contribute to the strengthening of their autonomy, to good government, and to the improvement of their living conditions. In other words, what we are going to do in Mexico and in the world, we are going to do without arms, with a civil and peaceful movement, and without neglecting or ceasing to support our communities.

Therefore . . .

In the world . . .

1. We will forge new relationships of mutual respect and support with people and organizations who are resisting and struggling against neoliberalism and for humanity.

2. As far as we are able, we will send material aid such as food and handicrafts for those brothers and sisters who are struggling all over the world.

In order to begin, we are going to ask the Good Government Junta of La Realidad to loan their truck, which is called "Chompiras," and which appears to hold eight tons, and we are going to fill it with maize and perhaps two 200-liter cans with oil or petrol, as they prefer, and we are going to deliver it to the Cuban Embassy in Mexico for them to send to the Cuban people as aid from the zapatistas for their resistance against the North American blockade. Or perhaps there might be a place closer to here where it could be delivered, because it's always such a long distance to Mexico City, and what if "Chompiras" were to break down and we'd end up in bad shape. And that will happen when the harvest comes in, which is turning green right now in the fields, and if they don't attack us, because if we were to send it during these next few months, it would be nothing but corncobs, and they don't turn out well even in tamales, better in November or December, it depends.

We are also going to make an agreement with the women's crafts cooperatives in order to send a good number of *bordados*, embroidered pieces, to the European countries that are perhaps not yet part of the union, and perhaps we'll also send some organic coffee from the zapatista cooperatives, so that they can sell it and get a little money for their struggle. If it isn't sold, they can always have a little cup of coffee and talk about the anti-neoliberal struggle, and if it's a bit cold then they can cover themselves up with the zapatista *bordados*, which do indeed resist quite well being laundered by hand and by rocks. Besides, they don't run in the wash.

We are also going to send the indigenous brothers and sisters of Bolivia and Ecuador some non–genetically modified *maiz*, and we just don't know where to send it so it arrives intact, but we are indeed willing to give this little bit of aid.

3. To all of those resisting throughout the world, we say other inter-continental *encuentros* must be held, even if only one other. Perhaps December of this year or next January; we'll have to think about it. We don't want to say just when, because this is about our agreeing equally on everything, on where, on when, on how, on who. But not with a stage where just a few speak and all the rest listen, but without a stage, just level and everyone speaking. Yet the *encuentro* should be orderly—otherwise it will just be a hubbub and the words won't be understood. With good organization, everyone will hear and jot down in their notebooks the words of resistance from others, so then everyone can go and talk with their compañeros and compañeras in their worlds. And we think it might be in a place that has a very large jail, because what if they were to repress us and incarcerate us, and so that way we wouldn't be all piled up—we'd be prisoners, yes, but well organized, and there in the jail we could con-tinue the intercontinental *encuentros* for humanity and against neoliber-alism. Later on we'll tell you what we shall do in order to reach agreement as to how we're going to come to agreement. Now, that is how we're thinking of doing what we want to do in the world. Now follows

In Mexico . . .

1. We are going to continue fighting for the Indian peoples of Mex-ico, but now not just for them and not with only them, but for all the exploited and dispossessed of Mexico, with all of them and all over the country. And when we say all the exploited of Mexico, we are also talk-ing about the brothers and sisters who have had to go to the United States in search of work in order to survive.

2. We are going to go to listen to, and talk directly with, without inter-mediaries or mediation, the simple and humble of the Mexican people, and, according to what we hear and learn, we are going to go about building, along with those people who, like us, are humble and simple, a national program of struggle, but one that will be clearly from the left: anticapitalist, anti-neoliberal, and for justice, democracy, and liberty for the Mexican people.

3. We are going to try to build, or rebuild, a different way of doing pol-itics, one that again has the spirit of serving others, without material

interests, with sacrifice, with dedication, with honesty, which keeps its word, whose only payment is the satisfaction of duty performed, like the militants from the left did before, when they were not stopped by blows, jail, or death, let alone by dollar bills.

4. We are also going to go about organizing a struggle in order to demand that we make a new Constitution, new laws that take into account the demands of the Mexican people, which are: housing, land, work, food, health, education, information, culture, independence, democracy, justice, liberty, and peace. A new Constitution that recognizes the rights and liberties of the people and that defends the weak in the face of the powerful.

To these ends . . .

The EZLN will send a delegation of its leadership to do this work throughout the national territory and for an indefinite period of time. This zapatista delegation, along with those organizations and persons of the left who join in this Sixth Declaration of the Lacandon Jungle, will go to those places where they are expressly invited.

We are also letting you know that the EZLN will establish a policy of alliances with nonelectoral organizations and movements that define themselves, in theory and practice, as being of the left, in accordance with the following conditions:

No to making agreements from above to be imposed below, but to make accords to listen to and to organize outrage. No to raising movements that are later betrayed behind the backs of those who made them, but to always take into account the opinions of those participating. No to seeking gifts, positions, advantages, public positions, from power or those who aspire to it, but to go beyond the election calendar. No to trying to resolve from above, but to build from below and for below an alternative to neoliberal destruction, an alternative from the left for Mexico.

Yes to having reciprocal respect for the autonomy and independence of organizations, for their methods of struggle, for their ways of organizing, for their internal decision-making processes, for their legitimate representations. And yes to having a clear commitment for joint and coordinated defense of national sovereignty, with intransigent opposition to privatization attempts of electricity, oil, water, and natural resources.

In other words, we are inviting the unregistered political and social organizations of the left, and those persons who lay claim to the left and who do not belong to registered political parties, to meet with us, at a time and place and in a manner in which we shall propose at the proper time, to organize a national campaign, visiting all possible corners of our Patria, in order to listen to and organize the word of our people. It is like a campaign, then, but very otherly, because it is not electoral.

Brothers and Sisters:

This is our word which we declare:

In the world, we are going to join together more with the resistance struggles against neoliberalism and for humanity.

And we are going to support, even if it's just a little, those struggles.

And we are going to exchange, with mutual respect, experiences, histories, ideas, dreams.

In Mexico, we are going to travel all over the country, through the ruins left by the neoliberal wars and through those resistances that, entrenched, are flourishing in those ruins.

We are going to seek, and to find, those who love these lands and these skies as much as we do.

We are going to seek, from La Realidad to Tijuana, those who want to organize, struggle, and build what may perhaps be the last hope this nation—which has been in existence at least since the time when an eagle alighted on a nopal in order to devour a snake—has of not dying.

We are fighting for democracy, liberty, and justice for those of us who have been denied it.

We are fighting for another politics, for a program of the left and for a new Constitution.

We are inviting all indigenous, workers, campesinos, teachers, students, housewives, neighbors, small businesspersons, small-shop owners, micro-businesspersons, pensioners, handicapped persons, religious men and women, scientists, artists, intellectuals, young persons, women, old persons, homosexuals and lesbians, and boys and girls to participate, whether individually or collectively, directly with the zapatistas in this national campaign for building another way of doing politics, for a program of national struggle of the left, and for a new Constitution.

This is our word as to what we are going to do and how we are going to do it. You will see whether you want to join.

We are telling those men and women who are of good heart and intent, who agree with this word that we are spreading, and who are not afraid, or who are afraid but control their fear, to state publicly whether they are in agreement with this idea we are presenting. In that way we will see once and for all who, how, and where, and when this new step in the struggle is to be made.

While you are thinking about it, we say to you that today, in the sixth month of the year 2005, the men, women, children, and old ones of the Zapatista Army of National Liberation have now decided, and we have now subscribed to, this Sixth Declaration of the Lacandon Jungle. Those who know how to sign, signed, and those who did not left their mark, but there are fewer now who do not know how, because education has advanced here in this territory in rebellion for humanity and against neoliberalism, in zapatista skies and land.

This is our simple word sent out to the noble hearts of those simple and humble people who resist and rebel against injustices all over the world.

Democracy! Liberty! Justice!

From the mountains of the Mexican Southeast

CLANDESTINE REVOLUTIONARY INDIGENOUS COMMITTEE, GENERAL COMMAND OF THE ZAPATISTA ARMY OF NATIONAL LIBERATION

NOTES

1. The *consulta* here refers to the independent referendum through which the zapatistas asked the Mexican people their opinion about specific issues related to the zapatista struggle. Those participating in the Consulta went to specific voting places to fill out ballots on a range of issues. In the indigenous communities, the votes were taken in meetings where they discussed, analyzed, and voted on the issues by a show of hands. The EZLN has organized two

National Consultas, the first in 1995, to define their future as a political force. The second was held in 1999, during the war of extermination, also about the future of indigenous rights.

2. *Finquero* refers to an owner of a large farm—a *finca*. *Fincas* are huge rural properties, which usually cultivate agricultural products and raise livestock for exportation. They are characterized by the practice of "miner" agriculture, which is an intensive and brutal exploitation of human labor and natural resources.

3. *Coyote* is a pejorative term for "middleman."

4. The horrific situation in Cuidad Juárez is being described as feminicide; see the Web page of WITNESS for more information: http://www.witness.org/option,com_rightsalert/ Itemid,178/task,view/alert_id,38/

5. *Porfirismo* refers to the period of time between 1876 and 1911 when the dictator Porfirio Díaz served seven terms as president of Mexico. During his terms of office, Díaz strengthened large, privately owned ranches, creating miserable conditions for farmers and Mexican workers, who were forced to labor in slavelike conditions on lands that had been taken from them.

6. *Hacendados* refers to the owners of the haciendas. Haciendas are large rural ranches that produce grains and livestock. They were introduced in Mexico with the Spanish conquest. Very often, the haciendas enlarged their borders by seizing the adjacent lands owned by the communities.

7. *Microchangarros* refers to small businesses.

8. Article 27 of the Mexican Constitution of 1917 grants peasant farmers the right to land. Article 27 created several legal concepts to protect the farmers' land from illegitimate sale and exploitation. It also established strict limitations on the usage and amount of property that could be owned in rural communities. President Salinas's reform in 1992 ended the agricultural land-distribution policy and allowed socially owned lands to reenter the open market without regulation.

9. As absolute ruler of Mexico for thirty-five years, Porfirio Díaz served as president from 1876 to 1880 and from 1884 to 1911. Díaz is usually credited with the saying "Poor Mexico, so far from God and so close to the United States!" ("*¡Pobre México! ¡Tan lejos de Dios, y tan cerca de los Estados Unidos!*")

10. *Capos* refers to drug-related crime bosses.

11. "The *piqueteros* of Argentina are organizations of unemployed workers who organize to fight for their rights and for social changes, using direct action, especially *piquetes*, or blockades. They are one of Argentina's strong social movements, and different *piquetero* organizations have different philosophies, strategies, and ideas. See http://www.zmag.org/content/ showarticle.cfm?ItemID=5406

A Penguin in the Lacandon Jungle

MEXICO, JULY 2005

(The zapatista is just a little house, perhaps the smallest, on a street called "Mexico," in a barrio called "Latin America," in a city called the "World.")

You're not going to believe me, but there's a penguin in the EZLN headquarters. You'll say, "Hey, Sup, what's up? You already blew the fuses with the red alert." But it's true. In fact, while I'm writing this to you, he (the penguin) is right here next to me, eating the same hard, stale bread (it has so much mold that it's just one degree away from being penicillin), which, along with coffee, were my rations for today. Yes, a penguin. But I'll tell you more about this later . . .

CONCERNING THERE'S NO PLACE FOR YOU IN THIS WORLD

What happens when, as happened more than a decade ago, a little girl (let's say between 4 and 6 years old), indigenous and Mexican, sees her father, her brothers, her uncles, her cousins, or her neighbors taking up arms, a ton of *pozol*, and a number of tostadas and "going off to war"? What happens when some of them don't return?

What happens when that little girl grows up and, instead of going for firewood, she goes to school, and she learns to read and write the history of her people's struggle?

What happens when that girl reaches youth, after twelve years of seeing, hearing, and speaking with Mexicans, Basques, North Americans, Italians, Spaniards, Catalans, French, Dutch, Germans, Swiss, British, Finns, Danes, Swedes, Greeks, Russians, Japanese, Australians, Filipinos, Koreans, Argentineans, Chileans, Canadians, Venezuelans, Colombians, Ecuadorians, Guatemalans, Puerto Ricans, Dominicans, Uruguayans, Brazilians, Cubans, Haitians, Nicaraguans, Hondurans, Bolivians, and et ceteras, and learns of what their countries, their struggles, their worlds are like?

What happens when she sees those men and women sharing deprivations, work, anguish, and joys with her community?

What happens with that girl-then-adolescent-then-young-woman, after having seen and heard the "civil societies" for twelve years, bringing not only projects, but also histories and experiences from diverse parts of Mexico and the world? What happens when she sees and listens to the electrical workers, working with Italians and Mexicans in the installation of a turbine that will provide a community with light? What happens when she meets with young university students at the height of the 1999–2000 strike? What happens when she discovers that there are not just men and women in the world, but that there are many paths and ways of attraction and love? What happens when she sees young students at the sit-in at Amador Hernández? What happens when she hears what campesinos from other parts of Mexico have said? What happens when they tell her of Acteal and the displaced in Los Altos of Chiapas?

What happens when she learns of the accords and advances of the peoples and organizations of the National Indigenous Congress? What happens when she finds out that the political parties ignored the death of her people and decided to reject the San Andrés Accords? What happens when they recount to her that the PRD paramilitaries attacked a zapatista march—peaceful and for the purpose of carrying water to other indigenous—and left several compañeros with bullet wounds on April 10? What happens when she sees federal soldiers passing by every day with their war tanks, their artillery vehicles, their rifles pointing at her house? What happens when someone tells her that in a place called

Ciudad Juárez, young women like her are being kidnapped, raped, and murdered, and the authorities are not seeing that justice is done?

What happens when she listens to her brothers and sisters, to her parents, to her relatives talking about when they went to the March of the 1,111 in 1997, to the Consulta of 5,000 in 1999, when they talk about what they saw and heard, about the families who welcomed them, about what they are like as citizens, how they also are fighting, how they won't give up, either?

What happens when she sees, for example, Eduardo Galeano, Pablo González Casanova, Adolfo Gilly, Alain Touraine, Neil Harvey, in mud up to their knees, meeting together in a hut in La Realidad, talking about neoliberalism? What happens when she listens to Daniel Viglietti singing "A Desalambrar" in a community? What happens when she sees the play *Zorro el Zapato*, which the French children from Tameratong presented on zapatista lands? What happens when she sees and hears José Saramago talking, talking to her? What happens when she hears Oscar Chávez singing in Tzotzil? What happens when she hears a Mapuche indigenous recounting her experience of struggle and resistance in a country called Chile? What happens when she goes to a meeting where someone who says he is a *piquetero* describes how they are organizing and resisting in a country called Argentina?

What happens when she hears an indigenous from Colombia saying that, in the midst of guerillas, paramilitaries, soldiers, and U.S. military advisers, her compañeros are trying to build themselves as the indigenous they are? What happens when she hears the "citizen musicians" playing that very otherly music called "rock" in a camp for the displaced? What happens when she knows that an Italian football team called Internazionale de Milan are financially helping the wounded and displaced of Zinacantán? What happens when she sees a group of North American, German, and British men and women arrive with electronic appliances, and she listens to them talking about what they are doing in their countries in order to do away with injustice, while teaching her to assemble and use those appliances, and later she's in front of the microphone, saying: "You are listening to Radio Insurgente, the voice of the voiceless, broadcasting from the mountains of the Mexican Southeast, and we are going to begin with a nice *cumbia* called 'La Suegra,' and we're advising the health workers that they should go to the Caracol to pick up the vaccine"?

What happens when she hears at the Good Government Juntas that a Catalan came from very far away to personally deliver what a solidarity committee put together as aid for the resistance? What happens when she sees a North American coming and going with the coffee, honey, and crafts (and the product of their sale), which are made in the zapatista cooperatives, when she sees that they haven't commanded any special attention despite the fact that they've been making them for years without anyone paying them any notice? What happens when she sees the Greeks bringing money for school materials and then working along with the zapatista indigenous in the construction? What happens when she sees a *frentista*[1] arriving at the Caracol and delivering a bus full of medicines, medical equipment, hospital beds, and even uniforms and shoes for the health workers, while other young people from the FZLN[2] are dividing up in order to help in the community clinics?

What happens when she sees the people from "Schools for Chiapas" arriving, departing, and leaving behind, in effect, a school, a school bus, pencils, notebooks, chalkboards? What happens when she sees Hindus, Koreans, Japanese, Australians, Slovenes, and Iranians arriving at the language school in Oventik (which a "citizen" compañero has kept functioning under heroic circumstances)? What happens when she sees a person arriving to deliver a book to the security committee with translations of the EZLN communiqués in Arab or Japanese or Kurd and the royalties from their sales?

What happens when, for example, a girl grows up and reaches youth in the zapatista resistance during twelve years in the mountains of the Mexican Southeast?

I'm asking because, for example, there are two *insurgentas* doing sentry duty here for the Red Alert[3] in the EZLN headquarters. They are, as the compas say, "100 percent indigenous and 100 percent Mexican." One is 18 and the other 16. Or, in other words, in 1994, one was 6 and the other was 4. There are dozens like them in our mountain positions, hundreds in the militias, thousands in organizational and community positions, tens of thousands in the zapatista communities. The immediate commander of the two doing sentry duty is an insurgent lieutenant, indigenous, 22 years old, in other words, 10 years old in 1994. The position is under the command of an insurgent captain, also indigenous, who, as it should be, likes literature very much and is 24 years old, that is, 12 at the beginning of the uprising. And there are men and women all over these lands who passed from childhood to youth to maturity within the zapatista resistance.

Then I ask: What am I saying to you? That the world is wide and far away? That only what happens to us is important? That what happens in other parts of Mexico, in Latin America, and around the world doesn't interest us, that we shouldn't involve ourselves in the national or international, and that we should shut ourselves away (and deceive ourselves), thinking that we can achieve, by ourselves, what our relatives died for? That we shouldn't pay attention to all the signs that are telling us that the only way we can survive is by doing what we are going to do? That we should refuse the listening and words of those who have never denied us either one? That we should respect and help those same politicians who denied us a dignified resolution of the war? That before coming out, we have to pass a test in order to see whether what we have constructed here over the last twelve years of war is of sufficient merit?

We told you in the Sixth Declaration that new generations have entered into the struggle. And they are not only new, they also have other experiences, other histories. We did not tell you in the Sixth, but I'm telling you now: They are better than us who started the EZLN and began the uprising. They see farther, their step is firmer, they are more open, they are better prepared, they are more intelligent, more determined, more aware.

What the Sixth presents is not an "imported" product, written by a group of wise men in a sterile laboratory and then introduced into a social group. The Sixth comes out of what we are now and where we are. That is why those first parts appeared, because what we are proposing cannot be understood without understanding what our experience and organization was before—that is, our history. And when I say "our history," I am not speaking of just the EZLN; I am also including all those men and women of Mexico, of Latin America, and of the world who have been with us . . . even if we have not seen them and they are in their worlds, their struggles, their experiences, their histories.

The zapatista struggle is a little hut, one more little house, perhaps the humblest and simplest among those that are being raised, with identical or greater hardships and efforts, in this street that is called "Mexico." We who reside in this little house identify with the band that peoples the entire barrio of below that is called "Latin America," and we hope to contribute something to making the great city that is called "the world" habitable. If this is bad, attribute it to all those men and women who, struggling in their houses, barrios, cities—in their worlds—took a place among us. Not above, not below, but with us.

A PENGUIN IN THE LACANDON JUNGLE

All right, a promise is a promise. I said you I was going to tell you about the penguin that's here, in the mountains of the Mexican Southeast, so here goes.

It took place in one of the insurgent barracks, a little more than a month ago, just before the Red Alert. I was on my way, heading toward the position that was to be the headquarters of the Comandancia General of the EZLN. There I was to pick up the *insurgentes* and *insurgentas*, the ones who were going to make up my unit during the Red Alert. The commander of the barracks, a lieutenant colonel *insurgente*, was finishing up the dismantling of the camp and making arrangements for moving the equipment. To lighten the burden of the support bases, who were providing supplies for the insurgent troops, the soldiers in this unit had developed a few subsistence measures of their own: a vegetable garden and a farm. They decided they would take as many of the vegetables as they could, and the rest would be left to the hand of God. As for the chickens, hens, and roosters, the alternative was to eat them or leave them. "Better we eat them than the *federales*," the men and women (most of them young people under the age of 20) who were maintaining that position decided, not without reason. One by one, the animals ended up in the pot and, from there, to the soldiers' soup dishes. There weren't very many animals, either, so in a few days the poultry population had been reduced to two or three specimens.

When only one remained, on the precise day of departure, what happened, happened . . .

The last chicken began walking upright, perhaps trying to be mistaken for one of us and to pass unnoticed with that posture. I don't know much about zoology, but it does not appear that the anatomical makeup of chickens is ideal for walking upright, so, with the swaying produced by the effort of keeping itself upright, the chicken was teetering back and forth, without being able to come up with a precise course. It was then that someone said, "It looks like a penguin." The incident provoked laughter, which resulted in sympathy. The chicken did, it's true, look like a penguin. It was missing only the white bib. The fact is that the jokes ended up preventing the "penguin" from meeting the same fate as its compañeros from the farm.

The hour of departure arrived, and, while checking to be sure nothing was left, they realized that the "penguin" was still there, swaying from one side to another, but not returning to its natural position. "Let's take it," I said, and everyone looked at me to see if I was joking or serious. It was Insurgenta Toñita who offered to take it. It began raining, and she put it in her lap, under the heavy plastic cape that Toñita wore to protect her weapon and her rucksack from the water. We began the march in the rain.

The penguin arrived at the EZLN headquarters and quickly adapted to the routines of the insurgent Red Alert. It often joined (never losing the posture of a penguin) the *insurgentes* and *insurgentas* at cell time, the hour of political study. The theme during those days was the thirteen zapatista demands, and the compañeros summed it up under the title "Why We Are Struggling." Well, you're not going to believe me, but when I went to the cell meeting under the pretext of looking for hot coffee, I saw that it was the penguin who was paying the most attention. And, also, from time to time, it would peck at someone who was sleeping in the middle of the political talk, as if chiding him to pay attention.

There are no other animals in the barracks . . . I mean except for the snakes, the "*chibo*" tarantulas, two field rats, crickets, ants, an indeterminate (but very large) number of mosquitoes, and a *cojolito*[4] who came to sing, probably because it felt called by the music—*cumbias, rancheras, corridos*, songs of love and of spite—that emanated from the small radio, which is used to hear the morning news by Pascal Beltrán on Antena Radio and then "Plaza Pública" by Miguel Ángel Granados Chapa on Radio UNAM.

Well, I told you there weren't any other animals, so it would seem normal that this "penguin" would think we were its kind and tend to behave as if it were one more of us. We hadn't realized how far it had gone until one afternoon when it refused to eat in the corner it had been assigned and it went over to the wooden table. Penguin made a racket, more chickenlike than penguinlike, until we understood that it wanted to eat with us. You should understand that Penguin's new identity prevented the former chicken from flying the minimum distance necessary for getting up on the bench, and so it was Insurgenta Erika who lifted it up and let it eat from her plate.

The insurgent captain in charge had told me that the chicken, I mean penguin, did not like to be alone at night, perhaps because it feared that the possums might confuse it with a chicken, and it protested until someone took it to their tarp. It wasn't very long before Erika and Toñita made it a white bib out of fabric (they wanted to paint it [Penguin] with lime or house paint, but I managed to dissuade them . . . I think), so that there would be no doubt that it was a penguin and no one would confuse it with a chicken.

You may be thinking that I am, or we are, delirious, but what I'm telling you is true. Meanwhile, Penguin has become part of the Comandancia General of the EZLN, and perhaps those of you who come to the preparatory meetings for the Other Campaign[5] might see it with your own eyes. It could also be expected that Penguin might be the mascot for the EZLN football team when it faces, soon, the Milan Internazionale. Someone might then perhaps take a picture for a souvenir. Perhaps, after a while of looking at the image, a girl or a boy might ask: "Mama, and who are those next to the Penguin?" (Sigh.)

Do you know what? It occurs to me now that we are like Penguin, trying very hard to be erect and to make ourselves a place in Mexico, in Latin America, in the world. Just as the trip we are about to take is not in our anatomy, we shall certainly go about swaying, unsteady and stupidly, provoking laughter and jokes. Although perhaps, also like Penguin, we might provoke some sympathy, and someone might generously protect us and help us, walking with us, to do what every man, woman, or penguin should do, that is, to always try to be better in the only way possible, by struggling.

Vale. Salud, and an embrace from Penguin (?).

From the mountains of the Mexican Southeast

SUBCOMANDANTE INSURGENTE MARCOS

NOTES

1. A *frentista* is a member of the Zapatista Front for National Liberation (FZLN).
2. The Zapatista Front for National Liberation was a Mexican sociopolitical organization allied with the Zapatista Army of National Liberation (EZLN). The FZLN was established in 1997 and disbanded in October 2005.
3. On June 19, 2005, the EZLN declared Red Alert. This action consisted of closing the Caracoles and the offices of the Good Government Juntas, suspending broadcast of Radio

Insurgente, urging members of national and international civil society to evacuate zapatista territories, and consolidating the insurgent military force of the EZLN. The Red Alert was called to facilitate and defend a comprehensive series of consultations with zapatista communities about the pending Sixth Declaration and the Other Campaign. The original text announcing the Red Alert can be found online, http://www.ezln.org/documentos/2005/redalerto60619.htm

4. A *pavo cojolito* is a kind of bird. In English, it is known as a Crested Guan. Its scientific name is Penelope-purpurascens.

5. The Other Campaign was first announced in "The Sixth Declaration of the Lacandon Jungle," June 2005. A civil and peaceful initiative proposed by the zapatistas, the Other Campaign is expressly anticapitalist and separate from party politics. Throughout a three-year process, the Other Campaign strives to establish long-term dialogue and alliances between organizations, collectives, and individuals "from below and to the left."

When the Word Appeared

OPENING WORDS READ BY THE EZLN AT THE SECOND
PREPARATION MEETING FOR THE OTHER CAMPAIGN

AUGUST 13, 2005

Community of Javier Hernández, Chiapas

As this is the meeting of Indian peoples and indigenous organizations, we are going to try to talk about what our way is like, among the indigenous, the Indian peoples. A small part of that is the history told by our Mayan ancestors as to how the world began. They said then, so our elder ones told, that in the beginning there was nothing, and in reality the world began to run when the word appeared. But the word did not appear just like that; the word, so say our elder ones, began by being thought inside oneself, by, they say, reflecting. By using the word, the first gods, those who made the world, began consulting among themselves, they spoke, they reached agreement, and they reflected.

And then, since they had made accords, they joined together, joined their thoughts, and that is when the world began to run. That is how everything began, with the word being thought within, or being reflected in the heart, which is a mirror within, for us to look at what we are. And therefore it was the word that met with another word.

The first word did not fight; it did not want to dominate or conquer another word, and that is because the first word that came out met a word that was like its sister, because it was equal yet different. It was as if they had the same root in the tree of the world, but were each a distinct branch or leaf. It was as if the first word was not alone, but there

was another word, and, according to the thinking of our Mayan ancestors, the world began being birthed when that one word and that other
word met each other and did not quarrel but rather met and reached
accord because they each respected the other and they spoke and they
listened.

Then there was accord, because the first word was not born alone.
Rather, it had an ear, and with an ear, and by listening, the first words
began to grow. They thought up the world and then they made it. They
did not just set about making the world with its rivers, its mountains,
its animals, its night, its day, its sun, its moon, its maize, its men and
women; instead, the first words thought first and then they made.

But then it came to pass that someone said he was better than the rest
and he wanted to rule—he wanted to have more and better than the
rest, and so he stole from them. He took by force and dominated their
work. He divested them of what they produced, or as is said, he *exploited*
them. And that is how the one who has more and better was born. He
was not born because he just arrived, but because of the deprivation and
the exploitation. And thus began, as is said, *the problem*. Because, as that
is how the one who wants to dominate came forth, so the one who did
not allow himself to be dominated also came forth. And so the history
of the world is the history of that struggle between those who want to
dominate in order to impose their word and their way, taking away the
wealth of others, and those who do not allow themselves to be dominated, those who rebel.

Those who rebel do not want to dominate; they want everyone to be
even, without there being those with more and those with less, without
there being those with reason to rob and exploit and those with no reason to be robbed and exploited. These rebels want us to be branches
and leaves on the tree of the world, each one in their own place and in
their own way. That is how our Mayan ancestors recount it, the indigenous Mayans who were the very first to people these lands. And so, it
was passed down to their sons and daughters, to the grandsons and
granddaughters, from one time to another, from one generation to

another. The way then remained among the Mayan indigenous who have various names and whose house extends to Yucatán and Guatemala, Campeche, Tabasco, Quintana Roo, and here in our state, which is Chiapas.

That way has remained with us. We zapatistas, or neozapatistas as they call us, have this way that first we think up the world that is and what to do from within, and then we take out the word and we seek other sister words and we look to find if there is accord speaking and listening, and so the word is made large and thus the world we are dreaming is also made large. But now, the beginning of the world is not up to us, but what *is* up to us now is that there are those who divest and exploit and there are those who rebel and want liberation. We chose to be by the side of those who are struggling for liberty, the side of those who are dominated and who are robbed and exploited.

This is history. The compañeros and compañeras from indigenous organizations already know it, because we have been walking together for a while. Together we saw that we must join together and reach accord, and that was how what is called the National Indigenous Congress was born. Accords and marches and mobilizations were made, and those who rule and dominate did not want to recognize our word. Each one thought once again, and new struggles were born to put our way in place, even if they did not recognize the laws of the rich. That is what we hope we shall talk about a bit with the brothers and sisters who come from other sides, from other Indian peoples, and from other indigenous organizations.

Comandanta Ramona

JANUARY 6, 2006

Transcription of a public announcement made by Subcomandante Marcos in Tonalá, Chiapas, at Cine Palacio, during the Other Campaign

Well, compañeros, compañeras. I'm going to ask you to listen to me carefully, and I'm going to respectfully ask you not to interrupt me until I'm finished. What we're doing with the Other Campaign is done so that everyone's voice can be heard—that's why it's important that we're all patient and listen to everyone. In my work as spokesperson for the Zapatista Army of National Liberation, there are moments that are very hard, like this one I'm going to tell you about right now. They've just let me know . . . that's why we interrupted this . . . that the compañera Comandanta Ramona died this morning. As everyone knows, she wasn't doing well but [inaudible] . . . thanks to the help of people like you, she was able to overcome it, and she had a kidney transplant. This morning she began vomiting, with blood and diarrhea, and while she was on the way to San Cristóbal she died on the road.

It's very difficult for me to talk about this, but what I can say is that the world has lost an exemplary woman. That the world, that Mexico, has lost one of those fighters that it needs, and a piece of our heart has been ripped out. In a few minutes the Caracol of Oventik is going to be closed, and we're going [to mourn] this compañera's death in private . . . In view of this, we're going to cancel our participation in today's and tomorrow's events, and right now we're going to go back there and wait for orders from the compañeros, the Comandancia, and the Clandestine Revolutionary Indigenous Committee . . .

Thank you for coming. Thank you for your words. We'll continue with this. We'll see to the circumstances. Comandanta Ramona was at the closing of the Plenary. Excuse me, when the Plenary began in La Garrucha. We were joking with her. Just a few days ago the compañeros saw her, the first of January. She sent me her greetings and joked [inaudible]. But right now what I remember is that day of the Plenary when she gave us an embroidery piece she'd made when she was convalescing from the operation she had ten years ago. She gave it to me and told me that she hoped the Other Campaign would be like that embroidery. That's what we have to do. Thank you, compañeros. We have to leave. Excuse us.

The First Other Winds

FEBRUARY 18–19, 2006

In the name of the Zapatista System of Intergalactic Television, "the only television which is read," we would like to express our gratitude to this space for the presentation of a special program, sponsored by "Huaraches Yepa, Yepa, the only globalized huarache" and "El Pozol Agrio, a delight for the palate."

We would like to take the opportunity to report that the channels on which SZTVI is broadcasting are for the exclusive and preferential access by the alternative media, and for all honest and principled persons on any part of Planet Earth. As an alternative to the tiresome (and inefficient) PPV system, the SZTVI is offering the NPPL (No Pay Per View) system as a gesture of courtesy for our compañeros and compañeras.

The following program will be rebroadcast by the *banda* of below to the left by methods that range from pirate radio to the very sophisticated (and practically impossible to jam) bathroom gossip. Now to you, with the program . . .

THE FIRST OTHER WINDS

PART I (CHIAPAS, QUINTANA ROO, YUCATÁN, CAMPECHE)

"We want them to lend wind to our words, that they
fly quite high and go very far."
—WORDS OF A MAYAN INDIGENOUS, SPOKEN IN THE OTHER CANCÚN,
IN THE OTHER QUINTANA ROO, IN THE OTHER SOUTHEAST, IN THE
OTHER CAMPAIGN, IN THE OTHER MEXICO

Walking over itself, with the excuse of a ski mask, the Other Campaign started the year by noting, from its first steps, what the response from above would be. The march that joint forces of the Other Campaign held in San Cristóbal de Las Casas on the first day of January of 2006 saw how the streetlights went out as they made their way. Almost simultaneously, step by step, the mass media's microphones, cameras, tape recorders, and notebooks were being turned off. La Otra's[1] first victory: More than indifference, the silence of above reflects fear, much fear. The joint steps of la Otra are not just a challenge to the economic and social system (and to the political class that lives off and with it), they are also another step, the change of pace and direction of those who have, up until now, been on the defensive, resisting, surviving, weaving history so they won't fall. La Otra is now a step toward the offense. And so a sound, which is still small, is rising up from the Mexico of below. And it rises up to then make itself a murmur, next a shout, and, finally, movement. With its journey, la Otra has a message for those of above: "*Ya basta*. No longer. Now we're going after you." A shiver runs down the system's spine: Instead of listening to those of above, those of below have chosen to listen to each other.

Chiapas

Above, a traveling stage set. Below, a yet incomplete heart and a growing indignation, seeking a way, a path, a direction, and a destination.

The stations of the Other Campaign follow each other, one by one, but the indigenous voice is repeated. From the first day, the Other Campaign has demonstrated that it is more, much more, than the EZLN. San Cristóbal de Las Casas, Palenque, Chiapa de Corzo, Tuxtla Gutiérrez, the Amate jail, Tonalá, Joaquín Amaro, San Isidro, Huixtla, Ejido Nuevo Villa Flores. Indigenous, most especially indigenous, and, along with them those who accompany their sorrows and rebellions: nongovernmental organizations, groups, collectives, families, individuals who work in the defense of human rights, gender struggle, economic projects, education, culture, defense of the environment, alternative communication, analysis, and theoretical debate. Mostly women, mostly young people. There they are, there they always were, even before 1994.

But something has changed: Their voice no longer carries just solidarity and support for zapatismo; now it speaks their history, their resistance, their struggle. The "this is what I am" with which the Sixth Declaration of the Lacandon Jungle began is now beginning to recount other histories and to name the other through their own voices. Indigenous organizations and Indian peoples—they are not zapatistas but neither are they antizapatistas—are demonstrating that their unfinished business is not just with those who rose up in arms in 1994 but also with the very roots of the Mexican nation.

The reappearance of the evangelical indigenous on the outskirts of San Cristóbal de Las Casas put an end to the illusion that la Otra Jovel is mestiza. In Palenque, something is emerging that may look like a symptom but is, in reality, a movement that is growing as la Otra moves through the Mexican Southeast: resistance against the high costs of electricity and against privatization. The first voices against the onslaught by the government, which is attempting to privatize the electrical industry, are from those who are dark of color and speak indigenous languages.

In Chiapa de Corzo and Tuxtla Gutiérrez, new voices appear with their own sound: market tenants, teachers, students, residents, nonindigenous campesinos. The tension line that joins the Southeast with the North surfaces in the first steps: David Meza, chiapaneco, who is used as a scapegoat to conceal the inefficiency of officials in the feminicide that set up camp in Ciudad Juárez, Chihuahua. The young man, 26 years old, is accused of murdering his cousin, Neyra Azucena Cervantes, 19 years old. Through torture, he is forced to sign a confession. He or the real murderers (without videos or tape recordings to verify their true identities) are still free and adding more deaths to the list of sorrows in northern Mexico.

The young students point out a truth: Education is bad and moving toward privatization, and when they leave there's no work. Injustice in Chiapas has the face and name of the indigenous, the campesino, the teacher, the journalist. But also rebel dignity: Section VII of the National Union of Education Workers (SNTE)[2] of the National Farm Workers

Union is contributing not only prisoners, but also mobilizations. In Tonalá, in Joaquín Amaro, in San Isidro, and in Huixtla, the civil resistance movement against the high cost of electric energy is appearing once again, but now the people there know they're not alone.

And throughout the coast of Chiapas, one can see the combined work of officials and companies in the destruction of nature. Work is now a luxury that you have to pay for, and poverty is a crime. Criticism is growing against the political class and the PRD as a renamed PRI, its corruption improved and magnified. Water is in short supply here, schools don't even have chalkboards, and Fox's messages about "educational excellence" sound like a bad joke. Old people are protesting against being treated like nonrecyclable products. All along the coast, the Sierra is an open wound that is far from being healed. Going up, we arrive at the Nuevo Villa Flores ejido and la Otra's most combative event, with the OCEZ-UNOPII[3] as host.

Halfway along, a blow to the heart forces the silence with which we grieve for those in the struggle whom we love. Comandanta Ramona has gone, leaving a multicolored embroidery as zapatista proposal for la Otra throughout the country. In the mountains of the Mexican Southeast, we zapatistas tear off a piece of the clothing we're wearing and, with this sorrowful tatter on our left shoulder, we name the one whom we now miss beyond all measure.

Meanwhile, as la Otra's journey progresses, the state government is moving the stage set of "Everything is calm in Chiapas," but just for the consumption of those who have accepted the *ley mordaza*.[4] For the photograph: equipment working on the highway. For the shadow: the scandal of the "disappearance" of the funds and aid earmarked for victims of the storms.[5] The government of Chiapas—when it can find time away from its work as real-estate consultant and public-image advisor to the "king of denim" (and emperor of pederasty and child pornography)— is persecuting and imprisoning dissidents and journalists, and, in addition, is building monuments in praise of themselves and of Fox. La Otra's journey is forcing them to redouble . . . their publicity expenditures.

Too late. It does not matter if they close their eyes and ears up above; below they have listened and seen. Now a wind lifts up and, from below and to the left, heads toward . . .

Quintana Roo

Above, a country of hotels. Below, Chan Santa Cruz[6] speaks once again.

Chetumal, Carrillo Puerto, Playa del Carmen, Cancún. Names that refer to tourist destinations, to large hotel companies, and to natural disasters. But the history of below recounts that the disasters have been brought about by pro-business governments. The privatization of large stretches of land and water was achieved through underhanded laws, seizures of ejidal and communal lands, and the destruction of nature. The campesino voice denounces seizure of lands and privatization of beaches with the Program of Certification of Ejidal Rights and Qualifications of Urban Plots (PROCEDE)[7] as spearhead. In Majahual, while the North American government is building a wall on the northern border, another is being raised by foreign companies to prevent access to a beach. The countryside no longer suffers from government inattention under these skies. Now it has an exceptional commitment, but in order to conquer/destroy it: high interest rates, low prices for what is produced, turning ejiditarios and *comuneros*[8] into small landowners under PROCEDE. The result is indebtedness, attachment, or buying and selling. And where before there was farming land, now there is, or will be, a shopping or tourism center, a residential area, or an airport.

Llover sobre mojado.[9] After Hurricane Wilma, wasn't the priority of Fox's PAN government to bring aid to the big hotel owners instead of to the humble people? Those up above who fear la Otra distributed blankets to the Maya of Nicolás Bravo so they wouldn't go to the meetings, while lumber is being looted by big companies with government permits, and the Mexican jungle is being destroyed with legal backing.

But nature and history have their guardians. Individually or in organizations, the defense of nature and of heritage supports their strongholds throughout Quintana Roo. Men and women are meeting, analyzing, discussing, agreeing to not remain silent or immobilized. They are thus undertaking a twofold struggle: one for the legal defense of nature and of history, and the other for creating awareness among the people of below and to the left. Hand in hand with these efforts, another artistic and cultural work is on the march, running up against the tackiness of Fox's cultural programs and looking below for other ears, other gazes.

In a corner of the corner that is the Mexican Southeast then appears the indigenous voice of the Union of Defense of the Mayan Race and of the Collective of Isla Mujeres. The *palabra morena*[10] of the smallest has best summarized the purpose of la Otra's first stage: lending wind to word, that it might fly high, that it might go far. The faltering initial steps of the alternative media in the caravan now have, from these distances, their own pace and firm definition: So that the ear can exist and increase, the word of the other is necessary. The direction of the other cameras and microphones has thus been reoriented, and, with these other men and women, now beginning to fly high are the voices of farmers, fishermen, construction workers, artisans, street vendors, indigenous, campesinos without land, residents, students, teachers, workers, researchers, men, women, young people, especially women and young people.

But in addition to voices, whispers, and shouts, la Otra hears silences. Here, in the Mayan lands of Quintana Roo, Chan Santa Cruz is taking back up the message of the *chiapaneco* mountains, echoing and so repeating: "May all the guardians of the land, the mother, awaken. May the watchkeepers awaken. May they awaken from the night of sorrow. The hour has come."

The wind then takes on new force, and, with the voice of the other as engine and fuel, reaches . . .

(Tomorrow, Yucatán and Campeche, as this first part continues.)

From the Other Tlaxcala

SUP MARCOS

PART II
MARCH 11, 2006

Yucatán

Above, a hacienda as political program. Below, Mayan dignity awakening the other.

On one side, that of above: the resistance of the powerful to losing privileges won through blood and fire since the era of the Conquest. On the other, that of below: ancient rebellion multiplying its colors.

The postmodern hacienda of the PAN's Yucatán is adding the establishment of maquiladoras to the tourism and oil. The weak scaffolding of government propaganda is being built on top of this: even though local economic powers are still thinking in the sixteenth century, Yucatán is exploiting these lands (and their people) using twenty-first-century methods.

This is the National Action Party's [PAN] political program: an *encomendero*[11] mentality running industry. More is missing; this is the "government of change." The real results are at odds with the fragile PAN stage set: land seizures, privatization of heritage, industrial exploitation, destruction of nature, migration. This truth is more visible in rural Yucatán: the destruction of the Mexican countryside is not the result of the governments' lack of skill; rather, it is their primary objective. It has to do with a strategic plan that entails, in simple and straightforward terms, a war, a war of reconquest. But this war is not just one-sided; the resistance is also resounding from below.

And then the guardians appear who are making it quite clear that the oblivion of the native people of these lands will not be legislated in their name. The Mayan artisans, who are resisting the seizure of memory-made-stone of their ancestors. Chichen Itzá: the fishermen of Puerto Progreso, of the Camarón Vagabundo, who denounced that they are turned into criminals if they work because of a law. They have to pay them to get permission to work, and not even then. In addition, the inspectors steal their catch. The ejiditarios of Oxcum, who note that they want to seize their lands for an airport. The *banda*[12] that suffers persecution for making and promoting another culture.

Indignation and fury look around, and, with Mayan language, color, and ways, they find others who also repeat, though separately, *"¡Ya basta!"* Also appearing here, along with residents, students, artisans, and academics, are homosexuals, their Oasis of San Juan de Dios, and their threefold struggle against AIDS: against the virus, against the society that discriminates against them and segregates them, and against the government that washes its hands of the problem. Others join in the struggle for respect of sexual diversity.

They all say, repeat, and insist: We're no longer going to allow it, *¡Ya basta!* Now it is not only pain that can be heard in the voices of below. The joy of someone who is beginning to realize that he or she is not alone, who, by being listened to and listening, finds the compañero, compañera.

But the peninsular rebel wind doesn't stop here. It goes on to . . .

Campeche
Above, destruction as government program. Below, the rebellion of colors.

In Bekal, the first voices resound, and from here they are beginning to sound the alert about the greatness of raising a popular movement throughout the country. The recounting is made: ejiditarios are harassed by corrupt leaders, by the government, and by the big owners. Now they have to pay to work their own land, pay to be poor. In the port of Campeche, the voice continues, and the listening is organized primarily by young people. The only common point with injustice is the number two: 20 wealthy families, 200 families of courtiers, and 200,000 poor families. The owners of the economy also own the politics; a powerful family has a candidate for each of the three parties: PRI, PAN, and PRD. They appropriate large expanses of land and beaches, and the campesinos and fishermen go on to become employees of tourism centers or immigrate to the United States.

Hand in hand with wealthy locals, Pemex contributes to the destruction of nature. In Campeche, a truth is made evident: Nature is being destroyed by the selfsame officials who are in charge of protecting it. The pirates and corsairs who once ravaged the Campeche coasts now hold public and private offices and appear in the society pages while 180,000 residents are surviving in conditions of extreme poverty. The sorrow reaches to Xpujil (Calakmul) and Candelaria. The old PRI politics (sometimes with the flag of the PT, of Convergencia, of the PAN, or of the PRD) are being repeated in the Mexican countryside: the buying of campesino leaders, division and confrontations between organizations, repression, persecution, imprisonment, death. Migration to the United States is the only door they find open. The situation isn't that different from what existed in the times of the *chicleros*.[13] Injustice is christened in these lands by Carlos Salinas de Gortari as Calakmul (Twin Pyramids)[14] in order to emphasize the zeal of the neoconquest of capital: These lands, with everything and the historical wealth they amass, will belong to the new lords of money.

And lies hold an important place in this war: The government social welfare programs do not arrive in full. Those monies remain somewhere else, but government progress is nonetheless announced with pomp and circumstance. The modern divestiture follows known paths: bank credits, increasing interest rates, the bank devouring all the work, and the debt somehow grows, PROCEDE eliminates legal impediments, and they are seized. Years of work and, in the end, the people have no land or anything . . . only rage.

But in the Campeche of below there are rebels who are not just from here, but also from the majority of the states of the Republic. And so rebellion takes on many colors throughout the state. As injustices multiply, intelligent and organized rebellions multiply as well.

The Other Campeche unites artisans, campesinos, cultural and theoretical analysis collectives, beekeepers, cooperative members, mostly indigenous. Many come from the ecclesiastical base communities and committed Christianity. All of them are in agreement about their indignation, rebellion, and rage. But they don't stop there; they form their organizations and educate themselves in the struggle, and there they identify the enemy and the compañero, the opportunist and the momentary passenger.

The wind resounds in the Other Campaign and repeats "No longer!" and the echo is so powerful it manages to reach the other country that, below and to the left, watches over the night in order to continue on its path, on another dawn, to Tabasco.

Intermission

Along its way and in its way, la Otra is beginning to turn into an option, into something else, into another alternative to despair. While up above the noise comes and goes (as does the money to simulate discussion and debate, where there are only e-spot ads), an echo sounds in the other voices of below, an echo that does not end, that is beginning to define itself in collective: La Otra is joining together struggles and thoughts. The "I am" is beginning to transform, step by step, into "We are."

Various points in common in the first winds:

- The brazen alliance between businesspeople and politicians from all parties.
- Seizure of lands.
- Privatization of the national heritage.
- Premeditated destruction of the environment.
- Repression, persecution, and imprisonment of those who fight for social good.
- High cost of living, especially that of electricity.
- Immigration to the United States.
- Educational crises at all levels and, in the end, the disaster of unemployment.
- Disgust with the political class and criticism of institutional political parties.

And so, bridges are beginning to be extended between those who—

below—are who we are. The first of these bridges, the struggle for our own: freedom for all political prisoners and the cancellation of all arrest warrants for social activists.

But that is not all. Proposals are also beginning to emerge:

- The general strike over payments to the Federal Commission of Electricity until fair rates are agreed according to the criteria that the rich pay more and the poor pay less or they don't pay.
- The generalized campesino rejection of PROCEDE. The national blockade against the official policy of destroying the environment.
- The national defense of our heritage in the face of its growing privatization.
- The building of a new option for future migrants that consists of a cry: Stay and fight!

Another First of May for the other workers, and the first signs of other realities and demands, which we will explain further along.

Video Clip: The Week Above and Below

There are differences, above and below, in looking at how the week transpired. Up above it's always Monday, even for those who are running as the electoral alternative.

Time and again they tell us that we don't have to go quickly, we have to stop, walk so slowly that movement is barely feigned.

Ah! It's so nice up above! Entertainment suitable for a wallet full of plastic, high culture, highways and wide streets for vehicles, second floors in order to reaffirm that we are above, television as an instant stage set in every Mexican home. Ah! Once again those naughty ones below, listening to one another, exchanging histories that look so nice in books and essays, but being talked about, how they offend. My friend, the democracy of those words of below is in such bad taste. What are we here for, the popular representatives, the opinion leaders, the columnists, the commentators, editors? Where do they get off dispensing with intermediaries in order to speak among themselves? And then, in addition to talking and listening, they dare to agree to rise up. Better that you turn up the volume on the television, my friend! Come on, just like that! How are the polls going? Good, we're in the lead.

What? The Other Campaign? A murmur, nothing to worry about . . . Or yes? I don't know why they're infuriated and promising us a jail. But who is advising them to try to dispense with us? They themselves? Why don't they wait? We can go on leading them, teaching them the caution and prudence which we learned and which, you'll see, is so comfortable! Red and black weekend? Excuse me, no, my friend, that color isn't registered, it's worthless. What do you mean they don't want to be registered? Don't tell me another politics is possible? And we—the whitewashed tombs of unhurried, exceedingly slow change—take no notice, because if we do, the investors will be frightened away from us. What is this about their not wanting investors? Or politicians? You see, my friend, they are *so* premodern. Let's hope they don't affect the polls. What would happen to our democracy then?

Yes, they look so pretty when they're silent, stopped, attentive to our word and our directions. Yes, ingrates. They don't know they can't do anything in such a hurry, so below, so to the left. Yes, little by little. Now, with the project for the Isthmus . . . What? The same as the Plan Puebla-Panama? No, my friend, if this is from the left. Bah! There will be a few indigenous peoples disappeared and a few effects on the land, but there will be jobs, maquiladoras, and a glimpse of service and tourism industry booms. Yes, modernity, but with a human face, our face.

That left—how can I say it—isn't it an ugly, poorly educated, vulgar left? Where is the high level of debate, our skill in dulling the edges of words, and our all remaining friends, happy, immobile? Yes, we say what debate is and what it is not. For example, all discussion that ends up in principled commitments is not high-level debate, it's for extremists, the desperate, resentful. Bah! They can't take anything, a few indigenous shot, kidnapped, tortured, stripped. No, my friend, don't look down there. What for? Here is the mature, calm, and prudent path. Do you see how we barely move? No, my friend, don't be distracted, look at me, listen to me, sit down, wait, don't move, like that, very quiet. Look, what you have to do is let me do. The rest are just that, the "rest," the "other."

Listen, my friend. Are there a lot of them? You say they're coming for us? For everyone? Also for the left that is faithful and loyal to the system? And are they going to take a long time? You know, the academy, the café, the automobile, the position, the symposium, the stroking we give and receive, the invitation to eat with that so-very-important politician/businessman/leader.

Another communication? All right, tell me why if the one that we have is the one that rules, the one that counts in the polls, the democratic and modern one. As if there's anything more important to report on other than what concerns me? Another art? What? And the exquisite selection of our tastes? Another culture? That, yes. The *charrapastrosos*[15] need their own things. They look so cute with all those things. What are they called? Yes, their idiosyncrasies, their crafts, their piercings, their tattoos, their hair sticking up and painted in scandalous colors, their *chido-guey-varo-rola*[16] things, their music. No, my friend, that's not rock. Real rock is neat and tidy, "nice," it's "your rock is voting," it's "better shut up," it's about that immobility that moves, jumps, and applauds, but thinking . . . Well, my friend, what for? If you're going to grow up and mature and you're going to be like us anyway . . . Or not?

What are you saying? An uprising? National? You mean it's not just a national mailbox of complaints? They're also joining together, organizing? But that's too fast—there should just be a few. What? Their number is growing? Listen, but is it true they're still going to be a while? My grant, my position, my editorial, my essay, my teaching post, my candidacy . . .

Unauthorized Interference

Chiapas, Quintana Roo, Yucatán, Campeche, Tabasco, Veracruz, Oaxaca, Puebla. Eight states and one single challenge: communication, another communication. Among the conclusions drawn from this first third of the trip around the country is that the slogan "All Mexico Is Tel-cel Country" is a lie. Slim needs to be put in jail, not just for exploiting, but also for lying.

One of the challenges is that of communication with all those who are fighting for this. Technology should also seek the path of below, so that the weaving of this network can be made visible in the Other Campaign. This is a job for right now. The alternative media should not be satisfied with keeping the words of the "others" up-to-date on their current channels. They should, we believe, seek out the others who don't have the ways or means to learn about this "other" that is growing below and to the left.

Little by little, the alternative media is coming to understand that the Sixth Committee of the EZLN is just their "back stage," a support team (big-nosed and ill-tempered at this point) that is helping this part of the "other" a bit in the beginning: making the word grow from below and building a collective ear for it. But the science and technology needed to link up the most distant compas are still lacking.

Provisional Final (only for the broad-minded)
Dawn has almost slipped away. The light from the sun is beginning to peek through the crevices, and we must return to the dim shadows that clothe us. The skin of desire and the tempest of her hair are still missing from my hands. A sigh still waits expectantly on lips. The gaze, and the cloud that envelops it, miss the light that is absent from them. Ah! The tricks of imagination: In the half-sleep dream, her thighs were a scarf around the cheeks and prison for the waist. Standing, the ride of desire ending, after a brief precipice, in a damp and mutual fall. And at the end there were no debts other than those one has with oneself. Ah, the longing to be drenched in her rain. To be sated by her and to make her desire increase.

Dawn breaks with the certainty that there could be no better photo than the one I take with my hands and lips, no better audio or video than that of awakening her gasps and moans, no better show or painting than that of skin joined together, no better meeting than that of our bodies.

Another communication? Another news report? Another art? Another culture? Another campaign? Who in hell would embrace that nonsense?

They are knocking on the door of the day. The shadow laces up his boots and desires. We must continue walking, listening . . .

From the Other Tlaxcala

SUP MARCOS

P.S. As of February 15, 2006, the Sixth Declaration and the Other Campaign have gained 1,036 political, indigenous, social, nongovernmental organizations, groups, and collective supporters, all of them from below and to the left. Without any advertisements other than their voices, nor any signatures traced other than those of their steps throughout the country, signed firmly and with a flourish. Here we are, we are the Otra, rebel dignity, the heart forgotten—until now—by the Patria.

NOTES

1. "La Otra" is the Spanish abreviation of "the Other Campaign." We chose to preserve the original Spanish phrase for purposes of clarity and becase this abreviation has entered the general vocabulary of zapatista discourses, in English and Spanish. We decided not to italicize the phrase because it is the abreviation of a proper name.
2. Section VII of the National Union of Education Workers (SNTE) is the regional teachers union for the state of Chiapas, Mexico.
3. Emiliano Zapata Campesino Organization—National Unity of Popular Organizations of the Independent Left (OCEZ-UNOPII).
4. *Ley mordaza* is a Spanish phrase that literally translates as "gag law," referring to a law that limits freedom of expression.
5. In the first week of October 2005, Hurricane Stan severely affected Chiapas, Guatemala, and El Salvador. In the southern region of Chiapas, it is estimated that more than 18,000 houses and 174 schools were destroyed. The hurricane left more than eighty-eight communities isolated, destroyed more than twenty bridges, and took out many highways.
6. Chan Santa Cruz is the Mayan town now known as Felipe Carrillo Puerto in what is now the Mexican state of Quintana Roo. This name also refers to the liberated indigenous Mayan state ruled from Chan Santa Cruz for much of the second half of the nineteenth century.
7. The Program of Certification of Ejidal Rights and Qualifications of Urban Plots (PROCEDE) was established in 1992 under the tenure of ex-president Carlos Salinas de Gortari. Part of

a comprehensive reform of Article 27 of the Mexican Constitution, PROCEDE promotes further privatization of land and natural resources by dividing collective ejidos into individual land plots.

8. Ejiditarios are members of ejidos, and *comuneros* are members of *comunales*. Both ejidos and *comunales* have distinct definitions according to Article 27 of the Mexican Constitution. Both are portions of collectively owned land with legal status, specific territorial limits, and representative bodies of governance. *Comunales* are exclusively indigenous and based on historical claims of land entitlement that usually date to pre-Colombian or colonial times. So far, *comunales* cannot be privatized, but ejidos can. However, changes made to Article 27 in 1992 permit *comunales*, with inalienable rights of communal ownership, to become ejidos. If a *comunal* community transitions to ejido status, its lands can be individually parceled and privatized.

9. This phrase literally translates as "rain on what is wet" and is comparable to the English saying "adding insult to injury."

10. *Palabra* means "word." *Moreno* refers to skin with a deep brown tone.

11. An *encomendero* is the manager of a colonial-era *encomienda*.

12. *Banda* usually refers to a gang of people, usually youth. North American and Mexican criminalization of youth has instilled the words *banda* and *gang* with a negative connotation, related to organized crime, antisocial behavior, or delinquency. Here, the word is used to question such authoritarian, ageist, and conservative reactionism.

13. A *chiclero* is a worker who harvests gum, *chicle*, from sapodilla trees. *Chicle* was a primary export of the sovereign Mayan state of Chan Santa Cruz—present-day Quintana Roo, Mexico—which maintained independence until it was invaded by Mexico at the end of the nineteenth century. Following the decline of indigenous sovereignty, the former Mayan state was overrun by North American and European companies seeking to profit from the area's natural resources. As the foreign-owned industry grew, indigenous *chicleros* were forced to harvest their ancient crop on lands that were no longer their own, in dangerous working conditions and for meager wages. By the mid-twentieth century, the advent of synthetic chewing gum marked the decline of the *chicle* industry, and the times of the *chicleros* came to an end.

14. *Calakmul* refers to one of the largest ancient Mayan cities known to modern archaeologists, located in the state of Campeche, Mexico. According to Cyrus Lundell, who named the site, *Calakmul* is a Mayan word that means "City of Two Adjacent Pyramids." In 1989, President Carlos Salinas de Gortari declared Calakmul a biosphere reserve. In an article by Hermann Bellinghausen—published in *La Jornada*, January 25, 2006—the municipality of Calakmul is currently dominated by the PRI. Bellinghausen reports that "the business of plundering precious woods continues with impunity. The 'ecological' aspect of the municipality only applies to the campesinos, who are prohibited from cutting down the trees. Only the big logging companies can do it, and these cut down countless trees."

15. *Charrapastroso* is a colloquial word that suggests a disheveled or unkempt characteristic.

16. This is a list of unrelated Spanish slang words.

Marcos and Durito on Bricks, Curtains, and Fish

JUNE 15, 2006

(Dialogue between Durito, Juan de Mairena, and a superfluous nose)

I must publicly apologize: The present text, in its basic corpus, does not belong to me. Rather, it is the transcription of a recorded tape. Said recording tape (or "cassette" for the rabble) has been surreptitiously extracted from the backpack of someone who looks extraordinarily like a beetle.

It could be seen as astonishing and scandalous that, in this digital age, someone would still resort to a "cassette" for recording and reproducing, but that would be nothing compared to the stupefaction that would arise from knowing that the individual in question is, in fact, a beetle. And from there deducing (it cannot be forgotten that it is a fortunate presentation that makes the audience and the reader feel very intelligent) that that beetle calls himself "Don Durito of the Lacandon Jungle" is a fairly regular, that is, light to moderate, step.

Accepting this small but thick package of facts, regardless of whether they take place in actual reality or in our bedeviled imagination, is an achievement for which I applaud you all. During these times of political platforms being defined in their proper dimensions (that is, as publicity "spots"); of "passes for the network" and polls that do indeed summon the entire nation (those having to do with what place the Mexican football team will have in the World Cup); of "deep" analyses of the "correlation of forces" by pedants who call themselves the part and the whole of "progressive intellectualism"; of situating the government spokesperson in policemen's penises (Atenco) and in grenade launchers (Atenco and Oaxaca); of the "high level" of columnists and editorial writers who comment on and analyze what is said by . . . other columnists and editorial writers. In sum, in these times of "political realism," the fact that there are still people (well, it seems as if some of them even have jobs) who allow room in their hearts for accepting the existence of a beetle who professes to the misunderstood profession of knight errantry is, to put it modestly, simply marvelous.

Not just because that means I'm no longer alone with the heavy burden of knowing of the existence of this strange being, but also and above all because it is irrefutable evidence that there are still people willing to be astonished by the marvels that walk below and that, therefore, are perceived only by those who know how to see the path and the way.

The beetle in question calls himself, as almost no one here will know, Don Durito of the Lacandon Jungle, I.C. of A.I. of I.I. (for its initials: Individuality Known of Invariable Anticapital of Unlimited Irresponsibility), Copyleft not of the Circle but Squared of Knights Errant, of which, incidentally, he is lifetime president and sole member.

Taking advantage of the fact that he is not present, I will divest Durito of all the paraphernalia flaunted by his form of address, and I will call him "Simply Durito."

Durito, without being invited, has traveled a good part of the lands of this unhealed wound that we call "Mexico" to be here with us in order to demand liberty and justice for the prisoners of Atenco.

He arrived, as is law, at dawn, carrying his baggage in one of those backpacks carried by the secondary-school/corner/with/degree/poorly/paid/job/and/or/unemployed/but/safe/getting by/safe kids.

He was not invited to this writers' meeting, despite the fact that he professes an exhilaration for the written word that the organizers would have had to reproach. Although perhaps they didn't invite him because they feared he wouldn't keep his word and would display that irresponsibility for which knights errant have been so famous ever since the time of the sad figure who exhibited said quality on the roads of Iberian La Mancha.

One cannot make serious plans with Durito. Not because he lacks formality (let us not forget that he is, yes, a beetle, but also a knight errant), but because he will suddenly grab his skateboard and head downhill, and I want you to see a security bubble here.

Yes, sometimes he just goes away. Other times he goes leaving a note which laconically states:

"My dear used-underwear face: Here I go, then. Don't get into (too much) trouble. Sincerely, Durito. Postscript—I took the tobacco."

Well, so as not to tire you out too much, I'll tell you that, when trying to recover my tobacco, I found a cassette in the backpack along with a note that read:

"For the new book, *Impossible Dialogues*. Listen: Tell the redundant nose to organize an auction between the publishing houses to see which one is going to get this best seller. Author's rights for the film, as well. *The Da Vinci Code* doesn't intimidate me."

End of note.

I don't know why Durito decided to give his new creature a title like this, but we won't worry about that now.

The dialogue we are presenting takes place between Durito, an individual about whom more will be known shortly, and the person who is making this presentation.

I said previously that I had transcribed a tape recording. When I heard it for the first time, I remembered the scene, since I had been there. It was in the "Comandanta Ramona" café, next to the "El Rincon Zapatista" shop. If someone wants to go there, it's very easy to find the place: Head out as if you're going there, but then make a U-turn where it says "U-Turns Prohibited," and then there are a lot of traffic lights, and, when you see a good number of cops from all the agencies, bored and acting as if they're keeping watch, there it is.

I will proceed . . .

It was dawn. The moon was the illuminated hip of desire, although without the longed-for cleft. In the dream, a long kiss, long and damp, was opening the flower of desire and was key for opening the closed and silent heart of time.

But, half asleep, I was picking up the mess, trying to digest some "vultures of the world, unite"–style beans, and looking to see if there was a carcass of some pecan ice cream left. I had been up late listening to an alternative radio station that calls itself "La Ke Huelga." During the program, the announcers had been digressing about dislocations.

And they moved from ankle dislocations to those of ideas, because for a bit, they had been talking about love in times of revolution, and then that they agreed we were for the mobilization for the Atenco prisoners, and they moved on to love in times of repression. From there, they went on to giving a lecture called "Measures Against Repression" or something like that, or what to do when the cops are already charging to shouts of "Against the left of below, the rule of law of above!"

I took note because of that thing about freezing. In addition to the quite classic, and proven to be effective, "Run until you see a sign that reads, 'Welcome to Guatemala,'" they provided other measures and advice.

For example, the psychology school recommended denial, or, when the club is already on its way to its destination, shouting "No!" most convincingly. The law school would recommend, I believe, the technique of legally overwhelming the cops, shouting "*Señor* police officer, you are violating such and such articles of the Constitution, which notes that no individual can be beaten by the police if a television program that presents him as a criminal has not previously intervened" (here the riot cop wonders if the one being presented as a criminal is he, or the aforementioned against whom the rule of law is being directed). The school of "instant recruitment" would advise slogans of "The uniformed peoples are also exploited" type, paradoxically, just before the tear-gas grenade explodes.

There was lengthy and abundant, good and ingenious information in the radio chat by those colleagues of "Ke Huelga," a station I highly recommend and which broadcasts at 102.9 megahertz FM. And I'll take the moment to send an embrace in solidarity to the compas of Radio Plantón, attacked yesterday by the police of the Oaxacan government, and to all the alternative media that, below and to the left, keep us informed and recharge our batteries.

Where was I? Ah, yes! Well, it so happened that at one of the little tables in the "Comandanta Ramona" café, the only table that didn't have books, newspapers, and magazines on top of it, said Durito was sitting with an individual who was known as Juan de Mairena and who, he said, was a great friend of the Spanish poet Antonio Machado.

Durito was bogged down in pancrema cookies and a cappuccino, with two pairs of his feet on top of the table, while Juan de Mairena, sitting quite properly, was elegantly taking a cup of tea of love.

The recording I have faithfully transcribed here picks up some parts of the dialogue that took place between these two individuals and the "heavy-duty" napkin.

It begins with the beetle speaking to me . . .

Durito: Listen, my dear antonym of a small nose, to the following arguments of Don Juan de Mairena:

"1. If every exception proves a rule, a rule with exceptions will be more of a rule than would be a rule without exceptions, which would lack the exception that would prove it.

"2. A rule will be that much more of a rule the more it abounds in exceptions.

"3. The ideal rule will contain nothing but exceptions.

> "(Continuing this chain of reasoning , until the vortex
> of stupidity is reached)"
> —ANTONIO MACHADO, "JUAN DE MAIRENA"
> (ALIANZA EDITORIAL, P. 40)

Me: It seems to me to be clever . . . and useless . . . reasoning.

Durito: That's true, but not completely. Sometimes questioning the obvious leads one to a linkage that will make one forget about the Tlalpan–Taxqueno crossroads. But other times one will find that that evidence is nothing but repetitious lies . . .

Me: For example?

Durito: The today, that created entity, cherished and adored by modern society, the one that is arranged around the media. Is it not true that "today" is no longer a present with a past and future, and it turns into the eternal? Before it, chaos. After it, nothing.

Me: I don't know where you're going.

Durito (with a complicit look at Mairena): The converse would surprise me. Look, Juanito, there's the capitalist system. Is it not true that it presents itself as eternal, omnipotent, and omnipresent?

Juan de Mairena: Certainly.

Durito: Is it not true that its presence is accepted as an inevitable, primary destiny, and later as the only one possible, and then later again as the best one we have had?

Juan de Mairena: "It is what happens always: A fact is noted, and afterward it is accepted as fate. Finally it is turned into a flag. If it is discovered one day that the fact was not completely true, or that it was completely false, the flag, more or less faded, would not stop waving." (Ibid., p. 77)

Durito: Right, waving a faded flag. That, and nothing else, is what the apologists for capitalism are doing. Now, what would happen if we were to question that whole construct?

Me (feeling the need to contribute something to the debate): Hmm . . . I don't know . . . we'd get bored?

Durito (looking at me disapprovingly): Besides that?

Me (with the urgent need to go "*cincuentear*"[1]): Hmm . . . We'd get into trouble?

Durito (applauding with those feet that were not on top of the table or occupied with the pancrema cookies): Correct! You got it right . . . We would have knowledge that would get us into such predicaments that you would forget about the Hidalgo metro[2] station at rush hour—

Me (*echándole mucha crema a mis tacos*):[3] Since we're on the subject of public transportation, I want to denounce that the other day I went down to the metro, and they sandwiched me—

Durito: Come on! Don't act like a rag doll!

Me: Yes, they sold me a sandwich with ham that was as skimpy as the governor of the state of Mexico's brain.

Durito (stating this to the above-mentioned Mairena): I am afraid, my dear sir, that we are getting off the subject. We were questioning the capitalist system. Or, better, questioning its omnipresence . . .

Me (focused on the issue): And the beans didn't agree with me. They wouldn't have passed inspection.

Durito (openly angry now): The level of debate is declining.

Juan de Mairena: Yes, yes, proceed.

Durito: Thank you, Don Juan. The elemental tools for questioning have to do with history. By studying it, we will see . . .

1. That the capitalist system has not existed forever.

2. That its origin has nothing to do with the spirit, the deity of choice, or idealism, but with dispossession, theft, exploitation, repression, and contempt, in sum: crime.

3. That its growth and development go hand in hand with that which gave it life.

Me (putting my spoon into the conversation and into a glass of past-its-expiration-date pecan ice cream): But this just leads to proving the omnipotence of capitalism, in that the bad who are seen as good always win.

Durito (opening another package of cookies): I have not finished . . . What are the founding and fundamental tricks of this system? Equality and liberty. Capitalism says and repeats unto death that it is based in an egalitarian society, and therefore, it turns itself into the guarantor of that equality. In capitalist society we are all human beings, and therefore, we are all equals. Equal before the law, for example.

Me (lamenting the inequality that makes Durito devour all the cookies while I'm left to sweep up the mess he leaves): But that's not true, or at least some are more equal than others. Here are the Atenco prisoners, and there are the Bribriesca children of Martha Sahagún. As if there were two laws: one for below and one for above.

Durito (throwing a fork at me for the obvious purpose of stifling the free expression of my ideas): According to capitalism, human beings are free, free to work, to become rich, to vote, to be an official, to express their thoughts.

Juan de Mairena: "The free expression of thought is an important, but secondary, problem to ours, which is that of freedom of thought itself. For one, we ask ourselves whether the thought, our thought, that of each of us, can take place with complete liberty, regardless of the fact that, then, we are allowed, or not allowed, to express it. Let us ask rhetorically: Of what use to us would be the free expression of an enslaved thought?" (Ibid., p. 179)

Durito: Good point, Don Juan. But let us go on questioning, even if they label us skeptics.

Juan de Mairena: "A devastating argument has been put forth against skepticism: The one who denies the existence of truth, assuming that is the truth, and affirms in the conclusion what was denied in the premise, contradicts oneself. I assume this argument will not have convinced any of the purebred skeptics . . . Skepticism is a vital, not logical, position, that neither affirms nor denies; it limits itself to questioning, and it is not frightened by contradictions." (Ibid., p. 47)

Durito: Cheers for that! Then let us ask: Are we equal? Are we free? And when do we ask these questions? Let us agree to ask them now, since it is above the affirmative response to both that entire edifices of ideas . . . and of bricks . . . are raised.

If we answer "yes"—excuse me if I'm being rude—then I don't understand what we are doing here. And I'm not referring to here, in this zapatista corner, or to that meeting of writers for liberty and justice for the Atenco prisoners, to which they did not invite me, but to this Mexico which, below and to the left, is trying to build a path and a way, without being clear about anything other than the agreed destination.

But we are here and there for something. Perhaps, within that infinite and chaotic universe, which is the "something," it is because we answer "NO!" to those questions: "Are we equal?" "Are we free?" And with this "NO!," we are not only putting in jeopardy the entire legal foundation of that which is called the "State of the Right" (a name that, obviously, is alongside what would be the "State of the Left"), we would also be starting to question the evidence that turns into tombstones for lack of critique. We would stop swallowing what they administer to us every day from above as if it were something true.

Juan de Mairena: "It is a normal tendency for men to believe something true when it proves useful to them. That is why there are so many men who are capable of falling for things." (Ibid., p. 67)

Durito: Then capitalist politics in the modern age would be the art of making the greatest possible number of persons swallow things. And nonetheless, it is increasingly difficult, or at least when more "others" appear who reject the indigestion those truths provoke. As if the politics of above is no longer what it was, and I'm not saying that nostalgically, but noting a fact. It is chaos now.

Juan de Mairena: "One must demand of the public man, and most especially of the politician, that he possess public virtues, all of which can be summed up in one: fidelity to one's own mask . . . a public man who is bad in public is much worse than a public woman who is not good in private. Joking aside . . . take note that there is no political imbroglio that is not an exchange, a confusion of masks, a bad comedy rehearsal in which no one knows his role." (Ibid., p. 81)

Durito: Excellent, Don Juan! You have precisely defined what politics in Mexico is now: a bad comedy in which no one knows his role. That is why there is so much mistrust of politics and so much reluctance to construct a new politics.

Juan de Mairena: "Politics, gentlemen, is an extremely important activity . . . I would never counsel being apolitical, but, as a last resort, scorn for bad politics that makes social climbers and cushy job-seekers with no purpose other than that of gaining profits and securing positions for their relatives. You should engage in politics, although I would tell something else to those who try to do so without you and, naturally, to those against you." (Ibid., p. 136)

Durito: Then another politics would be necessary. Necessary, urgent, merited. And it seems to me that here the role of critical thought, of the intellectuals, is very important.

Juan de Mairena: "It is said that intellectuals have not done anything useful in politics thus far. Intellectuals are confused with pedants." (Ibid., p. 54)

Me: Well, now, what's this about pedantry?

Juan de Mairena: "The specifically pedantic denies things when they are not the way we think them to be. But things are never the way we think they are; they are much more serious and complex." (Ibid.)

Durito: Then what would be the role of critical intellectuals? That of luxuriating spectators watching while society is being destroyed in the theater of politics?

Juan de Mairena: "But have you not yet noticed that almost always, when the curtain is lifted or opened in the modern theater, a room appears with three walls, lacking that fourth wall that the rooms we inhabit have? Why are you not amazed . . . by that terrible lack of verisimilitude? Because, without the absence of that fourth wall . . . how could we know what was going on inside this room?" (Ibid., p. 152)

Durito: I understand. The work of the intellectuals would be exactly that, taking down the fourth wall of the political space, showing it as it is, without anything being concealed, so we can all know what is going on in that room and act accordingly. Today there is a hidden injustice in the room of power: the one that killed Alexis Benhumea Hernández, the one that raped the Atenco prisoners, the one that is illegally keeping upright men and women imprisoned, the one that represses in Oaxaca and in all the corners of the Mexico of below and to the left. That is why . . .

The recording ends here. I have decided to bring his transcription here because I know quite well that there are writers and bright critics here who are willing to protest against the injustice that murdered Alexis, raped our compañeras, keeps social activists imprisoned, and chooses repression instead of dialogue.

Because there are, among these writers, those who produce plays and, through that, are raising the curtain that allows us to see not only what is going on up above, but also inside us. Because more than a few are also making poetry with the slippery bricks of words. Slippery, like fish.

"Poetry is," Mairena said, "the dialogue of man, of a man with his times. That is what poetry tries to make eternal, taking it out of time, difficult work that requires much time, almost all the time the poet has. The poet is a fisherman, not of fish, but of living fish, let us understand each other: of fish that can live after being caught." (Ibid., p. 106)

Cheers to these fisherwomen and fishermen who, with words, help us to look, to look at ourselves, and who are, along with us, demanding liberty and justice for the prisoners of Atenco.

From the Other Mexico City

SUBCOMANDANTE INSURGENTE MARCOS

NOTES

1. *Cincuentear* is an imagined word that translates as "to go fifty." In the 2004 edition of *EZLN—El Fuego y La Palabra*, by Gloria Muños Ramirez, Subcomandante Marcos explains the meaning of this curious verb: "The camps in that era were relatively humble . . . Well, it turns out that to do what they call 'primary' necessities, we had to withdraw a certain distance from the camp. To go urinate, we had to walk 25 meters; to defecate it was 50 meters, on top of having to make a hole with a machete and then cover the 'product' . . . Later, we constructed latrines in more distant areas, but the terms '25' and '50' stuck."
2. "Hidalgo metro" refers to a Mexico City subway station.
3. This phrase literally translates as "adding a lot of cream to my tacos," which is a figure of speech that suggests boasting.

Women Without Fear

MAY 2006

Words from the Sixth Committee of the EZLN for the public event "Women Without Fear: We Are All Atenco"

May 22, 2006

Good evening.

My name is Marcos, Subcomandante Insurgente Marcos.

For those of you who are familiar with zapatismo, it might not be necessary to explain what I'm doing here, at an event by and for women.

Of course you are not just women, but women who have decided to raise your voices in order to protest against the attacks the police have been making, and are making, on other women since May 3 and 4, 2006, in San Salvador Atenco, in the state of Mexico, in the Mexican Republic.

You are, here, there, and everywhere, women without fear.

My name is Subcomandante Insurgente Marcos, and I am, among other things, the spokesperson for the EZLN, a primarily indigenous organization that fights for democracy, liberty, and justice for our country, which is called Mexico.

As spokesperson for the EZLN, those others take voice through my voice, those who constitute us, who give us face, word, heart.

A collective voice.

In that collective voice is the voice of zapatista women.

And along with our voices and hearing is also our looking, our zapatista lights and shadows.

I am called Marcos, and among the numerous personal flaws I bear, sometimes cynically and cockily, is that of being a man, macho, male.

As such, I must bear, and often flaunt, a series of archetypes, clichés, proofs.

Not only in regard to me and my sex, but also and above all, in reference to woman, the female gender.

To those flaws that define me personally, someone might add the one we have as zapatistas, to wit, that of still not having lost the capacity for being astonished, for being amazed.

As zapatistas, sometimes we approach other voices that we know to be different, strange, and yet similar and appropriate.

Voices that astonish and amaze our ear with their light . . . and with their shadow.

Voices, for example, of women.

From the collective, which gives us a face and name, a journey and path, we go to great effort in choosing where to direct ear and heart.

And so, now we are choosing to hear the voice of women who have no fear.

Can one listen to a light? And if so, can one listen to a shadow?

And who else chooses, as we are today, to lend ear—and with it, thought and heart—in order to listen to those voices?

We choose. We choose to be here, to listen to and make echo for an injustice committed against women.

We choose to be fearless in order to listen to those who were not afraid to speak.

The brutality wielded by the bad Mexican governments in San Salvador Atenco on the 3rd and 4th of May, and which is still going on, to this very night, against the prisoners, especially the violence against women, is what summons us.

And not only that. Those bad governments are trying to sow fear through their actions, and, no, what is happening now is that they are sowing indignation and anger.

In a newspaper this morning, one of the individuals who, along with Vicente Fox and his cabinet, are priding themselves on "imposing the Rule of Law," Señor Peña Nieto (alleged governor of the state of Mexico), stated that what happened at Atenco had been planned.

If this were so, then it was planned, among other things, that those who were to be beaten, illegally detained, sexually attacked, raped, humiliated, were to be women.

We know, from the statements of those without fear who were detained, who are our compañeras, that they were attacked as women, their women's bodies violated.

And we also know from their words that the violence visited upon their bodies brought pleasure to the policemen.

The woman's body taken violently, usurped, attacked in order to obtain pleasure.

And the promise of that pleasure taken on those women's bodies was the benefit that the police received along with the mandate to "impose peace and order" in Atenco.

Certainly according to the government, they planned on having the body of a woman, and they planned, with extreme depravity, that their bodies would be plunder for the "forces of law."

Señor Fox, the federal leader of "change" and of the "Rule of Law," clarified for us a few months ago that women are "two-legged washing machines" (partial disclaimer, revolving payment plans and go to the customer service department).

And it so happens that up above, those machines of pleasure and work that are the bodies of women include assembly instructions which the dominant system assigns them.

If a human being is born woman, throughout her life she must travel a path that has been built especially for her.

Being a girl. Being an adolescent. Being a young woman. Being an adult. Being mature. Being old.

And not just from menarche to menopause. Capitalism has discovered they can obtain objects of work and pleasure in infancy and in old age, and we have "*Gobers Preciosos*"[1] and pedophile businessmen everywhere for the appropriation and administration of those objects.

Those above say that women should travel through life begging pardon and asking permission for being, and in order to be, women.

A path full of barbed wire that must be traveled by crawling, with head and heart against the ground.

And even so, despite following the assembly instructions, gathering scrapes, wounds, scars, blows, amputations, death.

And seeking the one responsible for those sorrows in oneself, because condemnation is also included in the crime of being women.

In the assembly instructions for the merchandise known as "Woman," it explains that the model should always have her head bowed. That her most productive position is on her knees. That the brain is optional and its inclusion is often counterproductive. That her heart should be nourished with trivialities. That her spirit should be maintained by competition with others of her same gender in order to attract the buyer, that always unsatisfied customer, the male. That her ignorance should be fed in order to guarantee better functioning. That the product is capable of self-maintenance and improvement (and there is a wide range of products for that, in addition to salons and workshops for *hojalatería*² and painting). That she should not only learn to reduce her vocabulary to "yes" and "no," but, above all, she should learn when she should speak these words.

There is a warranty included in the assembly instructions for the product called "Woman" that she will always have her head lowered.

And that, if for some involuntary or premeditated manufacturing defect, one should lift her gaze, then the implacable scythe of power will chop off the place of thought and condemn her to walking as if being a woman were something for which one must ask forgiveness and for which one must ask permission.

In order to comply with this warranty, there are governments that substitute the weapons and sex of their police officers for their lack of brain. And, in addition, these same governments have mental hospitals, jails, and cemeteries for irreparably "broken" women.

A bullet, a punch, a penis, prison bars, a judge, a government, in sum, a system, puts on a woman who doesn't ask for forgiveness or permission a sign that reads, "Out of Service. Nonreclyclable Product."

A woman must ask permission in order to be a woman, and it is granted to her if she follows what is shown in the assembly instructions.

Women should serve men, always following those instructions, in order to be absolved of the crime of being a woman.

Women confront this assembly process twenty-four hours a day, 365 days a year, from the moment they are born until the day that they die—at home, in the fields, on the street, at school, in the workplace, in transportation, in culture, in art, entertainment, science, government. But there are women who confront it with rebellion.

Women who, instead of asking permission, command their own existence.

Women who, instead of begging pardon, demand justice.

Because the assembly instructions say that women should be submissive and walk on their knees.

And nonetheless, some women are naughty and walk upright.

There are women who tear up the assembly instructions and stand up on their feet.

There are women without fear.

They say that when a woman moves forward, no men move back.

It depends, I say, from my "machismo-reloaded" perspective—a mixture of Pedro Infante and José Alfredo Jiménez.

It depends, for example, on whether the man is in front of the woman who is moving forward.

My name is Marcos; I have the personal flaw of being a man, macho, male. And the collective virtue of being what we are, we who are, zapatistas.

As such, I confess that I am astonished and amazed at seeing a woman raise herself up and seeing the assembly instructions shattering, torn into pieces.

A woman standing up is so beautiful that it makes one shiver just to look at her.

And that is what listening is, learning to look . . .

Cheers to these women, to our imprisoned compañeras, and to those who are gathered here.

Cheers for your having no fear.

Cheers for the valor that you pass on to us, for the conviction you grant us that if we do nothing to change this system, we are all accomplices in it.

From the Other Mexico City

SUBCOMANDANTE INSURGENTE MARCOS

P.S. Which Asks:

What punishment do those officials, leaders, and police deserve who attacked the women, our compañeras? What punishment does the system deserve which has turned being a woman into a crime? If we are silent, if we look the other way, if we allow the police brutality in Atenco to go unpunished, who will be safe? Isn't the release of all the Atenco prisoners thus a matter of elemental justice?

NOTES

1. This term has a double meaning. "*Gobers*" is short for *gobernadores*, or governors. *Preciosos* literally means precious or beautiful. However, the word also sounds like *preso*, prisoner, which suggests that the governors will soon be encarcerated or taken prisoner by the popular movements they so viciously repress. This mocking title was first bestowed on Mario Marín, the governor of Puebla. The title was later extended toward Enrique Peña Nieto (Mexico state), Ulises Ruiz (Oaxaca state), and any other politician that postures himself as enemy of the people and defender of the elite.

2. *Hojalatería* encompass a wide variety of products that can be made from thin sheets of iron or steel. An *hojalatería* is also a store where raw materials or products of *hojalata* can be purchased.

Other Intellectuals

Long ago, the Guadalajara dawn found Elías Contreras,[1] the EZLN's commissioner of investigations, sitting on one of the park benches in front of that cathedral which imposes its twofold power, the symbolic and the real, on the city of Guadalajara. Elías Contreras had come to this city to meet with the Ruso at his sandwich stall and, later, with the Chinese man Feng Chu in the public baths of the Mutualista, when he was involved in solving that unknown case of the *Mal* and the *Malo*.

For those who don't know, Elías Contreras was from an EZLN support base, a war veteran who helped the EZLN Comandancia General in what you call "detective" work and we call "investigation commission."

But before the Ruso's disconcerting sandwiches and the Chino's taciturnity, Elías Contreras had been sitting on one of the park benches in this city center of Guadalajara, scribbling sketches, odd phrases, complete paragraphs, and imprecise lines in his notebook, while waiting for the sun to mottle the eastern wall of the cathedral.

I hadn't known of the existence of that kind of trip log or campaign journal in which Elías Contreras, paradoxically, hadn't written anything referring directly to that case in which love, that other love, came to him just as love does come, that is, where one least expects it. In his case, accompanied by the confusion and fear that usually accompany an encounter with the other. The love that left him the way one always fears it will leave: by the irremediable path of death. Because, perhaps some might remember, La Magdalena fell fighting on our side, the zapatista side, against the *Mal* and the *Malo*. And she was our compañera in two ways: because she chose to be a woman and because she chose to be with us. But that's another history that we may, perhaps, find somewhere else.

Elías Contreras never said that he had fallen in love with La Magdalena, the transvestite who saved his life in the streets of Mexico City and who accompanied him in the pursuit of one Morales. He never said so openly, it's true, but anyone who learns to listen to words, silences, expressions, and manners also knows how to find secrets whose existence isn't even suspected. And Elías Contreras, the EZLN's commissioner of investigations, spoke of La Magdalena through his silence about her, as if words would hurt her. I believe—it's something that occurs to me now—that those feelings Elías Contreras harbored for La Magdalena were not returned in kind, and in some way that soothed the chaos provoked by that emotion.

But perhaps I might tell you about the now-deceased Elías Contreras's hidden love for La Magdalena, and what there was about it in his notebook, at another time. Or perhaps I won't recount anything, because there are people who not only leave the manifesto of their death as weight, but they also leave us the secrets of their lives.

Now I would like to tell you about some parts of the notebook Elías Contreras carried. The dawn often found us standing in front of the stove in his kitchen, and when our silences stretched out long enough, Elías would take the crumpled notebook out of his rucksack and pass it to me without even looking at me or saying anything.

I approached it as a clumsy intruder would. It took just a quick glance to realize that only the author would be able to decipher what was written or sketched there. As if it were a jigsaw puzzle whose complete picture was unknown to everyone except to the one who had designed the pieces.

Sometimes I would read a phrase out loud, and he, Elías Contreras, would begin putting the pieces together. As if talking to himself, he would rework an anecdote or an argument.

There were, for example, those simple and concise principles of the *guerrero* that Elías Contreras must have copied from somewhere in almost illegible strokes:

"1. The *guerrero* should always put himself at the service of a noble cause.

"2. The *guerrero* should always be willing to learn and should do so.

"3. The *guerrero* should respect his ancestors and care for their memory.

"4. The *guerrero* should exist for the good of humanity, live for that, die for that.

"5. The *guerrero* should cultivate the sciences and the arts and also, with them, be the guardian of his people.

"6. The *guerrero* should dedicate himself equally to things great and small.

"7. The *guerrero* should look ahead, imagining everything already complete and finished."

Not at dawn, but one afternoon—as the sun was leaping from one cloud to another until it concealed itself behind a mountain—with his notebook in my hands, I read to Elías Contreras the following sentence, which he himself had written:

"Resistance is averting, at just the right time, the fate that is being imposed from above, exerting the necessary force and thus destroying that disaster and those who are contriving it for us."

Upon hearing it, Elías Contreras said: "Guadalajara, during the time of the Ruso and the Chino." And he immediately told me that he had written that thought during the dawn when he was waiting in the center of the Pearl of the West.

Another sentence followed. I read it aloud:

"The great minds who sell themselves for money lack intelligence, as they lack courage, shame, and good manners. As the citizens say, they are mediocre, cowards, imbeciles, and bad-mannered."

"Up above," Elías Contreras told me, looking down bitterly, "they don't just invent a religion that values those who have instead of those who are. They also make some into their priests, who write and preach the doctrine of the powerful among those above and to those below. They are like priests, but also like the police and guards, seeing to it that we behave well, that we accept exploitation like meek little ones, our minds saying 'yes' or 'no' according to the order. In other words, the powerful also mess with thinking. And those priests of the thoughts of those of above are the great minds who sell themselves to money."

"The intellectuals of above?" I asked.

"Those," said Elías Contreras, commissioner of investigations for the EZLN, and—sitting on a tree trunk, looking toward the west—he repeated for me the argument he had constructed here in Guadalajara when he was following the trail of the *Mal* and the *Malo* in that still unfinished work of ours, of us, the neozapatistas.

I took the following notes from that argument, which Elías Contreras expounded to me in Tzeltal and which, therefore, has words for which there are no equivalents in the dictionaries of the dominant and dominating idioms:

THE INTELLECTUALS OF ABOVE

If the police and the armies are the stewards of the citizenry's good behavior in the face of seizure, exploitation, and racism, then who looks after good behavior in intellectual thought and theoretical analysis?

If the legal system, which sees the violent imposition of capital as being "rational and human," has judges, guards, police, and jails, then what are their equivalent in the culture of Mexico, in research and academia, in theoretical work, analysis, and in the debating of ideas?

Answer: The intellectuals above, who say what is science and what is not, what is serious and what is not, what is debate and what is not, what is true and what is false. In sum, what is intelligent and what is not.

Capitalism doesn't just recruit its intellectuals in the academy and in the culture; it also "manufactures" their sounding boxes and assigns them their territories. But what they have in common is their foundation: feigning humanism where there is only thirst for profits, presenting capital as the synthesis of historical evolution and offering the comforts of complicity through grants, paying for publicity and privileged colloquy. There is no appreciable difference between a self-help book and the magazines *Letras Libres, Nexos, Quién?* and *TV y Novelas.* Not in the writing, not in the price, not in their location in Carlos Slim Helu's Sanborns. Except, perhaps, in that more of the latter two are sold and read. In the contents? All offer the impossible mirror to those who above are what they are.

THE INTELLECTUALS IN THE MIDDLE

Those intellectuals in the fragile crystal towers of "neutrality" and "objectivity" are navigating, flirting discreetly or blatantly with the system, without caring about the color of the one holding political power. Looking above, these intellectuals answer the explicit or implicit question with which they start their work: "From where?" And other questions are tied to this question: "Why?"; "With whom?"; "Against whom?"

From the threshold of power, on their best behavior in the mandarin court of the current administration, these intellectuals are not in the middle, but rather in transit to above. They put themselves up for offer, with the tools of analysis and theoretical debate, at the banquets of political and economic power in Mexico, with a sign that reads: "Speeches made. Government programs justified. Businesspersons advised. Magazines produced at your pleasure. Entertainment provided for parties and for shareholder and cabinet meetings."

Next to those intellectuals are the ones who, slowly or quickly, lose their principles, give in, and desperately search for an alibi that will save them in front of the mirror. They are the prudent, mature, and sensible intellectuals who have put away the weapons of criticism for the blandishments of those who see their work on the right as being part of the left.

But the dishonest position of these intellectuals who belong to the system doesn't cease to amaze. The weak alibi of deliberate, rational, and responsible change isn't enough to sanctify that den of thieves that is the self-styled electoral left. They clothe themselves in the fragile transience of the media, and in that way they conceal not only their lack of principles, but also their renunciation of all critical analysis of the political class. Beset by the ghosts their prudence has created, they confirm their profound contempt for intelligence.

And there are the ones who say they belong to the radical left and are even zapatistas (certainly in the same way Guajardo says he's a zapatista). From the comforts of the academy they set themselves up as the new judges, the neo-commissars of good manners in the debate on what López Obrador's irresistible ascent in democratic modernity and in the polls really means.

They are the ones who say that any criticism of the political class promotes abstention and, with Thomist logic, that that's what will help the right. They are the ones who choose and edit national reality in order to present the unpresentable. The ones who remain silent in the face of the way the municipal president of Tulancingo, Hidalgo, of the PRD, treats indigenous and senior citizens . . .

They are the same ones who demand we swallow the millstone that we must support the macroeconomic program, at the same time the macropolitical changes.

They are the same ones who sell the illustrious "retirement to home." The increasingly lesser evil is the only comfortable option.

They are the same ones who shamelessly say that the government is protecting the Other Campaign so that it will attack López Obrador, while various police forces are photographing, watching, and harassing members of the caravan, state, regional, and local coordinators. The same ones who feel a profound contempt for their readers and who, without any shame whatsoever, say that Rosario Robles is a heroine one day and on the next, if they see her, they don't remember her.

They are the same ones who discredited the young students of the General Strike Council (CGH)[2] who, in 1999–2000, managed to keep the UNAM as a public and free university with their movement. The same ones who silently applauded the repression of young *altermundistas*[3] in that disgrace to the Jalisco calendar that is May 28, 2004.

They are the same ones who sigh with delight for the *segundos pisos*,[4] the bullet train, the Trans-Isthmus project, the co-investors in Pemex and in the electricity industry, Mexico's entrance into major-league baseball, the concerts in the Zócalo in Mexico City, the privilege of colloquy with officials.

Ah! Finally a high-class, *segundo piso* scene, so we don't see, or we pretend not to see, those of below, the provocateurs, the hyper, the *pelos parados*,[5] the rebels, the commoners, the wretched, those of below.

Who cares if the same ones are in the politics of above and if it's the same "macroeconomic" program as before? Who pays attention to those minutiae? Who is worried that the program represents the continuation and deepening destruction of the Mexican nation?

They are the ones who carry their leaking buckets of water to confront the promise written in Guanajuato: "There are still a lot of corn exchanges to set on fire." They're the ones with the thin skins who crack at the first criticism, and they scream their heads off, doling out labels like "intolerant," "Stalinists," "ultras," "outdated," "immature."

While the Other Campaign says, "Wake up," those intellectuals in the middle say, beseech, beg, implore: "Stay asleep."

THE OTHER INTELLECTUALS

From below and from the left, a movement that is creating itself, la Otra is also creating new realities. We neozapatistas think that these new realities, which are already emerging, and which will go on appearing further ahead, need another theoretical reflection, another debate of ideas.

This places demands on the other intellectuals. First, the humility to recognize that they are facing something new. And, second, to join in, to embrace the other, to learn about themselves through it, and to come to know the indigenous, the worker, the campesino, the young person, the woman, the child, the old one, the teacher, the student, the employee, the homosexual, the lesbian, the transgendered person, the sex worker, the street vendor, the small shopkeeper, the Christian base, the street worker, *the other*.

We think they should participate directly in the meetings of supporters in their states and, in addition, listen to what all the supporters throughout the country are saying. Thanks to the alternative media, the *other media*, it is possible to closely follow this beautiful lesson in contemporary national history. In their way and with their means, the other intellectuals will certainly produce analysis and theoretical debates that will astonish the world.

As zapatistas, we think that the Other Campaign can proudly say that it deserves this country's best intellectuals to be part of it. Now they will say, with their own work, whether they are deserving of the Other Campaign.

THE MISSING WORD

In the old and battered notebook of Elías Contreras, the EZLN's commissioner of investigation, there is an errant page, carefully folded, where it reads:

"There are stones that are still silent. When they speak the secrets they keep, nothing will be the same again, but it will surely be better for everyone. The being and not the having will be valued. Another hand will raise the flag, and the world will be scented, will be heard, will know, and will feel as it should be: the honourable home of those who work it."

ANOTHER VIGIL FOR SHADOW

Dawn. Above, the moon continues her pale disrobing of the blue that clothes her. The dark is forgiving of scars and generously offers her another veil for her shamelessness. Below, shadow curls up in the last corner of his sleeplessness.

Is that a wind rising up, or a bridge, seeking the faraway riverbank in order to complete its reach?

A sigh, perhaps.

And once again, the half-sleep and its illusions: a streamer, yearning and wrapped around an absent neck, longing rising and falling in the lower abdomen, the faint breathing of shadow in the ear of the night, desire clothing the dark of the half-light, a long and damp kiss on other lips, the hand writing a letter that will never reach its destination:

I would give anything to be entangled between your legs, to mingle our dampness, to exhaust myself in the cleft moon of your hips. I would give anything, except giving up doing what it's my duty to do.

Dawn breaks.

The sun is beginning to help the houses and buildings in their languorous bowing to the west.

The other Jalisco is honing word and tuning ear.

Outside they are asking:

"Are you ready?"

Inside, shadow carefully folds the longing, puts it in the left pocket of his shirt, close to his heart, and answers:

"Always."

From the other Guadalajara

SUBCOMANDANTE INSURGENTE MARCOS

NOTES

1. Elías Contreras is the name of a character in the book *The Uncomfortable Dead*, coauthored by Subcomandante Marcos and Paco Ignacio Taibo II. In an interview conducted by El Kilombo Intergalactico—January 13, 2007—Subcomandate Marcos explains that Elías Contreras was also the name of a zapatista reasearch group, launched after the March of the Color of the Earth in order to gather more extensive information about the state of social movements and civil society in Mexico. The research group was named "in honor of a support base compañero that died around that time."
2. The General Strike Council (CGH) was founded on April 20, 1999, by students, professors, and workers at the National Autonomous University of Mexico (UNAM). They were joined by supporters from the National Politechnic Institute (IPN), the Metropolitan Autonomous University (UAM), Chapingo University, various local unions, and individuals from throughout Mexico City. In opposition to reforms made by rector Francisco Barnés de Castro—which overturned student victories for free tuition gained in previous movements—the CGH voted for an indefinite strike at UNAM. The strike ended on February 6, 2000, when the Federal Preventative Police entered the university and arrested thousands of students.
3. *Altermundista* is an alternative to the term "antiglobalizationist." It suggests that the world can be altered and that an alternative world is possible. *Altermundistas* often describe their efforts as constructive, as opposed to negative or reactionary. They attempt to build toward a world beyond capitalism, neolibearlism, and injustice.
4. Construction of the *segundo piso*, a second level on the Miguel Alemán Viaduct in Mexico City, has been the source of extensive criticism and controversy.
5. *Pelos parados*—hair standing on end—is a figure of speech that suggests nervousness or hyperactivity.

How Big Is the World?

FEBRUARY 17, 2006

After a day of preparation meetings for the Other Campaign (it was September, it was dawn, there was rain from a far-off cloud), we were heading toward the hut where our things were when we ran into a citizen who all of a sudden came out with: "Listen, Sup, what are the zapatistas proposing?" Without even stopping, I answered: "Changing the world." We reached the hut and began getting things ready in order to leave. Insurgenta Erika waited until I was alone. She approached me and said, "Listen, Sup, the world is very big," as if she were trying to make me realize what nonsense I was proposing and that I didn't, in reality, know what I was saying when I'd said what I'd said. Following the custom of responding to a question with another question, I came out with:

"How big?"

She kept looking at me, and she answered almost tenderly: "Very big."

I insisted: "Yes, but *how big*?"

She thought about it for a minute and said: "Much bigger than Chiapas."

Then they told us we had to go. When we had gotten back to the barracks and had made Penguin comfortable, Erika came over to me carrying a globe, the kind they use in elementary schools. She put it on the ground and told me: "Look, Sup, here, in this little piece, there's Chiapas, and all this is the world," almost caressing the globe with her dark hands as she said it.

"Hmm," I said, lighting my pipe in order to gain some time.

Erika insisted: "Now you've seen that it's *very* big?"

"Yes, but we're not going to change it all by ourselves, we're going to change it with many compañeros and compañeras from everywhere." At that point they called the guard. Showing that she had learned, she shot back at me before leaving: "How many compañeros and compañeras?"

How big *is* the world?

In the Tehuacán valley, in the Sierra Negra, in the Sierra Norte, in the suburban areas of Puebla, from the most forgotten corners of the other Puebla, answers are ventured:

In Altepexi, a young woman replied:
More than twelve hours a day of work in the maquiladora, working on days off, no benefits, or insurance, or Christmas bonus, or profit sharing; authoritarianism and bad treatment by the manager or line supervisor, being punished by not being paid when I get sick, seeing my name on a blacklist so they won't give me work in any maquiladora. If we mobilize, the owner closes down and goes someplace else. Transportation is very bad, and I get back to the house where I live very late. I look at the light bill, the water bill, taxes, I do the sums and see there's not enough. Realizing that there's not even any water to drink, that the plumbing doesn't work and that the street stinks. And the next day, after sleeping badly and being poorly fed, back to work. The world is as big as the rage I feel against all this.

A young Mixtec indigenous:
My papa went to the United States more than twelve years ago. My mama works sewing balls. They pay her ten pesos for each ball, and if one of them isn't good, they charge forty pesos. They don't pay then, not until the contractor comes back to the village. My brother is also packing to leave. We women are alone in this, in carrying on with the family, the land, the work. And so, it's up to us to also carry on with the

struggle. The world is as big as the courage this injustice makes me feel, so big it makes my blood boil.

In San Miguel Tzinacapan, an elderly couple look at each other and answer almost in unison:
The world is the size of our effort to change it.

An indigenous campesino from the Sierra Negra, a veteran of all the dislocations, except the dislocation of history:
It has to be very big—that's why we need to make our organization grow.

In Ixtepec, Sierra Norte:
The world is the size of the swinishness of the bad governments and of the Antorcha Campesina, which is just prejudiced against the campesino and is still poisoning the earth.

In Huitziltepec, from a small autonomous school, a rebel television station is broadcasting a truth:
The world is so large that it has room for the history of the community and of its desire and struggle to continue looking out at the universe with dignity. A lady, an indigenous artisan, from the same round as the departed Comandanta Ramona, adds off-mike: "The world is as big as the injustice we feel, because they pay us a pittance for what we do, and we watch the things we need just pass us by, because there's not enough."

In the neighborhood of Granja:
It can't be very big, because it seems as if there's no room for poor children—they just scold us, persecute and beat us, and we're just trying to make enough to eat.

In Coronango:
As big as the world is, it's dying from the neoliberal pollution of the land, water, air. It's breaking down, because that's what our grandparents said, that when the community breaks down, the world breaks down.

In San Matías Cocoyotla:

It's as big as the government's lack of shame, which is simply destroying what we do as workers. Now we have to organize in order to defend ourselves from the government that is supposed to serve us. Now they see that they are without shame.

In Puebla, but in the other Puebla:

The world isn't so big, because what the rich already have isn't enough for them, and now they want to take away from us poor people what little we have.

Again, another Puebla, a young woman:

It's very big, so that just a few of us can't change it. We all have to join together in order to do it, because if not, we can't, you get tired.

A young artist:

It's big, but it's rotten. They extort money from us for being young people. In this world it's a crime to be young.

A neighbor:

However big it may be, it's small for the rich, because they are invading communal lands, ejidos, popular neighborhoods. As if there's no longer room for their shopping centers and their luxuries, and they're putting them on our lands. The same way, I believe, that there's no room for us, those of below.

A worker:

The world is as big as the cynicism of the corrupt leaders. And they still say they're for the defense of the workers. And up above they've got their shit together: whether it's the owner, the official, or the pro-management union leader, no matter what new things they say. They should make one of those landfills, a garbage dump, and put all of them in it together. Or not, better not, because they'd certainly pollute everything. And then if we were to put them in jail, the criminals would riot, because even they don't want to live next to those bastards.

Now it's dawn in this other Puebla, which hasn't ceased to amaze us with every step we take on its lands. We've just finished eating, and I'm thinking about what I'm going to say on this occasion. Suddenly, a little suitcase is sticking out from under the door, and it almost immediately gets stuck in the crack. A murmur of heavy breathing can barely be heard, of someone pushing from the other side. The little suitcase finally makes it through and, behind it, stumbling, something appears that looks remarkably like a beetle. If it weren't for the fact that I was in Puebla, albeit the other Puebla, and not in the mountains of the Mexican Southeast, I would almost swear it was Durito. As if putting aside a bad thought, I return to the notebook where the question that headed this surprise exam is already written down. I continue trying to write, but nothing worthwhile occurs to me. That is what I was doing, making a fool of myself, when I felt as if something were on my shoulder. I was just about to shrug in order to get rid of it, when I heard:

"Do you have any tobacco?"

That little voice, that little voice, I thought.

"What little voice? I see you're jealous of my masculine and seductive voice," Durito protested.

There was no longer any room for doubt, and so, with more resignation than enthusiasm, I said: "Durito . . . !"

"Not 'Durito'! I am the greatest righter of wrongs, the savior of the helpless, the comforter of the defenseless, the hope of the weak, the unattainable dream of women, the favorite poster of children, the object of men's unspeakable jealousy, the—"

"Stop it, stop it! You sound like a candidate in an election campaign," I told Durito, trying to interrupt him. Uselessly, as can be seen, because he continued:

". . . the most gallant of that race that has embraced knight errantry:

Don Durito of the Lacandona SA of CV of RL, and authorized by the Good Government Juntas."

As he said this, Durito showed me a decal on his shell which read: "Authorized by the Charlie Parker Rebel Zapatista Autonomous Municipality."

"Charlie Parker? I didn't know we had a MAREZ with that name—at least we didn't when I left," I said disconcertedly.

"Of course, I established it just before I left there and came to your aid," Durito said.

"How odd. I asked them to send me tobacco, not a beetle," I responded-protested.

"I am not a beetle, I am a knight errant who has come to get you out of the predicament you have found yourself in."

"Me? Predicament?"

"Yes, do not act like Mario Marín's 'precious hero' in the face of those recordings that revealed his true moral caliber. Are you in a predicament or not?"

"Well, predicament, what's called a predicament, then . . . yes, I'm in a predicament."

"You see? Perhaps you were longing for me, the very best of the knights errant, to come to your aid?"

I thought for barely an instant and responded: "Well, the truth is, no."

"Come, do not conceal that great pleasure, the huge joy and the unbridled enthusiasm that exist in your heart upon seeing me once again."

"I prefer to conceal it," I said resignedly.

"Fine, fine, enough of the welcoming fiestas and fireworks. Who is the scoundrel I should defeat with the arm I have below and to the left? Where is the Kamel Nacif, Succar Kuri,[1] and the so-and-sos and others of such low ilk?"

"No scoundrels and nothing to do with that ilk of swine. I have to answer a question."

"Come on," Durito pressed.

"How big is the world?" I asked.

"Well, there are a short version and a long version of the answer. Which do you want?"

I looked at my watch. It was 3 a.m., and my eyelids and cap were falling into my eyes, and so I said without hesitation: "The short version."

"What do you mean, the short version!? Do you think I have been following your tracks through eight states of the Mexican Republic in order to present the short version? *Naranjas podridas, ni mais palomas* not hardly, absolutely not, no way, negative, rejected, no."

"Fine," I said, resigned. "The long version, then."

"That's it, my big-nosed nomad! Take this down . . ."

I picked up my pen and notebook. Durito dictated: "If you look at it from above, the world is small and the color of the dollar: green. It fits perfectly in the price indexes and the valuations of the stock market, in the profits of a transnational, in the election polls of a country that has suffered from having its dignity hijacked, in the cosmopolitan calculator that adds capital and subtracts lives, mountains, rivers, seas, springs, histories, entire civilizations, in the miniscule brain of George W. Bush, in the shortsightedness of savage capitalism badly dressed up in neoliberal attire. Seen from above, the world is very small, because it disregards people and, in their place, there is a bank account number, with no movement other than that of deposits.

"But if you look at it from below, the world stretches so far that one look is not enough to encompass it; instead, many looks are necessary in order to complete it. Seen from below, the world abounds in worlds, almost all of them painted with the color of dislocation, poverty, despair, death. The world below grows sideways, especially to the left side, and it has many colors, almost as many as persons and histories. It grows backward, to the history that the world below made. It grows toward itself with the struggles that illuminate it, even though the light from above goes out. It sounds out loud, even though the silence of above crushes down on it. And it grows forward, divining in every heart the morrow that will be given birth by those who below are who they are. Seen from below, the world is so big that many worlds fit, and, even so, there is space left over, for example, for a jail.

"In summary, seen from above, the world shrinks, and nothing fits in it other than injustice. Seen from below, the world is so spacious that there is room for joy, music, song, dance, dignified work, justice, everyone's opinions and thoughts, no matter how different they are if below they are what they are."

I had barely been able to write it down. I reread Durito's response, and I asked him: "And what is the short version?"

"The short version is the following: The world is as big as the heart that first hurts and then struggles, along with everyone from below and to the left."

Durito left. I continued writing while the moon waned in the heavens with the night's damp caress . . .

I would like to venture a response. Imagining that I, with my hands, undo her hair and her desire, that I envelop her ear with a sigh, and, while my lips move up and down her hills, understanding that the world is as large as is my thirst for her belly.

Or, more decorously, trying to say that the world is as large as the delirium to make it "otherly," as the ear that is needed to embrace all the voices of below, as this other collective desire to go against the tide, uniting rebellions of below, while above they separate solitudes.

The world is as big as the prickly plant of indignation that we raise, knowing the flower of tomorrow will be born from it. And in that tomorrow, the Iberoamerican University will be a public, free, and secular university, and in its corridors and rooms will be the workers, campesinos, indigenous, and others who today are outside.

That is all. Your responses should be presented on February 30 in triplicate, one for your conscience, another for the Other Campaign, and another with a heading that clearly states: Warning, for those of above who believe, naively, that they are eternal.

From the other Puebla

SUP MARCOS, SIXTH COMMITTEE OF THE EZLN

NOTE

1. Jean Thouma Hannah Succar Kuri is a Lebanese-born Mexican businessman with American citizenship. Imbedded within the Cancún tourist industry, Kuri's wealth is estimated to be $30 million U.S. After publication of the exposé *Demons of Eden*, by Lydia Cacho, he was associated with Puebla-based Lebanese businessman Kamel Nacif Borge in a sexual-exploitation ring. In 2004, Kuri was detained in Chandler, Arizona, and extradited to Mexico. He is accused of child pornography, child sexual abuse, and statutory rape.

The Story of the Nonconformist Little Stone

READ BY SUBCOMANDANTE MARCOS AND
FIVE CHILDREN—KATY, GIOVANNI, MARCELO,
CARLITOS, AND PABLO—IN THE CARACOL
OF MORELIA, CHIAPAS
JULY 24, 2007

(In the other calendar: April in July)

This story will be narrated with special effects by the "Everything for everyone, cookies for us" Collective, composed of Katy, Giovanni, Marcelo, Carlitos, Pablo, and myself . . . that is, El Sup. The stories and legends of the zapatistas point toward a future that has its roots in the past and reveal their first lights in the present. Perhaps that's why our time and our calendar are somewhat mixed up, and we speak of things that took place centuries ago as if they had happened yesterday or, better yet, as if they were still to happen, and of distant places as if they were very near, just right around the hill. That's why our stories don't start with the traditional "Once upon a time . . ." and instead they start with "There will be a time. . . ."

We want to dedicate this story to zapatista children from autonomous schools and to all children in Mexico and the world, because this is the month of April, when we celebrate children's day.

(A girl, Katy, interrupts and starts arguing with El Sup: "It's not April, it's July."

"No way," responds El Sup, "July means Julio, and Julio is a compañero that supports us driving for the Sixth Commission."

"No, July is a month, and we're in the month of July."

"No, we're in the month of April and it's children's month."

"No, it's the month of July."

"It's April."

"It's July."

"April."

"July."

"It's April, otherwise what good is it to be a subcomandante?")

Well, after this brief argument about calendars, we've agreed that we're in the month of April and we're ready to go on with our story:

"There will be a time . . . when a little stone, a very tiny stone . . . like this (El Sup uses his hand to show the size). Don't you go thinking that I'm making a graphic reference to the size of my means of production, circulation, and consumption; I'm talking about the size of the little stone.

Well, this little stone was a rebellious stone, like many of the small, medium and large women that are listening to us or reading us. Let's say that it was a nonconformist little stone, because it kept nonconforming all the time. For example, this day that is yet to come, the little stone was laying on the ground, watching the clouds and the birds flying along the sun's path, and the stars and the shadows that dress up the moon. There's the little stone, thinking nothing at all. But all of a sudden—*boom!*, there's the nonconformance, and she starts whining and complaining: "Why did I have to be a stone when I could be a cloud, even if it was just a little one. If I was a cloud I could go anywhere I wanted and I could travel all the way to the place where Mrs. South Korea lives, or Mrs. India, or Mrs. Thailand, or Indonesia, wherever their homes are. If I'd been born a little cloud I would be able to see all that, but no, I was born a little stone and here I am . . . but I don't agree with that. I've thought it over and I've made up my mind to nonconform."

And so the little stone decided to make a lot of noise to make it known that it was nonconforming, because if you nonconform and don't do anything about it, no one will know what's going on and everyone will just go by without seeing you, or worse yet, a woman with her daughter will walk by and see you and say, "Hey, look, a little stone that's very happy to be a little stone. You should learn from it, and instead of wanting to run off with a poor zapatista who doesn't even have a job or a salary, you should fall in love with a member of the PAN or the PRI or the PRD, it doesn't matter which, cause they all make a lot of money."

So the little stone thought it made no sense to nonconform if no one knew about it, and it decided to make a sign that said "I'm nonconforming." And it also thought that the letters of the sign should be of many colors and in many sizes. So it said, "I need a lot of crayons and a ruler so the letters come out straight . . . and a piece of cardboard and some scissors, and a pencil . . . Shoot! And I also need to learn how to read and write, because I know what it's like to feel nonconformance, but I don't know how to write the word."

There's the little stone trying to figure out how to show its nonconformance. It spent a lot of time thinking and it finally said, "Dammit . . . nonconforming takes a lot of work. All right, first I need some hands and feet."

The little stone concentrated very hard and repeated to herself, "hand, hand, hand," but no hands appeared. Then she tried harder and started to push . . . mmhh . . . mmhh . . . and *pop!* . . . instead of a hand a little fart came out . . . *ffrrrttt!* How she blushed, the little stone, but then she saw that no one noticed and stopped worrying about it and kept on pushing . . . mmhh . . . mmhh . . . and when she started turning blue and purple, pop!, a little hand appeared on the left side. The little stone was very tired but she tried again and concentrated to get a right hand.

And she pushed and pushed and after a few little farts . . . *pop!*, a little leg appeared also on her left side.

"*Shht!*" thought the little stone, "now I really got it from below and to the left." And she kept on pushing to get a right hand and a right leg, but now it really seemed like she had parasites in her belly because the only thing that came out was a lot of little farts. The little stone was nearly fainting and she thought it was okay, that with a left hand and a left leg she could do a lot and do it well enough to nonconform. With great difficulty the little stone sat down and held her little left hand to her chin as if she was thinking very seriously. And it came to her that she had to learn the letters of the alphabet to write "nonconformance," and the numbers . . . and geography, because just imagine that instead of reaching South Korea she reached Washington D.C., and when she was giving her speech she said: "Dear stone compañeras of South Korea, through my voice speak zapatista stones . . . " *Boom!* Right there and then the Border Patrol, the FBI, the CIA, and the Marines would fall on her and arrest her and they would realize that she was an undocumented and landless stone . . . and missing a right hand and a right leg.

"I'm going to look for Mr. Owl," thought the little stone, because she had heard that the owl knows many things and has very big eyes and wears eyeglasses because he reads a lot. So there goes the little stone, limping and holding on to whatever she can until she reaches the tree where the owl lives. There she starts calling Mr. Owl: "*pst, pst*, hey, Mr. Owl, *pst, pst.*" Mr. Owl looked around and the only thing he saw was a little stone with a left hand and a left leg, so he didn't pay attention. The little stone got really mad because Mr. Owl was ignoring her, and she shouted, "Mr. Owl, I want to talk to you, if you keep ignoring me I'm going to throw a stone at your head." Mr. Owl finally looked at her and flew down to the ground and asked her what she wanted, saying that he was very busy. The little stone told him that she wanted him to teach her how to read and write, and how to do the arithmetic that Comandante Zebedeo is always talking about, and about geography, so she could find out where the homes of Mrs. India, Thailand, Indonesia, and South Korea were.

Mr. Owl laughed and said, "And how would I know all that!"

The little stone was surprised and said, "Everyone says you know many things, that's why you have big eyes and wear glasses."

"It's a lie," said Mr. Owl, "I have big eyes and wear glasses because I'm always watching the girls when they go take a bath in the river . . . Ha! But I do have a lot of books because everyone thinks I know many things and they're always sending me books. If you want, I can give you a bunch."

"Ok," said the little stone, and Mr. Owl filled up a huge backpack, just like the ones the compañeras and compañeros that come from other lands are always carrying, as if they brought their whole country on their backs.

So the little stone limped away dragging her huge backpack until she reached the shade of a tree and there she sat down and pulled out several books and started to look at the letters and the numbers. And she didn't understand a thing. So then she went to an autonomous zapatista school to see if she could learn with what they call "integral education," which means that you learn *everything* and learn it *well*, and not just one thing and badly. But when she got there no one talked to her, hardly anyone even looked at her, or just a little bit, because some mischievous boys wanted to grab her and throw her with a slingshot. But the zapatista girls defended the little stone and did a critical analysis on the mischievous boys and accompanied the critical analysis with a big stick and eventually the boys calmed down. And the little stone thought that this whole thing about autonomy was pretty good, and that the girls were also nonconforming.

So the little stone started to learn, but since she was a little stone she learned very otherly. For example, she learned a very other sort of geography, because according to her the homes of peasants in India, South Korea, Thailand, and Indonesia were closer to Chiapas than the White House or the homes of Mexico's bad government.

And the little stone was very happy learning and playing at the autonomous school. But one day the teacher asked the students what they wanted to be when they grew up. And everyone had to answer. And a girl said "I want to be an engineer," and another one said "I want to be a doctor," and another one said "I want to be a driverette," and another one said "I want to be a psychologist," and another one said "I want to be a lawyer," and another one said "I want to be a *subcomandanta*" and right there and then a macho laser beam came out of Sup Marcos and *buzz* . . . it disintegrated the girl . . . No, that's not true, nothing happened to her because El Sup didn't find out, 'cause otherwise . . .

Anyway, all the boys and girls spoke until it was the little stone's turn. The little stone had been thinking what she wanted to be and when the teacher asked her she said very happily and full of enthusiasm: "I want to be a cloud!"

The mischievous boys laughed and started making fun of her. "Ha! She wants to be a cloud and she's too heavy!" said one of them.

"Yes, she's too fat!" said another one. And they teased her a lot. But the girls got really mad and brought out the big stick of critical analysis and the mischievous boys finally calmed down.

But the little stone was very sad. "Yes, it's true," she said, "I'm very fat and heavy, I'll never be a cloud." But the zapatista girls and boys encouraged her and told her not to worry, promising to help her. And one of the girls said, "I have a sister that's a *miliciana*[1] and she can teach you how to exercise so you lose weight." "Alright," said the little stone, who started feeling a little better. And the zapatista girls and boys called the *miliciana* to teach the little stone some exercises. And the *miliciana* said she would, but that she first had to inform her command.

Her command finally gave her the order and the *miliciana* said that, since the little stone wanted to be a cloud, she would give her airborne troop training. So the training program started and there was the little stone running up and down, doing sit-ups and push-ups and eating a lot of *pozol* in order to get really strong. The little stone spent many days exercising but she didn't lose any weight. The zapatista children saw her nearly fainting and told her, "all right, little stone compañera, you're not losing any weight, you're like a rock. We need to think of something better to help you out." The girls and boys walked away and the little stone ran off to eat a lot of candies, cookies, and chocolates. Then the zapatista children came back and joined her to eat candies, cookies, and chocolates, and so they spent a lot of time. They were all stuffed when they said, "Listen, little stone, we've thought it over and we have a plan to make you fly like the clouds."

The little stone was laying down trying to digest all the junk she ate and she just sighed, "ok." Then the boys and girls took out a balloon and they filled it up with air and tied it to the little stone's belly with a string and she started to float, not a lot, but enough a little. They all clapped and the little stone didn't clap because she only had a left hand, but everyone could see that she was happy.

"Let's go up to the hill, said the boys and girls, and from there we'll throw the little stone so she can fly."

"Wait," said a girl, "we don't even know which way to throw her." And she asked the little stone, "Which way do you want to fly?"

And the little stone said, "I want to go rain in Asia, Africa, Oceania, Europe, and all over America, but first I'm going to Asia."

"*Mmmh*, now we're really screwed," said a boy, "cause we don't know which way that is."

"Let's go ask El Sup," said a girl.

"I'm not going," said a boy, "because El Sup doesn't like children and he cuts off their head with a dull machete so it takes a long time, and he makes sure it's rusty so it gets infected." The children started arguing about whether or not that was true.

And they went on until a girl said, "I know, let's bring some cookies for El

Sup, that way he won't cut off our heads." "Ok," said the children, and a group of them went to look for him at the General Command of the Zapatista Army of National Liberation. There they learned that El Sup was very mad because, he said, a beetle had stolen the tobacco for his pipe.

The boys and girls went up to him very scared, and a 5-year-old girl called La Toñita, who wasn't afraid, said, "Hey, Sup."

El Sup answered growling as if he was very mad: "*grrrr, grrrr.*"

La Toñita said, "We brought you some cookies," and then El Sup calmed down a bit, though not a lot, but enough. Then they sat down next to him and they all got stuffed with animal cookies.

Then they asked El Sup, "Hey, Sup, where's the house of Mrs. Asia?"

El Sup shook the crumbles off his shirt and took out his pipe, but he didn't light it up because, he said, a son-of-a-such-and-such beetle (that's what he said, cause he has a really foul mouth) had stolen his tobacco. And he said, "Well, you go straight that way, and when you get to the crossroads where there's a poorwill bird you'll see a road that goes to the right and another one that goes to the left. Don't take the one to the right, take the one to the left, and keep following it until you see a sign that says 'Welcome to Asia,' and there you are."

"Ok," said the boys and girls, and when they were about to leave El Sup told them to take a lot of *pozol* because it was far away. The boys and girls were very happy when they got to where the little stone was waiting for them, hanging from the balloon, and she was already turning purple because the string was too tight. They loosened it a bit and they told her that they knew which way was the home of Mrs. Asia.

The little stone said, "All right, but there's a problem. How am I going to make it rain, if I'm a little stone?"

The boys and girls got together again to think about it and came to an agreement, and then they went to get a bucket of water and they tied it to the little stone so it could throw water whenever it wanted to rain. Then everything was ready and they went to the hill. And then they gave so many speeches that it seemed like a meeting of the Other Campaign. And finally the speeches were over. And they thought about it and they painted a sign on the balloon that said "The Other Cloud," so the rest of the world knew what it was. And the little stone was really nervous and said goodbye to the children and they sort-of wanted to cry, but the little stone told them not to cry because as soon as she ran out of water she would come back for more. All right, said the children, and put it on the edge of the hill. But the little stone didn't move because it was heavy, not a lot, but enough. So the children started blowing really hard and the balloon started to move, and then the wind blew and it took off flying.

And it went . . . far away. It crossed the border with the United States and the U.S. Air Force mobilized because, they said, there was an unidentified flying object, and many warplanes surrounded the little flying stone and their commander spoke to the pilots over the radio and asked them what it was and the pilots said it was a stone tied to a balloon carrying a bucket of water and a sign that read "The Other Cloud." The commander got really mad and asked them what they'd been smoking and whether they were drunk and told them to come back immediately because they were all going to be arrested. The warplanes left and the little stone made ugly signs at them with her left hand.

And wherever the little cloud went, I mean, the little stone, people looked up at the sky and took out their umbrellas and their raincoats because they thought it was going to rain. And when she reached Asia the peasants from those countries were very happy because they got good rains for their cornfields and they started to dance.

And one day the autonomous zapatista school received a letter and all the children got together to read it, and everyone was very curious because the letter had many stamps with very strange signs. The girls and boys opened the letter and it was from the little stone and it read like this:

Dear Compañeras and Compañeros, Zapatista Boys and Girls:

I hope you are in good health and studying hard. After my brief greeting I move on to the following: Look, my little compañeras and compañeros, the water in my bucket is running out and I will soon be back. But I want to make it clear that I no longer want to be a cloud, because I'm dizzy. So I've thought it over and now I want to be a tree. See to it. That's all I have to say.

Sincerely,

The Airborne Zapatista Little Stone

And now the zapatista children are trying to figure out what to do to make the little stone become a tree, and I think that now they're really screwed because God only knows how they're going to go about it.

Tan-tan.

Thanks a lot.

For the "Everything for all, cookies for us, even if they're animal cookies" collective,

Katy (11 years old)
Giovanni (12 years old)
Marcelo (6 years old)
Carlitos (9 years old)
Pablo (7 years old).
El Sup (515 years old)

NOTE

1. A miliciana is a member of a militia.

ABOUT THE CONTRIBUTORS

SUBCOMANDANTE INSURGENTE MARCOS is a spokesperson for the EZLN, an insurgent indigenous organization that is part of a larger Mexico-based movement for democracy, indigenous autonomy, and a new way of doing politics. Marcos first joined the indigenous guerrilla group that was to become the EZLN in the early 1980s. He is a prolific writer, and author of several books translated into English, including *Story of the Colors* (Cinco Puntos), which won a Firecracker Alternative Book Award, and *Our Word Is Our Weapon* (Seven Stories Press), and with Paco Ignacio Taibo II, *The Uncomfortable Dead: A Novel of Four Hands* (Akashic Books).

LAURA CARLSEN is the director of the IRC Americas Program at www.americaspolicy.org

ABOUT THE EDITORS

CANEK PEÑA-VARGAS studied Latin American History and Education at the Gallatin School of Individualized Studies, NYU. He is a member of Estación Libre—a collective of people of color who work in solidarity with the zapatista movement—and Visual Resistance, an art collective based in New York City. He is also a member of the Regeneración Child Care Collective. In the summer of 2005, Canek traveled to Chiapas to study the Mayan language of Tzotzil and assisted in research at autonomous clinics in the zapatista Caracol of Oventik. An aspiring educator, Canek currently works at an after-school program in East Harlem.

GREG RUGGIERO is editor at large for City Lights Books. Ruggiero has been involved with publishing zapatista writings and communiqués since February 1994. Some of titles he has produced include *Our Word is Our Weapon* (with Juana Ponce de Leon), *Zapatista Encuentro, The Other Campaign, I Scatter Flowers of War*, and an audio CD of Subcomandante Marcos reading selections of his works in English. Greg travels to Chiapas frequently and is currently working on a project involving zapatista music recorded by the indigenous-operated radio network, Radio Insurgente.

LINKS FOR MORE INFORMATION

EZLN | http://enlacezapatista.ezln.org.mx/
This page presents all the EZLN's letters, stories, and communiqués as they release them and features a daily blog of the Other Campaign as it travels across Mexico. To join an e-mail list that sends out news and translations, see http://www.eco.utexas.edu/facstaff/Cleaver/chiapas95.html

Radio Insurgente | http://www.radioinsurgente.org/
To hear the voice of the indigenous rebel communities in Chiapas, tune into the zapatistas' clandestine shortwave and FM radio broadcasts here. Past programs are also available for downloading. An incredible resource for those interested in hearing not just Subcomandante Marcos, but the insurgent women, men, and young people who are struggling together for democracy, dignity, and justice in Mexico.

Enlace Civil | http://www.enlacecivil.org.mx/
To get a deeper sense of the indigenous struggle in Chiapas and the ongoing human-rights abuses and paramilitary attacks suffered by the communities there, take a look at Enlace Civil's excellent Web page.

Chiapas Independent Media Center | http://chiapas.mediosindependientes.org/
San Cristóbal is a magnet for independent journalists, indigenous advocates, human-rights activists, and other intellectuals, artists, and cultural workers. This superbly maintained bilingual site is an invaluable resource for news regarding the autonomous zapatista communities.

Rebeldía Magazine | http://www.revistarebeldia.org/
This Mexico-based Spanish-language publication runs a broad range of zapatista-related articles, and their Web page is excellent.

OTHER ZAPATISTA BOOKS AVAILABLE FROM CITY LIGHTS

The Other Campaign: The Zapatista Call for Change from Below
Subcomandante Marcos
Introduction by Luis Hernández Navarro
Edited by Greg Ruggiero
978-0-87286-477-1 | 176 pages, $8.95

The Other Campaign is a collection of Zapatista texts—in English and Spanish—that articulate a vision for "change from below," a call to create social change outside and beyond the limits of electoral politics.

First World, Ha, Ha, Ha!: The Zapatista Challenge
Edited by Elaine Katzenberger
978-0-87286-294-4 | 200 pages, $13.95

In this collection, writers from Mexico and the United States provide the background and context for the Zapatista movement, and explore its impact, in Mexico and beyond.

"The Mexican Zapatista Army's march in 1994 provoked a national crisis in the country, challenging current trends in Mexican politics and management or social concerns. The Chiapas uprising was a direct attack on current world order: in this collection U.S. and Mexican writers document the background for the movement and reveal its philosophies and impact." —*Midwest Book Review*

The Fire and the Word: A History of the Zapatista Movement
By Gloria Muñoz Ramírez
Introduction by Subcomandante Marcos
Epilogue by Hermann Bellinghausen
978-0-87286-488-7 | 300 pages, $16.95

An illustrated history of the Zapatista movement based on interviews with the movements original organizers. Also available: *El Fuego y la Palabra* (978-0-87286-465-8). "The most complete version of the public history of the Zapatistas." (Subcomandante Marcos)

"In the Zapatistas we have not one dream of revolution but a dreaming revolution." —Naomi Klein